Terror of the

# TOKOLOSHE

The Untold True Story of Southern Africa's Hairy Invisible Ghost-Rapist

# S.D. TUCKER

Typeset by Jonathan Downes, Jessica Taylor
Cover and Layout by SPiderKaT for CFZ Communications
Using Microsoft Word 2000, Microsoft Publisher 2000, Adobe Photoshop CS.

First published in Great Britain by CFZ Press

**CFZ Press**
**Myrtle Cottage**
**Woolsery**
**Bideford**
**North Devon**
**EX39 5QR**

© CFZ MMXIIi

# ISBN: 978-1-909488-10-6

*"Africa semper aliquid novi"*
- Always something new out of Africa
Pliny the Elder

The region defined as 'southern Africa' for the purposes of this book.

# CONTENTS

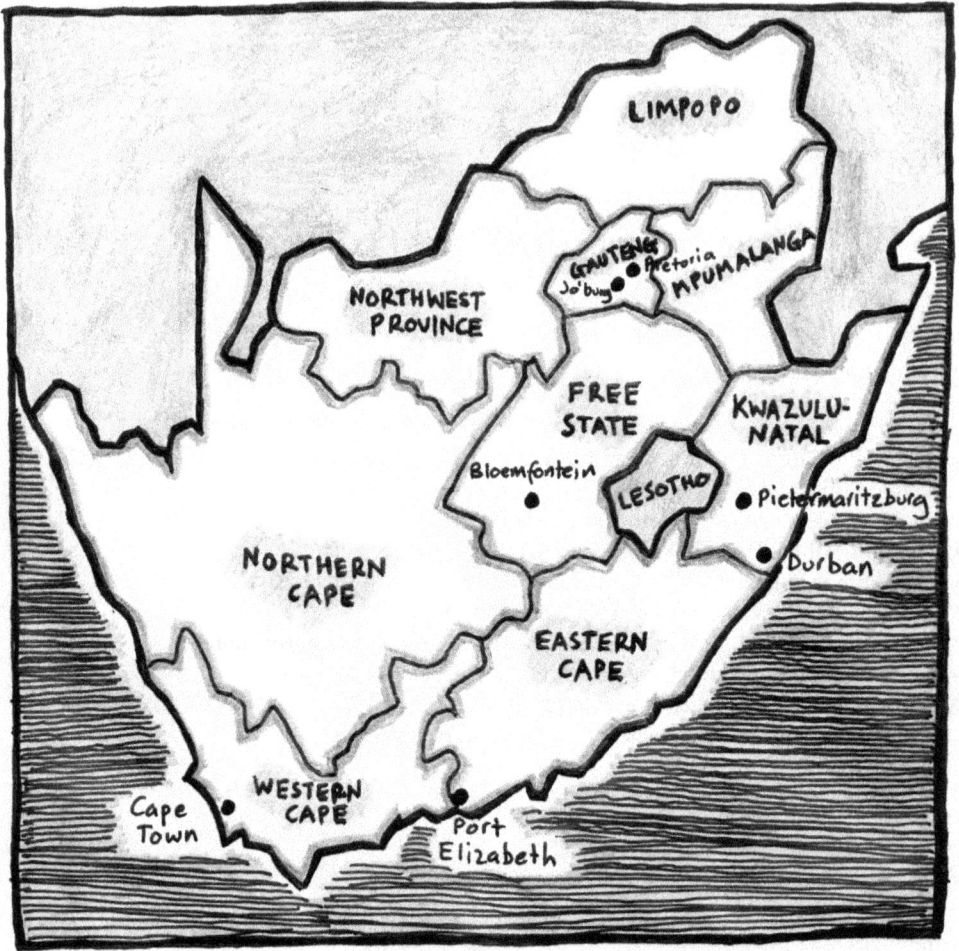

The Provinces and main cities of South Africa,
the main nation discussed in this book.

# *Introduction:*

## The All-Purpose African Entity

The word tokoloshe [1] is an unfamiliar one to most Western readers, but not to most people in the southern part of Africa. There, the term is as well-known and well-understood as the words 'fairy', 'ghost' and 'demon' might be in cities such as London, New York, Paris or Amsterdam. In South Africa, especially, knowledge of the tokoloshe is a part of everyday existence for people of all walks of life, whether they believe in the hairy little beasts or not. This is all very well; but most readers of this book will probably never even have heard of such a being before. So, the question very naturally arises - what on earth is a tokoloshe? Sadly, there is no easy answer to such an enquiry.

Perhaps it would be best to start off by looking at an eye-witness account from somebody who has been lucky (or unlucky, perhaps) enough to have actually bumped into one herself. It comes from the mouth of a black South African woman named Flora Nthshuntshe, and concerns what happened to her one bright moonlit night in 1916 when, still a teenager, she was walking back home to her parents' house in the Northern Cape Province town of De Aar. Suddenly, she said, she saw a "strange-looking object" coming towards her from the distance. At first, she was not entirely sure whether it was an animal or a child. Apparently, it was neither. It was a tokoloshe.

Mrs Nthshuntshe takes up the narrative from here:

> "He was short and fat with a fur cape or animal skin round his shoulders. His eyes were like lights, yellow, shining brightly and looking evil. He looked hard and very angrily at me, but otherwise took no notice ... he was evidently going to something much more important and was in a great hurry. I shook with terror and watched him hurrying up the street. I wondered if any evil would befall me or my people, but I think his thoughts were elsewhere and he was too concerned with thinking about something else to worry about me." [2]

Given what the hideous monster looked like, perhaps this was just as well.

The description is a fascinating and eerie one; even if we don't believe a word of Mrs Nthshuntshe's claims, we can still get a good picture of what a tokoloshe is meant to be from looking at her story, can't we? Clearly, he is conceived of as being some kind of supernatural and demonic little man with glowing eyes; the southern African equivalent of a troll or goblin, maybe. If only it were that simple.

Unlike trolls and goblins in the modern West, tokoloshes are widely believed in today, rather than simply being known of from fairy-tales, right the way across the southern tip of Africa, particularly in the countries of South Africa and Zimbabwe, but even as far north as Zambia and Malawi. As such, encounters with them are still being reported even now; and with a disturbingly high level of frequency, too. However, he does not always manifest in the form of a bright-eyed little man in a hurry, as reported to us by Mrs Nthshuntshe. Indeed, when examining contemporary tokoloshe reports in the African news media, it might occur to the average Westerner simply to think of a poltergeist. This is because, commonly these days, tokoloshes are meant to manifest as invisible beings (this invisibility supposedly being achieved by virtue of a magic pebble which they either swallow or keep hidden inside their mouths) which create havoc in households by producing rappings, moving around objects, smashing things up and throwing stones about, just like Western spooks are supposed to do. Right. So tokoloshes are actually ghosts, then? Not exactly.

**Furry Fairies?**
Another commonly-reported form of present-day tokoloshe manifestation does not involve the hurling around of pebbles and household furniture but, rather, something altogether more disturbing in its nature; namely, the forcible rape of sleeping women in their beds at night. Dozens of accounts of this kind of misdeed supposedly taking place can be read of in southern African tabloid newspapers in any given year, such tales apparently being given wide credence by their readerships. Here, of course, the tokoloshe sounds less like a poltergeist, and much more like the notorious incubi and succubi of Medieval Europe - sex-demons which were also once believed to have their way with their own unwilling victims after dark. Perhaps this makes our current conundrum a little clearer; tokoloshes, obviously, are simply African demons, then. Or are they?

Amazingly, tokoloshe-rapists are sometimes said to get their victims pregnant. When such unfortunate women give birth, however, it is generally to disabled babies, or still-born foetuses - which, it is often alleged, are really tokoloshe-children in disguise. This idea is genuinely believed in. People have actually been taken to court for abusing or killing disabled infants in the mistaken belief that they were really tokoloshes, as we shall see later. This all parallels, quite closely, the old European idea of the 'changeling' - the notion that the fairies would steal away healthy children from their parents and leave them with weak, sickly ones to look after instead. Given this fact, could we be justified then in saying that tokoloshes are actually some kind of strange African fairy-folk? Sometimes, perhaps. Frequently, the idea of the 'goblin' has indeed become confused in many people's minds with that of the tokoloshe, as we shall discover when we come to examine a strange breed of creatures known as chikwambos later on. Except …

Very often, tokoloshes are alleged to be something called 'familiars' - that is to say, the demonic servants of witches, whom they keep satisfied by doing their evil bidding and also by acting as their willing sex-slaves. Accounts of how witches recruit these devilish vassals, however, differ. Some say that they just conjure them up like spirits, others that they re-animate the corpses of pygmies and murdered children for such a purpose. Given this fact, it appears that the idea of the zombie must be thrown into the whole mix, too.

Other people, though, think that the witches themselves are actually the tokoloshes, and that they can shape-shift into them at will, in order to cause death and destruction. However, yet other people say that tokoloshes are actually some kind of magical baboons - something which has even led some to suggest that they are really nothing more than genuine zoological animals which have been 'mythologised' somehow by having various unlikely tales attached to them. Then again, it is in fact nowadays possible to buy tokoloshes in certain African market-places; you can pick them up in bottles, and they sometimes seem to be more like magic potions than they are supernatural beings as such. On occasion you can purchase them as 'seeds' and then plant them, in order to bring love and success, as 'good-luck goblins'.

Clearly, then, the tokoloshe has many forms, more than one of which may be accepted simultaneously for him by the same individual. In this way, he really is like the fairies of Western folklore, which were sometimes the spirits of the dead, sometimes demons, sometimes fallen angels and sometimes miniaturised gods. Also like the European fairies, the tokoloshe has a wide number of variant names, such as hili, gilikango, chikwambo and mubobobo, all of which sometimes mean basically the same thing, and sometimes something slightly (or even radically) different, as we shall eventually see. When the term tokoloshe is translated into English, meanwhile, it is usually as 'gremlin', which isn't terribly helpful, seeing as such creatures were entirely fictional entities invented by Allied fighter pilots during WWII in order to jokingly account for technical malfunctions occurring with their planes - whereas the tokoloshe, quite clearly, is the subject of actual widespread belief across much of southern Africa.

This may right now all seem to the reader, perhaps, like an absolute mess. Maybe it is not, however. It might initially seem useful to us to view the tokoloshe through the prism of certain specific Western paranormal entities and figures of folklore with which we are probably more familiar, as I have tried to do above, but possibly this is not quite the right way to go about matters. In this book, I hope to show how the apparently incoherent figure of the tokoloshe is actually no such thing. For sure, precisely what a tokoloshe looks like or is capable of doing alters from person to person and situation to situation, but that is, I would submit, exactly the point.

The tokoloshe is no one single thing in and of itself; rather, it is a kind of generalised spiritual being whose presence can be invoked in order to explain all manner of different phenomena, whether these be inherently supernatural in their nature or not. It is, as the title of this introduction implies, a kind of 'all-purpose African entity'. Have you just given birth to a dead child? Blame the tokoloshe. Perhaps, on the other hand, your wife has gone off you? That'll be because she's getting enough loving from the tokoloshe, who's more of a man then you ever were. Seen a ghost and had pebbles hurled at you by invisible hands? More tokoloshes, not poltergeists. Having bad luck? It's hardly surprising, seeing as a malicious witch has sent out her pet tokoloshe to get you. What you need to do is to buy a bottled tokoloshe of your own to counteract the negative effects of this deadly curse. The list is almost endless.

In a society in which the uncanny is widely believed in, in which witch-doctors and native healers enjoy wide credence, and where the efficacy of magic is, for many, a simple fact of life, the tokoloshe fulfils an important role. Some people, such as the South African academic Nhlanhla Mkhize, have openly proposed that the tokoloshe is essentially little more than a convenient 'social fiction' in southern African countries; pointing out, for example, that to children he fulfils the role of adult authority at one remove. For instance, in African childhood folklore the tokoloshe frequently instructs kids not to tell anyone that they have seen him and expects to be obeyed, punishes those who do disobey him by slapping them in the face, and then offers small rewards and treats such as coins and apples to those children who are wise enough to do as he says. In other words, in this particular guise the tokoloshe, far from being an evil being, actually helps to socialise the young [3]. He is also a figure through whom any number of difficult issues - sexuality, race, gender, disability and more - can be explored by proxy, bringing certain taboo topics out into the open, where they can be discussed more frankly than might otherwise be the case. As I hope to show, this is apparently the main purpose of the tokoloshe in the minds of most of those southern Africans who choose to believe in him. Westerners, too, once did exactly this same kind of thing with their own supernatural entities such as witches, fairies and demons, of course - all of whom could kill, steal away healthy babies, cause sterility and molest sleepers, at least according to those who genuinely believed in such things during the past.

**Fine, Upstanding Members of Society**
Nonetheless, I would say that the average southern African, in spite of the multifarious nature of the beast, has a fairly clear image of what a tokoloshe would look like if he or she was actually to come across one. No doubt you would like to have such an image in your head, too; although, then again, perhaps not. After all, the first thing that you would notice about a tokoloshe if you were indeed to see one would undoubtedly be its penis. Tokoloshe penises are proverbially large - so large, in fact, that the creature is obliged to walk around everywhere with it slung over his shoulder, so that it doesn't just drag along the ground and weigh him down (or perhaps even trip him up!). Fortunately for his observers' modesty, however, most tokoloshes are said to cover up their phenomenal members with a type of sheepskin cloak termed a kaross, in order to protect it from coming to any harm. No doubt this is what Flora Nthshuntshe's tokoloshe was hiding beneath the animal-skin cloak which it was wearing around its own shoulders, as we read about earlier. This penis is not notable only because of its size, however. As we shall see in a future chapter, the tokoloshe is able to use this incredible instrument of his to open doors with, and to act as a kind of 'periscope' in order to keep a look-out for his enemies. He can even send it underground; pity the poor blackbird who mistakes that for being a nice, fat earthworm ...

Why does the tokoloshe have such monstrous genitals, though? Primarily, they are the mere tools of his trade, given that his most commonly-reported form nowadays is probably that of the supernatural rapist-figure; either that or the eager sex-slave of a malicious witch. A more scholarly explanation, however, might be that the figure of the tokoloshe actually has its origins way back in pre-history, in the guise of some now long-forgotten god-figure who once represented the concept of male virility and fecundity; an archaic African version of the Greek

Devils in the traditional form of Pan-like horned and goat-legged beings leading witches around in a merry dance at the Sabbat; this seems to be what certain white South Africans originally conceived the tokoloshe as looking like.

fertility god Priapus, perhaps, who was notoriously depicted in ancient art in possession of a massive and permanent erection. [4]

Curiously, certain ancient Trickster-gods, too, were once depicted as having gigantic penises, which sound rather similar in nature to that of the tokoloshe. Wakdjunkaga, for example, the hero of a cycle of Trickster-stories told by the North American Winnebago people, is described as having "intestines wrapped around his body, and an equally long penis, likewise wrapped around his body with his scrotum on top of it" [5] - and, at other times, he is spoken of as having coiled his dick up like a Cumberland sausage and then carried it around with him in a box on his back [6]. During the course of his adventures, it is furthermore revealed that Wakdjunkaga's penis has yet more amazing qualities; for example, he is able to detach it and send it shooting out across a lake like a guided torpedo until it ends up being firmly lodged between the legs of a chief's daughter, where it then gets stuck, despite everyone's best efforts to pull it out [7]. Eventually, however, Trickster is himself tricked by a cheeky chipmunk which persuades him to probe up inside a tree through its hollow with his snake-like member, before then biting most of it off, leaving him with the mere stub of a thing which modern man now has to put up with for a penis today [8]. Tokoloshes, too, are sometimes spoken of as being able to perform similarly amazing penile acts.

The Classical fertility god Priapus, depicted holding the caduceus (staff/wand) of Mercury, as seen in a fresco found at Pompeii, and opposite in a terracotta figure from the late 18th Century. Did the tokoloshe also have its large-penised origins in some similar, long-forgotten African fertility deity?

The general interpretation of this kind of ability upon Trickster's behalf, though, is that his penis in these stories is deliberately being depicted as a kind of independent entity beyond Wakdjunkaga's control, as it becomes hard and aroused, etc, without his consciously willing it to do so. In this sense, Trickster becomes a figure representative of the mental state of early man, who will, presumably, have had less control over his animal instincts and appetites than modern man is meant to have (before the chipmunk has bitten his penis down to size and thus given mankind his more developed sense of contemporary sexual restraint, of course).

Given these similarities between the genitals of Wakdjunkaga and the tokoloshe, then, perhaps it could even be speculated that the latter is actually some kind of diluted survival of some original, and now long-forgotten, African Trickster-god? Certainly, various African cultures did have Trickster-gods of their own - Edshu of the Yoruba people (left) and Ananse of the Ashantis perhaps being the most famous - so this idea might not be entirely implausible. Maybe some vestiges of the tokoloshe's possible original identity as a Trickster-deity can still be seen in things such as his insatiable sexual appetite, and the amusing and childish pranks, which he is sometimes said to play upon his unwilling dupes during his frequent manifestations in the form of a poltergeist? This is all purely idle speculation, of course, but the idea might bear some thinking about, at least.

Either way, it is a well-known fact that, because of this fearsome piece of weaponry, and also on account of the tokoloshe's alleged penchant for biting off sleeping people's toes and then eating them, many women in southern Africa place piles of bricks beneath their beds at night in order to try and raise themselves up high enough off the ground so that the tokoloshe's penis will be unable to enter them whilst they sleep (a wholly illogical idea, given its length). This idea is now so widespread, in South Africa especially, that it has apparently become colloquial to say of somebody who is considered to be 'hard' or intimidating that "he's so mean he makes the tokoloshes sleep on bricks", or some such variant [9].

This all implies, however, that all tokoloshes are male, and their victims female. In general, this is indeed the case. I think that most people would claim that there are no female tokoloshes; however, they would be wrong. In certain areas, rumours of female tokoloshes are indeed abroad - these

14

horrible, baboon-like beings making up for their lack of a huge penis by virtue of having gigantic hairy breasts instead, apparently [10]. It has to be said, though, that I could find very few references to the idea of female tokoloshes in any of the sources available to me, so I am presuming that this particular aspect of the belief is quite rare. If not absolutely all tokoloshes are male, though, then neither are all their victims female; there are, for example, a few cases of homosexual tokoloshes in existence, although this concept is probably not exactly a traditional or common belief.

For instance, a 14-year-old boy claimed to have been forcibly masturbated during the night by one in 2004 [11], a bizarre idea which is not actually entirely without parallel - or, at least, not without parallel within the pages of dubious South African tabloid newspapers. The mixed attitude of the public towards the notion of man-on-tokoloshe action, however, can perhaps best be seen in the response of listeners to the words of a man who was interviewed by the South African radio station OFM one evening in March 2009, who claimed that he was being raped on a nightly basis in his home by a rampant gay tokoloshe.

The station received several complaints about the broadcast, making the contrasting points either that homosexual tokoloshe-rape was a real and traumatic phenomenon, which did not deserve to be belittled by the mocking and sceptical tone of the man's interviewer, or saying that OFM were simply gaining cheap publicity by broadcasting the words of a mentally ill person for wider public ridicule and entertainment [12].

Being raped by a tokoloshe cannot be something that many persons would desire, however, given the being's general appearance. He is notoriously - indeed, proverbially - ugly. If someone should ever accuse you of 'looking like a tokoloshe', then there is no way that this could be construed as being in any way a compliment (unless the person who says it should happen to be looking at your penis at the time, I suppose...) Indeed, the ugliness of the tokoloshe is so notorious that one folk-remedy for ridding yourself of his unwanted attentions would be to hang up a mirror in your room. Then, if a tokoloshe should happen to come in looking to rape you in the night, he would catch sight of his reflection in the glass, and become so frightened by his own hideous appearance that he would instantly flee away from it in terror! [13]

### The Nature of the Beast

What do they look like, then? Generally, much like Flora Nthshuntshe said that her tokoloshe did back in 1916. Namely, when they are seen, tokoloshes are generally described as being little brown, hairy, dwarf-like figures of less than one metre in height, much like brownies or boggarts (types of hearthside fairy) were in old European tradition; although, unlike the Western brownie or boggart, the tokoloshe appears to have only the one buttock - as, curiously, some Western demons were occasionally said to have, too. A variant form, however, has the tokoloshe as being a 'little old man' rather than a hairy monster, as such. Occasionally, he is also alleged to possess only one arm and one leg, or to look something like a miniature bear - some sources specifically speak of the monster resembling a teddy-bear, and the pet-name 'Tokoloshe' is apparently given to their cuddly toys by some southern African children - with hair coming out of his ears. They are also supposed to speak with a lisp and, sometimes, to have large, outsized heads; occasionally with a bony ridge running across its top, which they rather unkindly use to head-butt cattle with, killing them. Other people, however, say that tokoloshes have a big hole in their head, for whatever reason. Some informants, meanwhile, speak of their arms and legs being short and muscular, and totally out of proportion to their torso, too. In his right hand, he is sometimes said to carry a big stick, which he uses to vanquish his foes. Some descriptions even say he has horns, like the stereotypical image of the Devil. These are the basic 'templates' of the tokoloshe's appearance, then; it seems that witnesses and those who believe in him mix and match from these various details from description to description.

Occasionally, however, it is possible to come across a description of a tokoloshe which conforms to none of these characteristics, as with a wholly aberrant case from March 2012, in which workers on a place called Blaukrans Farm some 50km north-west of the small town of Khorixas in the Kunene region of Namibia began reporting that a tokoloshe in the form of an unnaturally large monitor lizard was on the loose there. Blaukrans Farm, it seems, was no stranger to the supernatural. In September 2011, it was reported in the Namibian press that a 13-year-old boy on the farm had been forcibly French-kissed by a dreadlocked tokoloshe with a "smelly tongue" and a woman's neck been scratched by a demonic figure known as a 'Night-Walker' there, for example, whilst there was also a rumour going around the place that a tokoloshe wearing a chain had been released onto the property by the creature's former owners - so the idea of evil spirits being on the rampage there was no novelty whatsoever to the isolated place's terrified inhabitants.

The most recent scare on the farm, though, centred around a series of alleged sightings of a gigantic monitor lizard moving around on top of people's roofs in the middle of the night. Perhaps the strangest thing to occur during this panic, however, was that one witness claimed to have seen a piece of burning wood floating out of one of the farm-houses of its own accord [14]. That, of course, sounds like the actions of a typical tokoloshe in the form of an invisible poltergeist - but a tokoloshe in the form of a colossal monitor lizard? As far as I know, this particular aspect of the report is unique; but the people involved seemed to have had no problem in believing that the lizard was a tokoloshe, even though it was much more scaly in its nature than it was remotely hairy. A tokoloshe, then, is pretty much whatever you want him to be, it seems. I even found one case, to be detailed further in a future chapter, wherein the demon was conceived of by one man as being a kind of miniature Cyclops made from porridge!

It is a fact, however, that actually seeing a tokoloshe is generally viewed as being a characteristically 'black' experience, and sightings of him by whites are very rare indeed. The following description, though, given by a European woman named Phylis Beard in 1921, seems fairly typical of the way that white South Africans who had never actually seen him themselves, once tried to depict the tokoloshe rather patronisingly as being a funny little demon, of comically unlikely provenance:

> "Mr Tokoloshe is an imp from Hades barely thirty inches in height; he has a head the size of a large pumpkin, a whiff of a nose, small snake-like eyes, hands like the claws of a vulture, with the hairy nether limbs and feet of a goat. In fact, had he a tail and a pair of horns, he would have resembled old Lucifer to a T. The owl is his most intimate friend, who is supposed to announce the coming of His Terrible Majesty by doleful hoots and shrieks." [15]

Quite how much Mrs Beard has exaggerated, or added to, the appearance of the tokoloshe as actually reported to her by her black South African informants here must remain a moot point, of course; did she introduce the idea of the goat-legs simply in order to make him conform to traditional white European ideas of what demons and devils were meant to look like, for instance, in order to better please her readership?

But, if exaggeration there was, then this picture, too, of the brute has fed into some more modern descriptions of the tokoloshe. After all, he is nowadays occasionally associated with the idea of Satanism - an "imp from Hades" indeed - which would certainly not have been the case prior to Christianity having arrived in southern Africa with the nineteenth-century European missionary-movement.

Given the variety of different physical features which the tokoloshe is claimed to have from source to source, though, it is quite evident that no one single 'definitive' picture of him exists in the popular mind, beyond perhaps the basic template of a hairy dwarf with a giant male member. Occasionally, this fact seems to be referred to by informants who specifically describe him as being a shape-shifter who is able, for example, to appear as a handsome man to women at night in order for him to facilitate his raping-sprees - like European incubi were also meant to be able to do. However, if the tokoloshe were to be caught in this act by a real man, he would still appear his usual ugly self, as his handsome form would actually just be an illusion. Occasionally, meanwhile, they are said to manifest purely as inexplicable dancing lights, like fairies and ghosts sometimes did in the West. Usually, though, the tokoloshe is said to be invisible, like a poltergeist. As such, actual recorded eyewitness sightings of the entity are few and far between.

Whilst usually invisible, however, if a tokoloshe is ever seen by anyone, the best thing to do is meant to be simply to ignore it; under no account should you point at or try to speak to a tokoloshe, as it is said that he will become annoyed and take his revenge. Indeed, sometimes it is alleged to actually be impossible to engage a tokoloshe in eye-contact at all, for whatever reason.

The main exception to this rule comes with children, whom tokoloshes are meant to try to befriend by giving sweets and playing with them. If a child has an 'invisible friend', it is sometimes presumed by adults to be a tokoloshe and such a relationship discouraged, as if it continues on into adulthood some people believe that there is a risk that the child may be influenced by the entity into becoming a witch. (However, other sources contradict this idea by implying that tokoloshes in fact hate kids and delight in scratching children in their beds whilst they sleep, leaving behind festering wounds).

Maybe these ideas are simply attempts by people to account for the spirit's general invisibility, however. Notions that the tokoloshe can hear every word that a person says, and will slap you with unseen hands should you say his name out loud, meanwhile, are also very suggestive [16]. This idea seems quite similar to that old notion from European fairy-lore wherein you were not supposed to refer to the fairies by name, instead using euphemisms such as 'the Good Folk', at pains of offending them and thus drawing down unnecessary supernatural misfortune upon yourself. The tokoloshe, evidently, wishes to remain unknown as much as it remains unseen. Such widespread taboos only act to reinforce the creature's sense of occult mystery, perhaps.

**A Watery Grave**
So, then; that is what the tokoloshe looks like - namely, however you want him to, albeit within certain broad parameters. But where did he come from in the first place? Speculation about ancient and now long-forgotten fertility-gods and Trickster-figures being mere conjecture, the earliest place that we can trace the tokoloshe back to for sure is beneath the water. The name tokoloshe has its etymological origins in the Xhosa language in the word uthikoloshe, which term was once used to refer to a kind of dwarf-like water-sprite or god formerly worshipped by that tribe. Echoes of this ancient origin of the entity can still be found in occasional folk-beliefs which place the ultimate lair of the tokoloshe-race either in or near rivers, lakes or pools. Sometimes, the tokoloshe is even said to lurk within the riverside den of a monitor lizard, with which reptiles the spirits are said to be good friends, and even occasional dancing partners! [17] (Maybe this aspect of the myth was what allowed the people on Namibia's Blaukrans Farm to misinterpret the large monitor lizard, which they saw there as being a tokoloshe, as mentioned earlier?) However, in more urban areas, this idea seems to be less common nowadays, with most town and city-dwellers apparently preferring to believe that tokoloshes usually hide within the homes of witches and wizards, rather than underwater.

The tokoloshe, though, was originally a river-deity of the Xhosa people of what is now South Africa's Eastern Cape Province, and was apparently known to some other Bantu peoples who lived in certain of the eastern parts of what we now call South Africa, Swaziland, Lesotho and Zimbabwe, too. Of this we can be absolutely certain. There is an old Zimbabwean folk-tale, for example, which tells of a beautiful maiden, the daughter of a tribal chief, who was once desired by a tokoloshe water-god living in a stream, but who rejected him and instead wore on her arm nine metal bangles in order to symbolise that she had already been taken by a human lover, who had given the decorations to her as a token of his love. This made the tokoloshe so angry that when the girl next came down to the water to bathe, he cut off her arm and threw it into the river. An interesting little old folk-tale, of course, but evidently not one with any semblance of actual truth to it; or is there?

Amazingly, in 1924 a severed bone from a human arm was actually found right next to the same river - which would seem most likely to have been either the Tsambe or the Mutare - in Zimbabwe's eastern Manicaland Province, surrounded by nine metal bangles of traditional native workmanship, by a certain Captain A Valentine, who was prospecting for gold in the region surrounding what is now the city of Mutare, but which was then known as Umtali. It was discovered a mere four feet above the water-level, and ten feet away from the then limits of the riverbank, the stream presumably having changed course slightly as the years went by. The mummified arm and the decorations were handed in to Harare (then Salisbury) Museum in 1935, and are apparently still there, whatever the actual truth of their origin may ultimately prove to be. [18]

Such ancient legends are amongst the earliest references to the tokoloshe that we have available to us; as such, it seems safe to say that he has lived in the water for a lot longer than he has been going around raping people or helping out witches. Even during the earlier days of his existence, however, as the story above implies, the tokoloshe was conceived of as having at least some kind of dangerous sexual component to his persona. One common myth about him, for instance, used to be that he had an uncontrollable habit of seducing any native girls who were foolish enough to go down to rivers or pools in order to bathe or wash their clothes [19]. If such people drowned, I'm sure it was said that it was probably all just down to him gathering in yet more new members for his ghostly harem.

During the heyday of British colonialism in South Africa, during the late nineteenth and early twentieth centuries, it seems that the idea of the tokoloshe as being a river-sprite was still the prevalent one amongst the native peoples, at least in Eastern Cape Province, the traditional Xhosa heartland of tokoloshe belief. For example, a curious tale is told by a woman named Estelle Hamilton-Welsh, the wife of a British colonel, of her experience (sadly undated, but it can have occurred no later than 1913) one day whilst trying to cross a river near to the town of Umtata (now Mthatha) in her horse-drawn cart during a storm. Two brave men of the Cape Mounted Rifles - a kind of paramilitary border-patrol force maintained by the British authorities prior to WWI - crossed over the water with their steeds before her, in order to ensure that it was safe to do so during the bad weather conditions. Apparently, it was. However, when Mrs Hamilton-Welsh then tried to cross the river herself, she was unable to do so as the horse pulling her cart suddenly sat down in the middle of the water and refused to budge, putting the white woman in danger. One of the soldiers tried riding back into the river to help her, but his animal refused to go anywhere near the seated one, so this proved impossible.

Fortunately, a local black man was passing by who said that he would wade into the river without a horse and try and rescue the woman himself, which was of course dangerous, but added that he would accept no responsibility if Mrs Hamilton-Welsh should be drowned whilst he did so. She did not drown, however, and, when he got her back safely to dry land, the passer-by explained that the horse's bizarre behaviour was only to be expected, seeing as the white merchant who owned it had very foolishly christened him with the name Tokoloshe, perhaps as some kind of a joke, despite being specifically warned not to do so. "The white man has no business to give the name of our water-god to a horse," he apparently explained.

"He might know that trouble would ensue. The god resents his having his name." [20] And well he might, I suppose; perhaps we can hardly blame the river-god here for trying to gain his revenge as soon as the insulting animal and its arrogant white masters had entered into his watery domain.

A rather more amazing South African case of a water-dwelling tokoloshe trying its best to do evil, though, is supposed to have occurred in 1893, near to a river in the Mount Ayliff district in East Griqualand (now Eastern Cape Province). Here, a District Surgeon named HB Maunsell had been sent out by the British authorities, together with a native black constable, to investigate some curious goings-on at a kraal - a kind of circular mud-walled or palisade-enforced enclosure for cattle, often to be found as the central hub-point of an African village or family-community - near to the Umzimvubu River. Stones, it seems, were being hurled around at people by invisible hands, causing some disquiet. Maunsell soon discovered that these events had begun after a 15-year-old girl living on the kraal had gone down to a stream which ran into the Umzimvubu one day in order to fetch back some drinking water for her family. Lying down at the edge of the stream to have a drink herself, however, she was most disturbed to see a "little old man" lurking beneath the water. It was the tokoloshe!

The girl screamed and ran away, followed by the tokoloshe, who seemed to have taken something of a fancy to her. When she got back home, she fainted. Coming around, she then allegedly began vomiting up bizarre substances such as iguana bones and skeletal dog-toes, hairs from a dog's tail and, more suggestively, grey hairs from an old man's head and small white pebbles of the sort normally seen by the river, the tokoloshe's lair. Soon, poltergeist phenomena began bothering the girl in her hut. She would be asleep on a mat when her blankets were pulled off from her, and then thrown across to the other side of the room by unseen forces. Worst of all, however, were the stone-showers themselves; these occurred inside the girl's hut, and involved pebbles and rocks - some of them as large as a man's hand - falling down from the thatched roof and either landing harmlessly on the floor or striking down upon the people inside with great force, and harming them. Weirdly, upon closer inspection, it was found that the thatching had no holes in it, meaning that the stones had to have been materialising inside the hut, at ceiling-height, and then falling down spookily from there. Discovering that the girl at the centre of this haunting had been visited by a local witch-doctor in order to be treated for some unspecified ailment not long before she had seen the tokoloshe in the river, Maunsell's somewhat unlikely conclusion was that this man had hypnotised the girl and all her family and neighbours into seeing the ghostly phenomena going on, for reasons entirely unknown. He had no doubt, however, that they were all totally sincere in their account of what they said had occurred. [21]

We shall encounter similar stories involving stone-showers later on in this book, when we come around to examine the numerous surprising connections which exist between tokoloshes and poltergeist manifestations; it seems to be a curious fact that, in cases such as the one detailed above, the realms of myth and reality apparently coincide. Poltergeist phenomena really do occur, in my view; and, in southern Africa, it seems to be tokoloshes who are generally blamed for causing them. Another thing which undeniably exists, however, is mental illness - and it seems that, in the land of the tokoloshe, such maladies are sometimes conceived of as being caused by malign supernatural entities which dwell in rivers and pools. There is even a specific culture-bound syndrome known in South Africa as uthukwase, and as mashawe in Zambia, wherein people who have been looking down into swirling water begin to become 'self-hypnotised', almost, into believing that they have been possessed by the river-gods; including, presumably, water-dwelling tokoloshes.[22] In much of southern Africa, as in the *Jaws* films, it seems, it is never quite safe to go into the water.

### Tokoloshes Today

It is a long way, however, from the tokoloshe's original identity as a mischievous and powerful water-sprite to the dreaded figure which is so prevalent in the popular culture of countries such as South Africa today. Perhaps this is as a result of the spread of belief in the being passing outwards from its original heartland in what is now the Eastern Cape Province of South Africa, the traditional home of the Xhosa people, and into the rest of the country and beyond. Take a Xhosa river-god out from his native environment, it seems, and eventually he will mutate into the incoherent being we now have today, as he adapts to the new conditions of life and beliefs of the people in different parts of the country. This is a process which apparently only really began to occur on any wide scale during the twentieth century, and can be related quite closely to the spread of black migrant workers who during this period moved around from region to region in search of work, especially clustering around the gold mines near the city of Johannesburg in what is now Gauteng Province, where their labour was sorely needed. As different black and other racial groups began encountering one another and mixing upon a more regular basis due to these important social changes, it seems that belief in the tokoloshe began noticeably to increase in places other than just the main Xhosa and Zulu heartlands in the east. [23]

Maybe this is why, very occasionally, he is conceived of as actually being a miner, a kind of dwarf who lives underground and seeks out precious metals, another idea which has parallels with certain European fairy-entities, such as gnomes, kobolds and knockers, all of whom were also once said to have dwelled within the earth's subterranean zones.[24] Could this belief, perhaps, include a kind of coded reference to the migrant workers who poured into other areas of South Africa to work down the gold and diamond mines, inadvertently upsetting traditional local ways of life as they did so? Maybe. We cannot really hope to know for sure. However, many modern tokoloshe myths in southern Africa do indeed seem to explore issues surrounding forms of migrant labour in some way.

For example, Isak Niehaus - a South African sociologist whom we shall meet again numerous times throughout this book - studied beliefs relating to witchcraft in a South African village called Green Valley, in Limpopo Province in the north-east of that country, in the 1990s. He found that the alleged witches in the area only began supposedly making use of tokoloshes during the 1960s, after the white South African government of the time had begun initiating the forced migration of labour for certain of their black subjects in the area. It was speculated locally, apparently, that migrant-workers from Green Valley who had been made to go out and work in the Witwatersrand area outside Johannesburg (home to many of South Africa's famous gold mines) had encountered tokoloshes there and then brought them back to their home village with them once their work in the region was over. Before the era of forced migration, however, it seems that nobody in Green Valley had ever even heard of these evil beings. [25]

It is possible, then, to view the distorted contemporary South African idea of the tokoloshe as having its genesis to some extent as being a kind of useful negative symbol of the 'other' - of pollution of traditional village communities by the strangeness of the wider world outside. Locals go away from their home-village and come back bringing tokoloshes with them; a variation on the old 'country boy goes away to the big city and comes back with a head full of new-fangled ideas' trope, maybe.

Presumably, during this period in South African history, numerous black labourers from all areas of the country would have encountered Xhosa workers, and learned of the tokoloshe from them. When they returned back home, however, this 'foreign' belief would not necessarily have been welcomed, and so the tokoloshe soon began to get a bad name for itself.

Perhaps some people did not approve of such strange new non-local gods, and so set out to spread nasty rumours, equating the tokoloshe with witches and demons - and thus, by an extremely roundabout way, the Xhosa river-god ended up being what it is today, namely, a nasty little poltergeist-rapist.

This, at least, is one possible theory; that the image of the tokoloshe shifted in the popular mind during the twentieth century, becoming some kind of way for people to deal with unpleasant social realities through fiction, and to express disapproval of the old apartheid policies concerning forced black migrant labour through a kind of convenient fairy-tale bogeyman figure.

Now, however, the era of forced migration for the black population has, thankfully, long-since ended; and the tokoloshe cannot just stand still and refuse to develop with the modern-day, post-apartheid society which now surrounds it. In the age of the entertainment-state, the tokoloshe, much like vampires, werewolves and aliens have been in the West, has now, predictably, been co-opted for use in the entertainment media.

Disreputable tabloid newspapers such as South Africa's *Daily Sun*, for example, regularly carry stories about tokoloshe attacks, many of them clearly invented, and no doubt thought of by many of their readers simply as being amusing rubbish.

One front-page story from May 2007, for example, has the dramatic headline 'TOKOLOSHE!'('It has knocked out this woman! Now the creature of evil is trapped!'), and even purports to show a close-up photograph of a tokoloshe, standing ominously over an unconscious woman's head. [26]

OPPOSITE: A tokoloshe stands over its victim, ready to pounce; this pathetically obvious fake photo from the front cover of a 2007 edition of South Africa's popular tabloid the 'Daily Sun' does, nonetheless, give a good enough indication of what the creature is generally supposed to look like. Beneath that sheepskin kaross lurks something terrible ...

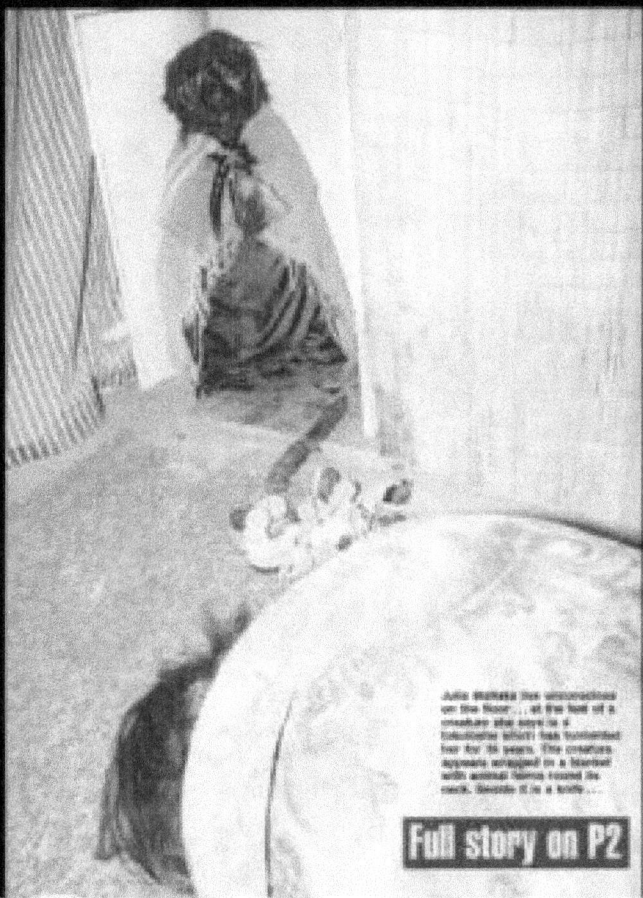

# It has knocked out this woman! Now the creature of evil is trapped!

# TOKOLOSHE!

Julia Matlala lies unconscious on the floor... at the feet of a creature she says is a tokoloshe which has tormented her for 16 years. The creature appears wrapped in a blanket with animal horns round its neck. Beside it is a knife...

Full story on P2

TWO OUTCASTS–
...a boy nobody wanted ...a man who saw no evil
HARRY SHUSTER presents
A MIGHTY AFRICAN ADVENTURE!
TOKOLOSHE
THE EVIL SPIRIT
G
Starring Sidney James & Saul Pelle
with a special guest appearance of Chief Gathsa Mangosuthu Buthelezi
Written & Directed by Peter Prowse Produced by Harry Shuster
an Artists International Distribution Ltd. release
TECHNICOLOR® TECHNISCOPE®

It is a comically obvious fake, but is evidently not a one-off. In April 2011, after the same newspaper had printed a defamatory story about it, the Youth Wing of the ruling ANC (African National Congress) Party not only demanded that the publishers retract their claims and apologise, but also released a public statement in which they sarcastically undertook to "humbly advise their editorial team to continue focusing on reports of witchcraft and tokoloshes" instead of serious political news.[27] Perhaps as a result of such negative comments being made about them by prominent public figures, the *Daily Sun's* owners apparently decided to lay off from carrying so many tokoloshe stories for a while, but in 2012, backed up by market-research which showed that "well over half" of the newspaper's readers loved reading about such things, decided to start printing them again. As the organ's publisher Deon du Plessis put it succinctly, "In this market a tokoloshe every now and then makes the world go round." [28] He, however, did not appear to think that these stories were real himself, though ...

Whilst clearly not everyone in southern Africa believes in the tokoloshe, then, it appears that everybody knows what they are, or are meant to be - amongst them, apparently, the famous Carry-On and *Hancock's Half-Hour* actor Sid James, a native South African, who in 1971 appeared in the film *Tokoloshe, the Evil Spirit*, playing the role of a blind man who helps out a young Zulu boy who has been cursed by a witch-doctor to suffer the attentions of one of these demons. Also starring the Chief of the Zulus, Mangosuthu Buthelezi, playing himself, the film must have helped to spread the notion of the tokoloshe even further, a process only helped by subsequent tokoloshe-inspired movies such as 1999's *A Reasonable Man*, starring Nigel Hawthorne, of *Yes Minister* fame, as a white judge presiding over a case wherein a black man has been accused of murdering a small child under the mistaken impression that it was a tokoloshe, and the more recent, rather schlocky-sounding *Blood Tokoloshe*, in which the notion of the tokoloshe as a demonic, killer-familiar rears its ugly head. (You can see the inadvertently amusing trailer for this no-budget masterpiece - tagline: 'Under your bed, waiting to be fed' - on YouTube; it's well worth a look!)

More pleasantly, perhaps, the tokoloshe is also now a popular children's cartoon character, in the form of a figure named Prince Thabo, described by his creators as being "a tokoloshe for the new South Africa", a kind of benign superhero figure. Created by the author Greg Doolan, initially for a series of books, in the first such tale, 'Prince Thabo's Calling', he is shown being taught magic and then, whilst wearing a special invisibility-ring, being sent out by the elders of his tokoloshe-clan to frighten a little girl by playing poltergeist. However, the young goblin fails in this task, and is therefore rejected by his tribe, after which he decides to dedicate his life to doing good.[29] Needless to say, of course, in these books and cartoons, Prince Thabo's gigantic penis is kept discreetly veiled from impressionable children's view, thereby allowing him (and his author) to escape being placed upon the South African

---

**OPPOSITE: A poster for one of Mr Sidney James' lesser-known movies, 1971's 'Tokoloshe: The Evil Spirit'. Sadly, none of the other 'Carry On' regulars seem to have seen fit to appear in the film with him. What would a tokoloshe have done to Barbara Windsor – or Kenneth Williams, for that matter?**

---

equivalent of the Sex Offenders' Register. From fertility-god to friendly childhood ghost, then; from being worshipped to being used to shift toys and sugary breakfast cereals during commercial breaks. Such is the fate even of the tokoloshe when exposed to the new, far more powerful, god of the contemporary capitalist marketplace.

It is obvious, then, that the original conception of the tokoloshe as being a water-deity has now become, in many respects, fairly outdated, in spite of its occasional vague resurfacing. As southern African society has changed, the tokoloshe has changed with it, again and again, until we arrive at the current point of the creature's evolution: as being nothing less than the 'all-purpose African entity', as we said earlier. He is, in short, whatever you want him to be, whether visible or invisible, benign or malignant, physical or incorporeal, obscene or sanitised. It is time now, then, to examine in more detail some of the more popular modern interpretations of the fiend in order to work out why exactly he has developed in the particular ways that he has. It is a strange and fascinating story, which deserves to be far better known than it actually is.

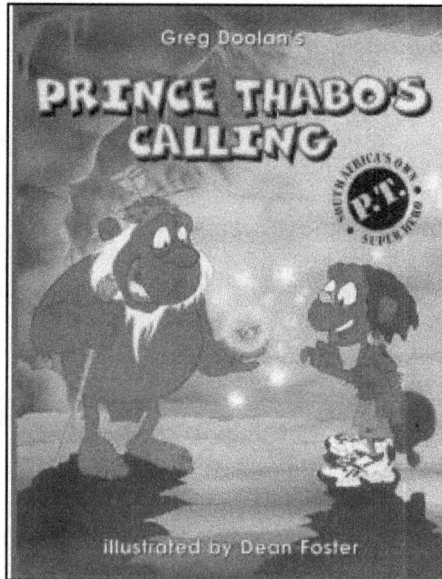

The cover of the first of South African author Greg Doolan's popular children's books about a friendly infant tokoloshe named 'Prince Thabo'. As seems nowadays to be obligatory for such characters, Thabo wears a baseball cap and ridiculously elaborate US-style sneakers. I'm sure he thinks it makes him look 'cool', but it doesn't.

# Chapter One

## A Familiar Story: Tokoloshes and Witchcraft

In 2010, a rather worrying story appeared in Lesotho's press. A frail, diabetic woman of 64, Mamorero Khobai, from the village of Phomolong in the Qoaling region, was attacked by a neighbouring family, and beaten to a pulp - and all for being, allegedly, an evil witch.

Mamorero, it seems, was going to the toilet one morning when she saw a car speeding towards her house. A man named Thabo Khiba jumped out, ran towards her swearing, and claimed that she had been bewitching his wife, Matšeliso. He grabbed her by the neck and started slapping her around, and was soon joined on the scene by Matšeliso's sister and her mother, named Malineo. Malineo was holding a knife and a stone and, after Mamorero had been knocked down to the ground, this angry woman started jumping on the prone grandmother, and smashing her face in with the rock. According to Malineo, Mamorero had cast a spell upon her daughter Matšeliso, meaning that she was being haunted at night by both the astral body of Mamorero's granddaughter Refiloe, and a malicious tokoloshe (or perhaps both ghosts were meant to be differing aspects of one another, the report is not quite clear in this respect).

It was her view that, as such, Mamorero was a witch, and that she was sending out her spirits to torment Matšeliso because she was married whilst Refiloe was not. In fact, Refiloe had just had a baby out of wedlock, and was currently a single mother, a cause of shame in local culture. Jealous of Matšeliso's good fortune, the old woman and her grandchild had thus been colluding to make poor Matšeliso's life a misery - at least in Malineo's view. The young girl had begun having nightmares, and was waking up at night to find the tokoloshe strangling her, as well as giving her instructions to go into some bushes outside, where she would presumably then come to some harm, upon pain of death. Mamorero ended up in hospital due to the severity of her injuries, and Thabo Khiba was ultimately arrested and charged with assault, as well as having his house surrounded by an angry mob seeking to teach him a lesson for picking on a defenceless old woman like that [1].

This is an unedifying story, certainly; but it also raises some interesting questions for us. If Mamorero was a witch (which she wasn't, obviously), then how on earth was she controlling a tokoloshe and making it go out and perform her bidding for her? If a tokoloshe is supposed to be a demon, water-god or evil spirit, then why would it have been under an old woman like

Mamorero's control? Well, the answer lies in yet another similarity between modern African folklore and that of Europe in centuries past; namely, in the unpleasant figure of the witch's familiar.

## Sympathy from the Devil

The definition of a familiar is quite simple; it is a demon or some other kind of spirit, whether malevolent or otherwise, which is under the control of a human being, and which performs various tasks to help them out, either of its own volition or under compulsion from its human master. One pleasant type of familiar from European folklore was that breed of hairy fairy known as the brownie, which was meant to perform certain tasks around the household or farmstead at night, such as sweeping up or helping to bring in the crops. The physical similarities between brownies and tokoloshes have already been alluded to by us, and a further connection can be found in the fact that there is, in fact, an account in existence of a tokoloshe washing up dishes and cleaning a South African woman's house for her, much as friendly European brownies were meant to do, though it is sadly vague in its nature [2]. (Perhaps this element of the myth was why one young South African boy claimed to have once seen tokoloshes in the form of "creatures like monkeys wearing aprons" fleeing from out of his house one night - most appropriate clothing for one's domestic staff! [3])

However, whilst there are these very occasional reports of tokoloshes being friendly to members of the general public, mostly their role as helpful household entity is restricted to one specific category of person; the witch. Witches in Europe, of course, were once often claimed to have their own little helper-demons called familiars bestowed upon them by the Devil in return for signing over to him their immortal souls, as well. The alleged workload of a stereotypical witch was heavy, what with all those people to kill and spells to cast, so it seems that Satan was meant to have taken pity upon his followers and given them some free household help. Brownies may have been one pleasant variety of European household familiar, but the evil figure of the witch's demon-familiar was one which loomed rather larger in the popular mind of Medieval and Renaissance man. Generally, these European familiars appeared in the form of ordinary-looking and common animals, such as cats, dogs, hares, toads, bats, birds and insects, but sometimes little black or brown hairy men not unlike tokoloshes were reported as being amongst their number too. For example when, in 1653, a small boy from the village of Benenden in Kent began to wake up in the night suffering from nightmares and shouting out things like "Father! Father! Here comes a black hairy thing will tease and kill me!" it was not a difficult matter for a local diviner to conclude that a suspected witch named Bess Wood had sent out one of her pet hairy humanoid demons to torment the child. [4]

Frequently, these spirits were said to be shape-shifters, and appeared composite in form, having the qualities of many different animals at once, such as in the following description of a familiar named 'Vinegar Tom', extracted from an alleged witch named Elizabeth Clark by England's notorious

---

**OPPOSITE: Some horned demons with faces rather like those of apes torment sinners in Hell, as seen in this illustration from a sixteenth-century French manuscript.**

---

**A demon-familiar in the form of a weird half-hedgehog, half-owl creature; from an English witch-trial pamphlet dated 1579.**

'Witch-Finder General', Matthew Hopkins. Tom, apparently, was "like a longlegg'd greyhound with a head like an ox, with a long tail and broad eyes", and yet who was also able to transform himself into "the shape of a child of four years old without a head" [5]. Obviously, such confessions were frequently produced under conditions of extreme pressure and are often somewhat less than reliable to say the least, but this description of Vinegar Tom does at least show what familiars were sometimes conceived of as looking like. Hairy, non-existent animals with the ability to shape-shift and appear in humanoid form are not exactly a modern African invention, then.

Accounts of European familiars and demons appearing as apes and bears, meanwhile - the two animals which the tokoloshe is most frequently said to resemble - were also hardly unknown during the Renaissance. You only have to look at an artistic depiction of Hell from the time in order to be able to spot images of hairy bipedal imps with monkey-faces roasting sinners alive on spits and so forth, for example, something which was occasionally mirrored in accounts from real-life English witch-trials. In 1579, for instance, the Berkshire witch Elizabeth Style claimed to have first met her pet familiar sitting beneath a tree in some woods, "sometimes in the shape of an ape, and otherwhiles like a horse", whilst a 1566 Chelmsford witch-trial featured testimony from an Agnes Brown that she had witnessed her neighbour's demonic familiar in the form of "a black dog with a face like an ape, a short tail, a chain and a silver whistle ... about his neck, and a pair of horns on his head." [6] (One query, though: would most English common-folk of this period have known what an ape looked like?)

Matthew Hopkins himself, likewise, once claimed to have been bothered at night by a familiar in the form of a ghostly bear, which had been sent out to try to kill him by the witches he was then investigating, an assertion which we must of course treat with much suspicion given the man's self-serving desire for social advancement and power at the expense of innocent people's lives. But for him to have presented this alleged assault to the public at large as being a plausible one to have occurred does show that European familiars, too, were once thought of in the popular mind as being able to take on the form of bears [7]. Higher demons in the hierarchy of Hell, too, could adopt this guise, apparently; in 1646 a labourer named John Winnick from the Cambridgeshire village of Molesworth, for instance, confessed to selling his soul to a powerful demon which appeared to him in the barn where he was working in the form of "a Spirit, blacke and shaggy, and having pawes like a Beare, but in bulk not fully so big as a Coney [i.e a rabbit or hare]." This weird mini-bear offered him money and two imp-familiars in the form of a cat and a rabbit if Winnick would agree to forsake God and bow down and worship him instead, a condition to which he supposedly agreed [8].

Even Satan himself would sometimes appear in the form of an ape - or goat, dog or toad, depending upon his mood - at the notorious witches' sabbats, unholy ceremonies to which sorceresses were supposed to fly away on broomsticks every so often in order to display their fealty to their satanic master. As well as kissing the bare arse of the Devil whilst he was in animal form, the witches were also meant to have sex with him either whilst he was still in the shape of a beast, or after he had transformed himself into a black man; his penis was often spoken of as being unnaturally large and hard, too, just like a tokoloshe's, and his semen was often freezing cold and painful to the touch. As this idea implies, the notion of demon-on-human sex (often termed 'demonialitas' or 'incubism') was central to the old European witchcraft-mania, and the familiars bestowed upon witches by Satan were frequently spoken of as having to provide sexual services to their new owners as part of their reward for selling their souls and turning against God. This is also a persistent - indeed, perhaps the most persistent - element of the modern association of tokoloshes with witchcraft in Africa as well, as tokoloshes, too, are said to perform various sexual activities for their witch-mistresses, their gigantic genitals allegedly providing them with much illicit satisfaction.

**Familiar Relations**
For example, the South African sociologist Isak Niehaus collected a tale about a female teacher/witch who kept a tokoloshe in bed with her in order to act as her lover. When her husband got beneath the sheets with her at night, he claimed that he could feel a furry creature lying there between them, which reacted angrily to his presence by slapping him unconscious [9]. Once a witch has experienced tokoloshe-sex, it seems, she cannot ever go back to coupling with human males, as this yarn seemingly symbolises. A tokoloshe's genitals just provide so much more pleasure than a human's can; a tokoloshe will ruin any woman for normal men, apparently. Witches can have other familiars who provide them with sexual services as well, though, such as the impundulu - a kind of bird-spirit looking something like a small ostrich, with beautiful, soft and velvety feathers, whose very touch is said to create uncontrollable sexual desire in a woman, whether she be a witch or not. The other main feature of the impundulu, meanwhile, is its unnaturally thick and long tongue, which it uses to pleasure its witch-mistress with; what the penis is to the tokoloshe, the tongue is to the impundulu, it seems [10].

This all probably sounds quite comical to Western ears, of course, but perhaps it should not. After all, during the European witch-panic of the 1500s and 1600s, accounts of witches supposedly engaging in bizarre sexual acts with their familiars were just as common as such tales are in southern Africa today. To give but a few examples from English witch-trials, for instance, we can read of a woman named Margaret Bayts who had, supposedly, been given two pet imps by Satan which followed her around everywhere she went hidden beneath her skirt. They pleasured her whilst she went about her housework, and also of one of her neighbours was bewitched so that she became bothered by two invisible butterfly-demons which began living inside her vagina, causing certain sensations to be felt by her whilst they fluttered about in there. One other English 'witch' of the period, meanwhile, testified that she had allowed the Devil to send out two gigantic flying beetles to her in her bed at night, so that they could engage in horrible insect-threesomes with her [11]. A woman named Margaret Legat, likewise, who was accused of being a witch by the villagers of Playford near Ipswich in 1645, was allegedly witnessed allowing a demonic mole to crawl beneath her skirt and begin suckling food from what are termed delicately her "secret parts", presumably thereby also giving her oral sex in the process [12]. These testimonies, I would submit, are no more absurd than their modern African equivalents concerning tokoloshes are. Indeed, probably they are even more so!

But why is there this sexual association in existence between the witch and her pet tokoloshe? What caused such an idea to develop in the first place? Well, obviously, if you are talking about a demon which is notorious for having a massive penis cohabiting with a single woman - as most witches stereotypically are - then rumours such as this are bound to spring up. However, there is a further layer of meaning to this notion; namely, it lies in the idea that witches, by definition, lack something which is sometimes known in South Africa as maitshwaro - or a sense of good conduct and character, and feelings of solidarity and shared humanity with one's fellow humans. In short, witches are supposed to be wholly evil, and as such to be completely dominated by their desire for base things such as money, power, revenge ... and, of course, non-loving sex [13]. Thus, their alleged craving for tokoloshe-penis is simply another way of characterising them as being immoral and governed entirely by their lower instincts. By having sex with well-endowed animal-like beings, they are metaphorically characterised as being beast-like themselves, and thus dangerous and disgusting. To put it crudely, they will shag anything - even big, hairy, baboon-demons - so watch out!

It has often been noted by scholars that witches are habitually depicted as being inversions of prevailing societal norms - they are frequently supposed to walk backwards, have reversed feet or to sleep upside-down like bats, for instance - and this is just yet another instance of that particular motif at play. As women, their traditional 'moral' role in southern African society would be to have sex in order to procreate, to raise the next generation of children and thereby to fulfil their expected status as loving mothers. Tokoloshes, though, do not get their lovers pregnant (unless it is with dead or disabled children, as we shall see later), so the sex that the

---

**OPPOSITE: A 1639 pamphlet concerning the antics of the well-known English fairy-familiar Robin Goodfellow, here depicted as being a little tokoloshe-like; he is hairy and has a massive erection, for instance.**

---

# ROBIN

## GOOD-FELLOW,

### HIS MAD PRANKES AND MERRY IESTS.

Full of honeſt Mirth, and is a ſit Medicine
for Melancholy.

Printed at *London* by *Thomas Cotes*, and are to be ſold by
*Francis Grove*, at his ſhop on Snow-hill, neere the
Sarazens-head. 1639

witches are thought of as having with their familiars is conceived of as being purely for carnal pleasure, thereby setting them up as being a danger for traditional notions of society and the family-unit. Probably in the case with which we opened this chapter, for instance, such ideas were at play somewhere inside the heads of those involved; the granddaughter and alleged sorceress Refiloe, for example, was a single mother, implying to those who might disapprove of such a state of affairs that she had an uncontrollable, witch-like sexual appetite. Furthermore, the idea that her grandmother Mamorero was sending out tokoloshes purely in order to destroy the happiness of a more traditional family-unit, in which a mother had married the father of her child instead of having it out of wedlock, is also highly suggestive of the idea of witches being thought of as being implacably opposed to the way that normal society is meant to work.

**Feed Me!**
Indeed, so opposed are witches meant to be to societal norms that it sometimes seems almost as though the tokoloshe is actually the witch's baby. Instead of looking after human children and raising the next generation of people, African witches are seen as inverting the role of motherhood by raising evil demons, which will go out to try and destroy society instead. In return for receiving the tokoloshe's sexual services, and as reward for them going out and causing mischief, illness and even death for those whom the witches decide to curse, their mistresses feed their spirits and cook for them by leaving them out gifts of milk, butter and food. This again, is just like many ordinary Europeans used to do for brownies in order to thank them for helping out around the household, and just as European witches supposedly once did in order to placate their own familiars, too. Putting salt in this food, however, will apparently prove harmful to the tokoloshe, which seems to be a further crossing-over point with European conceptions of demons and evil spirits, which were also meant to have an aversion to salt for whatever reason.

Interestingly, witches can also nourish their tokoloshes by breast-feeding them; another unnatural perversion of the traditional female role as mother-figure, which is also paralleled by the old European belief that witches had secret, hidden extra nipples which they used to suckle their own familiars with, too (actually, when discovered by their prosecutors,

A horned demon-familiar with the face of an ape and the body of a dog, and with a chain and whistle tied around its neck, as depicted in an English witch-trial pamphlet of 1566.

**A demonic familiar in the form of a headless bear as depicted in an English pamphlet from 1613. There are few claimed visual forms of the tokoloshe which have not had their parallels in the European demonology of the past.**

these 'secret nipples' were usually just quite ordinary things like moles, scars, freckles and skin-tags - or even, in those cases where demons were said to suckle at the witch's genitals, perhaps, over-large clitorises). For example, from English witch-trial records alone, we can read accounts of women allowing familiars in the shape of cats and even hedgehogs to suck the milk from their breasts, just as if they were their beloved children [14]. Supposedly, familiars drank not just milk from these 'witch's marks', as they were known, but also warm blood for sustenance, as if they were vampires.

Where the modern African witch is also a real mother, though, it seems that it is a fair bet that at least some of her offspring will be said to turn out to be witches, too. For example, it is believed amongst some of the Sotho people of South Africa and Lesotho that, once a witch has given birth, she will throw each of her new-born babies against a wall in order to test out

**Imps in the form of little black humanoids – like tokoloshes – pay homage to their master Satan in this old English woodcut. They, too, appear to have erections, some of which are rather pointy in their nature.**

whether they have inherited her powers or not. If the infant manages to cling to the wall like a bat, instead of just falling down to the floor in pain, then that baby will also grow up to be a witch, apparently. Accordingly, the mother-witch from then on begins suckling her chosen child with a secret stash of magical breast-milk which is intended to encourage her offspring's own supernatural abilities to grow. Her normal babies, meanwhile, just get her average normal milk to feed on [15]. It seems likely that such beliefs have fed into modern myths about the tokoloshe, too, influencing the form they now take.

Some people who are not actually witches misguidedly feel that they can control the tokoloshe with offerings of food left out for it as well, however. In April 1999, for instance, two car thieves were arrested by South African police in the town of Groutville in KwaZulu-Natal Province. Inside their stolen car, the officers found a human skull left out on a plate. Upon looking inside this macabre object, a piece of bloody animal-meat was found. The thieves said that it was an offering for the tokoloshe, which they had invoked in order to protect them from harm or being caught by the law during their crime-spree. Evidently, however, this precaution did not work [16]. Usually you need specifically to be a witch in order to be able to control a tokoloshe properly, then, it seems.

Clearly, therefore, the tokoloshe, in its role of familiar, is conceived of as being under the direct control of its witch-mistress (or, sometimes, wizard-master). Strangely, this feat is supposed to be quite easy to achieve; the witch is said to be able to keep her tokoloshe docile and obedient simply by cutting the fringe of long hair, which is meant to hang down over its eyes. This gives her power over the entity, much as Delilah tamed Samson by depriving him of his strength-giving locks. In this conception of the beast, then, the tokoloshe is less evil in and of itself than it is a means of doing evil at the behest of someone who is so disposed; like a kitchen-knife in the hands of a murderer, perhaps. Because of his widely believed association with witchcraft, however, it seems that the tokoloshe can easily be blamed by the average person for any misfortune which they suffer, be it illness, crop failure or the death of cattle, whether these things actually occurred entirely naturally or not. This is yet another crossover with former European conceptions of witches and their familiars, who were also once blamed for causing such appalling and damaging things.

Of course, though, as in the case with which we opened this chapter, blaming a tokoloshe for your misfortune is perhaps only an intermediary step in this whole chain of reasoning. Once Malineo had decided that her daughter Matšeliso was being strangled in the night by a tokoloshe, she then had to follow this up by inventing a theory about who had sent it out to do her harm, settling ultimately upon the entirely innocent figure of poor old Mamorero. The idea of a tokoloshe, with all of its magical powers to do evil, then, being under the control of a supposed 'witch', is only a means to an end; it allows a person to create themselves a convenient scapegoat to take any anger they might have about their misfortunes out upon. This is one of the standard sociological explanations as to how and why belief in malicious witchcraft develops and is then sustained anywhere, of course.

**The Discovery of Witchcraft**
Perhaps we should just pause for a moment here, however, in order to give a little context to this whole situation, and discuss the extent of witchcraft beliefs in modern-day Africa. It may not be terribly politically-correct to say it, but belief in the reality of magic in the continent seems to be endemic. Obviously, not everyone in sub-Saharan Africa believes in the literal reality of witchcraft, but many do, something which has allowed witch-hunts to become common in certain African countries over recent years. The numbers are shocking; for example, in South Africa's Limpopo Province alone, between 1985 and 1995, 200 people were lynched after being accused of practising witchcraft, whilst between 1994 and 1998 in Tanzania, an astonishing 5,000 alleged sorcerers were killed by mobs [17]. In societies where poverty, lack of education, warfare, crime, disease, social unrest and various other unpleasant realities of life are much more prevalent than they currently are in the West, traditional witchcraft beliefs seem to have flourished. A common way of explaining people's belief in witchcraft, even of the most absurd kind, is that it provides desperate and powerless people with some degree of hope in their everyday lives in a world without the welfare state safety-nets, and levels of economic development which we now take for granted here in the West.

This, it would seem, is a reasonable theory to apply to the state of affairs in Africa today.

In addition, of course, belief in the reality of witchcraft has also been aided by the activities of certain evangelical churches active across the continent, whose pastors promulgate the idea of a heated battle between God and Satan raging on invisibly behind the scenes of everyday life. This notion, being spread around by figures of authority such as self-styled 'prophets' and preachers, has had much influence upon the upsurge of belief in, and persecution of, African witches in the modern day. Furthermore, the continuing high status of witch-doctors in African society is another contributory factor towards many indigenous people's belief in magic and so forth. It is important to note that witch-doctors are not witches in the sense we have so far been talking about them above, however. They are not inherently evil, are not supposed to be in league with the Devil, are very often male, and are generally meant to do good for their clients, even though some can 'turn rogue', and begin casting black magic spells if they so wish.

Known by such names as inyangas, marabouts, tsikamutandas and sangomas, they are consulted by ordinary people for help, providing such services as healing the sick, contacting dead ancestors, telling the future, interpreting dreams and providing advice and good luck charms, as well as being used to cast out demons or counteract the adverse effects of evil spells. Witch-doctors can make use of tokoloshes, according to popular belief - indeed, some people say that they live inside the witch-doctors' huts and homes, hiding away in the darkness behind their magical paraphernalia during the daylight hours [18] - but would perhaps be just as likely to be hired in order to perform a kind of traditional exorcism in order to dispel one. The powers of these shaman-like holy men are widely accepted in sub-Saharan Africa, and everyone from Prime Ministers to high-flying businessmen consult them, not just the ignorant and uneducated poor. Some accounts of their doings even imply that some of them might have genuine powers. The prominent position of witch-doctors in modern African society, then, only reinforces the general social consensus that magic and witchcraft - whether black or white in nature - is genuinely real and a force to be reckoned with.

However, the above discussion being very short, is - of course - a little oversimplified in its nature. I don't want to paint a picture of every African country as being poor and chaotic, or of every black African as being a rabid believer in the reality of witchcraft, because self-evidently these stereotypes are not in any way true. But nonetheless, social conditions across much of the continent seem to be such that belief in magic and demonology is still as strong over there as it was over here in the Middle Ages. In such a world, belief in witches, and in their tokoloshe-servants, is not perhaps as weird as it might initially appear to most European or American readers upon first picking up this book. After all, if most people around you think that tokoloshes are real, then wouldn't you probably do so, as well? These are widely socially-sanctioned beliefs and, whilst they might appear to be amusing to us, it does not necessarily mean that the people who hold them are stupid. They are merely taking their cue from the beliefs and structure of the wider society around them - just as you would most probably have done had you been unfortunate enough to have been born in Medieval Europe at the height of the witch-burning craze.

**Double Trouble**

How does an African witch get hold of a tokoloshe, though? Does he or she conjure it up like a spirit, or create it from scratch using esoteric and macabre magical practices? Accounts of this particular aspect of witch-lore are, as might be expected, highly inconsistent and contradictory in their nature. Obviously, evangelical pastors who preach to their congregations about the dangers of tokoloshes often tend to say that they are sent up to aid witches from Hell by the Devil. But others claim that sorceresses manufacture them by means of some kind of magical animal fat which they use to rub down the corpses of ordinary domestic dogs and cats with, thereby miraculously transforming them into tokoloshes somehow (some descriptions of tokoloshes do indeed claim that their faces have certain unspecified cat-like features about them - particularly a bizarre toilet-dwelling sub-species of tokoloshe known as pinky-pinky which we shall examine in more detail later) [19].

Other people, however, say that it is the corpse of a child that is transformed by the application of magical fat, and not of a pet. Yet others, meanwhile, maintain that tokoloshes are essentially some form of pre-existing spiritual entities, and that they are inherited by witches from their mothers (perhaps a reflection of the occasionally-voiced opinion that they are essentially ancestral spirits associated with representatives of certain tribes and clans, like the Irish banshee) [20]. More rarely, it is claimed that a witch taking some kind of magical plant-root into their house and planting it causes the root to transform itself into a tokoloshe, which sounds a little like certain old European beliefs involving the creation of homunculi (tiny artificial men) from the vaguely human-looking mandrake-root [21]. A downside of some of these processes, though, is that in return for the creation of a tokoloshe, a member of the witch's family must die within the year for some unspecified reason [22]. Another possible disadvantage of creating a tokoloshe for a sorceress, meanwhile, is that killing one is supposed to lead to the death of its witch-controller as well, or at least to rob her of her magic powers, such is the supposed strength of their mystical connection to one another.

This last belief speaks of an associated idea, namely the notion that the tokoloshe is actually the witch herself, but in alternative form, the two being simply differing aspects of one another, much like the relationship between a werewolf and his human counterpart was said to be in old European belief. At night, according to this opinion, the witches smear themselves all over in their magical animal-fat and then assume the form of a baboon-like tokoloshe, going out to do mischief - most commonly in the shape of an ape or monkey, raping those men and women whom the witch most desires. At other times, though, it is alleged that the relationship is reversed and that the tokoloshe transforms itself into a double of the witch, allowing the sorceress to fly away into the night to do evil whilst the transformed tokoloshe remains tucked up inside her bed until morning, thereby averting suspicion away from her. Apparently, these tokoloshe-doubles are meant to be quite convincing; one story, for example, is told of a young South African man who was going out with the daughter of a well-known local witch. Presumably, he did not suspect that the younger woman was a witch too, as he turned up in her bedroom one night wanting to sleep with her. Whilst having his way with her, however, he was somewhat disturbed to find that, whilst she looked entirely normal, her skin felt unusually hairy and cold to the touch. When he began speaking to her and his girlfriend's voice responded to him coming from outside the room, he realised that he was actually having sex with a disguised tokoloshe and fled away from the house, terrified [23].

There are several interesting aspects to such unlikely accounts. For one thing, we have here yet another similarity with old European witchcraft beliefs, as it was once believed that, when European witches were off out flying to worship the Devil at their sabbats, Satan would provide them with magical dolls or dummies, often termed supposita, or sometimes eidolons, which they could place inside their beds at night. Seeing as these supposita were the exact doubles of the witches themselves, if their husbands should happen to awake during the night then they would be unable to tell the difference, thereby providing the evil sorceresses with the perfect alibi [24].

Another parallel with old European witch and werewolf-beliefs, meanwhile, comes in the idea of African witches rubbing themselves down with 'magical fat' in order to facilitate their hideous transformations into tokoloshes. European witches, too, were meant to make use of special ointments, which they would spread over their bodies in order to effect their transformations into animals, or to enable them to fly through the air to their secret sabbats. This is also similar to some accounts in existence from Medieval and early Renaissance werewolf trials, wherein the accused confessed to rubbing themselves down with certain ointments and salves, supposedly given to them by the Devil and then boiled up in the fat from murdered children, which enabled them to become wolves. Seeing as these mixtures apparently often contained substances such as henbane, deadly nightshade, belladonna and opium, some scholars and commentators have speculated that stories of people rubbing themselves down with such things and then thinking that they had become animals could actually have been based in fact. After all, many of these ingredients are notorious hallucinogens! [25] Maybe some modern African witches really do rub themselves down with strange substances in order to transform themselves into tokoloshe-baboons, then; in their own minds, at least ...

**Shamanic Strangeness**
Furthermore, we have in the idea that the witch and the tokoloshe-baboon are simply two differing aspects of one another some interesting echoes of ancient shamanic practices. The idea of therianthropy, or people being able to transform themselves into animals, has a long history. However, it was not always the case that such a transformation was believed in as taking place physically, in a literal sense. For example, the Naga people of north-eastern India once believed that their shamans were capable of becoming leopards. This did not mean that they thought that they were physically able to shape-shift, but rather that, during altered states of consciousness, some part of their souls was able to be projected out into the leopards. When a sleeping shaman was tossing and turning about, for example, it was said that his leopard-twin was being hunted in the night; and if the leopard should get harmed, then his human 'brother' would find that exactly corresponding wounds would suddenly appear upon his own body, too, from out of thin air. The human and the beast, it might be said, were thus imagined as being 'psychic twins' [26].

According to the famous scholar of religion Mircea Eliade, such shamanic practices would once originally have had the function of allowing a shaman to go into a kind of trance or ecstasy during which they felt that their souls would exit from their bodies and then wander through the Otherworld in the form of their animal-counterpart, or 'tutelary spirit'. From ancient times, Eliade says, such animal spirits were seen as being psychopomps, or 'soul-guides', for people when they passed on into the afterlife. By turning his spirit temporarily into that of an animal through ecstatic practices, then, the shaman thus essentially becomes his own psychopomp, taking on the animal-spirit's powers and abilities in order to be able to navigate safely the land of the dead [27]. It seems likely that in such ancient ideas lie the ultimate origins of the European werewolf myth - and, perhaps, that of the tokoloshe as being the witch's baboon-double, too.

The notion that, by killing a tokoloshe you kill its witch-mistress also has parallels with shamanism and more specifically with a phenomenon known as 'sympathetic wounding'. Many readers will no doubt be familiar with old folk-tales about a werewolf having its paw chopped off and then, later on, an old woman being found with her own corresponding hand having been severed as well, thereby revealing that she was in fact the fiend in alternative form. This is what is meant by the term 'sympathetic wounding'; you injure a monster/spirit, and the same wounds are later found upon the body of its human counterpart also, just like was meant to happen with the Naga people's leopard-shamans. Shamans, it is said, were once meant to challenge each other to psychic duels in the shape of their respective animal-souls, the loser taking his wounds and eventual demise back to his own human body once the spectral fight had finished. Was this form of astral combat, perhaps, the ultimate source of the 'sympathetic wounding' myth found both in old European tales of werewolves and in certain modern African stories of tokoloshe-witchcraft?

Maybe. After all, we can find examples of this kind of motif being associated specifically with witches as well as with werewolves in European records far more often than we might initially presume to be the case. For example, the famous Scottish witch Isobel Gowdie, who confessed to her supposed crimes in 1662, claimed that she and her coven could transform themselves into small animals like cats and crows. She, however, liked to shape-shift into a hare, in which disguise she said she had once nearly been torn apart by the teeth of some hounds. Other witches known to her, she said, had actually been bitten by dogs whilst in animal-form, however, and their wounds still remained visible upon them as clear evidence of their guilt [28].

Many scholars view such tales from the European witch-panic as being remnants of ancient shamanic beliefs and practices, which had altered somehow over time and shifted around to reflect new, contemporary concerns and ideas about witchcraft. European witches, prior to (and after) the witch-panic of the 1500s and 1600s, were not necessarily always conceived of as being evil, after all. Rather, they were thought of by many ordinary folk as being much more like African witch-doctors are today - indeed, the phrase 'witch-doctor' is actually a native English term, not the anglicised version of a pre-existing African word, and was once used to describe a breed of benign 'white' witches who formerly lived in the British countryside. Other terms for them included 'wise women' and 'cunning folk', and, whilst they were thought of as being able to provide curses, they were generally consulted to provide healing potions for ailments and suchlike, as with African sangomas and inyangas today. In such figures - far removed from the demonic stereotype of witches propagated by the

Medieval and early Renaissance Church and its allies - many modern scholars, most notably Emma Wilby, have seen echoes of an archaic shamanic past. Perhaps the alleged ability of certain women such as Isobel Gowdie to shape-shift into animal form, then, would once have been viewed positively by people, as being able to be used for good, before such notions were later defined as being very definitely 'demonic' by the Medieval Church.

If this is true, then it seems possible that a similar process has perhaps now begun to occur in modern-day Africa, too. After all, many witch-doctors - being, as they are, essentially shamans - are supposed to have had the magical ability to transform themselves into a wide variety of native animals, from lions to crocodiles. It is just that, nowadays, perhaps due to white European and evangelical Christian influence, such abilities are viewed in a more negative way than they once were in the past. Astonishingly, belief in 'evil witches' - as opposed to in the more neutral concept of magic itself, *per se* - is actually on the rise in southern Africa today, due to a variety of social, economic and religious factors. This can be seen in the fact that, around the turn of the twentieth century, witch-killings did not usually take place in countries like South Africa. The number of persons publicly accused of being witches and of performing black magic was actually lower than it is today back then, and offenders were often simply fined money or grain by tribal chiefs rather than being burned, lynched or torn to shreds by frenzied mobs [29].

Now, however, the public mood towards the notion of witchcraft has changed quite dramatically, and tales of people transforming into baboons, tokoloshes or other creatures are likely to be less tolerated by the general public than they once were. As such, the practice of therianthropy is nowadays usually ascribed in the popular mind to evil witches rather than to potentially benign witch-doctors, the original beneficial and religious functions of such abilities being now long-since forgotten. The southern African belief in the ability of witches to transform themselves into sexually-rapacious baboons, then, might initially seem insane to Westerners coming to the idea fresh, but it is not so; it most likely evolved from out of older, much more archaic, beliefs, rather than simply being conjured up from out of nowhere. That, at least, is my own theory about the matter.

**I Walked With a Zombie**
There is one final contrasting body of opinion regarding tokoloshe-manufacture, though, which is particularly interesting, viewing them, as it does, as being artificial but corporeal creations, something like zombies, on behalf of evil sorcerers, rather than as spirits or demons or anything like that. According to this particular belief, after stealing a fresh corpse from its grave, the witch or wizard who wishes to transform the dead body into a tokoloshe is said to remove the eyes and tongue from its head and then thrust a heated iron rod into its skull, thereby somehow causing the body to shrink down to dwarf-size. After this, a secret powder of some kind is blown into the empty mouth of the body whilst certain magical incantations are said, thereby imbuing the tokoloshe-zombie with both some kind of life and a sense of total obedience to its master or mistress [30]. The witches and wizards involved can then either choose to keep the zombie for their own usage, or sell it on to others in order to make themselves a handsome profit.

Amazingly, advertisements for such tokoloshe-zombies sometimes pop up in the African press. A 2010 news report from Botswana, for example, about the nefarious activities of a local sorcerer named Dr Imrani, is most instructive. Dr Imrani takes out regular advertisements in Botswana's newspapers, claiming that he can lengthen people's penises ("10 to 25cm within a day!"), give them semi-permanent erections, or cause their spouses to return through magic, as well as offering what are termed "short boys and rats to gain good life". These 'short-boys', he explained to a curious reporter who went to seek him out after seeing his ads, were nothing less than tokoloshes.

He defined these as being the corpses of the dead, which he went out to local graveyards at night to fetch, using his magical powers in order to call them forth from the grave. Occasionally the corpses of particularly devout Christians refused to resurrect themselves, he explained matter-of-factly, but in general the dead bodies would do exactly as he said. Once a dead body had dug itself up from out of the ground, Dr Imrani said that he would then carry it away and breathe more life into it, at the same time whispering certain instructions into its ear on behalf of the clients who had commissioned him to create them a tokoloshe. This treatment, apparently, had the effect of shrinking down the corpses, leading to him giving them their nickname of 'short boys'. Once he had performed this task, the tokoloshes would become his clients' property, performing slave-labour for them at night such as laying bricks or performing farm-work. In this way, entire undead labour-forces could be created from tokoloshes, saving smart businessmen money on wages and administration. Zombies, it seems, are the ideal employees; they work long hours without complaint, never get sick or take a day off, and don't even have their own trade union [31].

At this point, the reader might begin to feel a little puzzled, however. Little stakhanovite zombie-men do not sound much like the tokoloshes which we have been discussing so far. They are not hairy, they are not horny, and they don't have to lug their massive swollen balls around over their shoulders with them everywhere they go. So how are they tokoloshes, then? The answer lies, apparently, within an old and now fairly well-known African folk-tale.

In his popular book *Indaba, My Children*, the prominent Zulu sangoma and spiritual leader Credo Mutwa explained to his public that the common perception of a tokoloshe as being a kind of hairy sprite, which lives in pools or rivers and is controlled by witches and wizards, is in fact entirely false. Fortunately, however, he knew exactly how the first tokoloshe had been created, and revealed the secret to the world by telling an entertaining little story. Mutwa's tale is set long, long ago, "before the Bantu had moved south of the Zambezi" (the Zulu equivalent of 'once upon a time', perhaps), when there lived in the land a murderous tyrant named Kambela, who raped and killed all the wives and daughters of a local witch-doctor named Mulundi before then throwing their dead bodies into the river to be eaten up by the crocodiles. Perhaps unsurprisingly, Mulundi at once swore revenge upon the evil chieftain.

Knowing of the old wizard's strong magical powers, Kambela became scared and began hiding himself away inside his kraal, with all of the gates shut up and a stockade placed all around it, guarded by his fierce warriors. However, just outside this stockade grew a large marula tree, whose branches extended over into the compound. It was from this tree that

Mulundi's tokoloshe - the first one ever created in all of history - dropped down to gain its master's revenge. Jumping from the branches onto his enemy's roof, the tokoloshe managed to make use of its tiny body to squeeze through the gaps in the grass thatching and down into the room below. The evil Kambela, lying drunk in this hut, awoke suddenly in the middle of the night to find a hideous dwarf squatting down over his body. It wore a mask and costume made up entirely from the skin and fur of some slaughtered baboons, and around its neck the monster carried the decomposing severed head of a woman. In its hands were a bow and an arrow with a poisoned tip. Before Kambela could scream for help, the tokoloshe loosed his arrow into the chief's bowels, killing him instantly, before letting out a loud sound of insane laughter into the night sky. Kambela's soldiers came rushing in to see what had happened, but could find no sign of the murderer, no footprints, and no indication of how the killer could have entered the place, the tokoloshe having scrambled away back out up through the gaps in the roof. All they could see was their dead leader, lying on the floor with the arrow in his flesh.

The first tokoloshe, then, was a murderer, albeit of someone who probably deserved it. But how did the wizard Mulundi create it in the first place? According to Credo Mutwa, the answer was quite simple. First, the witch-doctor had captured a particularly small pygmy and then kept him prisoner, forcing him to endure an extreme diet so that he would grow extremely skinny. Then, he transformed him into a brain-dead zombie by rather uncharitably sticking a large awl (a kind of pointed spike, generally used for making holes in wood and leather) into his head, presumably through his ears, and removing certain parts of his grey-matter. After the pygmy had been killed in this way, the newly-created tokoloshe-zombie no longer had any will of his own and was thus primed to do Mulundi's bidding.

The wizard's work was not finished yet, however. Wishing to make the zombie's appearance as disturbing as possible, he tore the hides off from some dead baboons, sewed them together and covered his tiny slave in them, as well as digging up some body-parts from their graves and festooning them all about him, hence the rotting head which dangled down from the being's neck. Once Mulundi had first done this, other witch-doctors, liking the idea, then copied it for their own ends and, ever since, tokoloshes have been on the loose in southern Africa, either killing their owners' enemies by giving them heart-attacks due to the horrifying baboon/corpse-costumes they wear, or working on their farms for the rest of their 'lives' for free [32]. And that, says Credo Mutwa, is the story of how the tokoloshe got its baboon-skin; a fable altogether more gruesome and unsettling than anything that is to be found in any of Kipling's *Just So* stories ...

Mutwa's legend, however, seems to have several competing, variant versions of it abroad amongst southern African folk-tale tellers and rumour-mongers. For example, one old belief amongst some Africans was that, whenever twins were born, the first one to come out was a genuine human child, but the second was in fact some kind of evil spirit attempting to enter

**OPPOSITE: A witch's menagerie of demon-familiars, from a 1621 drawing. They have various forms, but one of them could be viewed as looking suspiciously like a mutant ape or tokoloshe ...**

into the world in corporeal form by fooling its unwitting 'parents' into looking after it. According to legend, sangomas on the lookout for new zombie-slaves would get hold of these second twins somehow, and then raise them as animals, hoping to make them vicious and inhuman in their nature. These kidnapped children, allegedly, were forced to commit unspeakable acts by the witch-doctors, such as torturing small animals or killing other kidnapped babies, so that they would later do their master's evil bidding without any moral protest once they were old enough. The sangoma would then wrap these beast-children up in furs and animal skins (presumably from baboons) and make use of them in his rituals, telling people that they were really his army of evil tokoloshes [33]. This myth itself sounds rather similar to yet another witch-doctor's familiar from South African legend, meanwhile, the notorious chitukwane, or 'thin child' - the reanimated zombie-corpse of a mutilated infant used by the sorcerer to perform his or her nefarious bidding after nightfall [34]. The modern idea of the tokoloshe-as-zombie, it seems, has merged over time with both of these myths, incorporating their details into its own, ever-expanding narrative.

### Zombies Ate My Porridge

These are all very nice (or not) little folk-stories, of course, but there is more to the original African version of the zombie-myth than this. Today in the West, our view of what zombies are, what they look like and how they act, has been irredeemably corrupted forever by Hollywood films and Japanese videogames, ever since the release of George A Romero's seminal film *Night of the Living Dead* in 1968. Subsequent depictions of zombies in our popular culture, from movies such as *The Evil Dead* and *28 Days Later* to popular video games such as *Resident Evil, Plants vs Zombies* and *Zombies Ate My Neighbours*, have generally depicted them as being relentless - if somewhat dozy - flesh-eating hordes. This, however, is an idea largely of Romero's own invention. Originally, the idea of the zombie that sprang up in Africa several centuries ago now was nothing like this media construct. Far from shuffling awkwardly through post-apocalyptic cityscapes with their limbs hanging off and mumbling 'braa-aiins...' emptily to themselves, the first African zombies did not feast on human flesh at all; amusingly, they actually wandered through the night in search of free porridge instead!

Credo Mutwa's version of how zombies were created is not the only one in existence, after all. An alternative South African belief relating to zombie-manufacture is that witches are able, somehow, to capture what is termed a person's seriti - their 'shadow', or part of their soul. Once they have done this, they are then able to gradually begin possessing various different parts of a person's body until they end up in control of his or her entire being. At this point, they would call the zombie out to them, and cause a fake magical double to appear in their house instead, playing dead in order to fool the victim's family. The grieving family would then bury their relative's corpse - which, in actuality, was nothing more than the stem of a fern tree which had had an illusory spell cast upon it - leaving the witch free to exploit their new zombie without his friends and kin asking awkward questions about what had happened to him [35].

But what would the witch do with her new creation once she had enticed the zombie away from his or her family? Simple. Once a witch had a zombie, she would use it as a slave; and one zombie alone was usually not enough. Witches, you see, would create themselves entire labour-forces from these creatures, using them to look after their cattle, plough their fields and do all their housework for them. During the day, they would be hidden away from sight in valleys and caves, or on top of cliffs, but at night they would emerge and do their owners' bidding. In order to hold more power over them, witches would cut out part of their tongues so they could not speak, shrink them down in size so that they stood no more than a metre tall, and alter their appearance, making them all look like one another, even rendering them entirely sexless. Zombie-slaves had no gender, and no sense of individual identity, either.

Again, this all sounds silly at first glance; and yet, examined more closely, it seems obvious that the original African zombie-legend is in fact some kind of ingenious supernatural metaphor for the old master-servant relationship, which used to exist between black labourers and their white masters during colonial times. The witches stand in for the white farm-owners and industrialists, and the zombies for their vast black workforces. Zombies' tasks, after all, are mindless and repetitive, and their similarity in appearance has echoes of the impersonal nature of being part of a massive, low-status labour-force. The zombies' tiny stature and severed tongues, too, seem like some kind of allegory for the blacks' former lack of power and voice in their own countries. The witches and wizards, meanwhile, have an easy time of it by comparison. All they have to do is issue their zombie-slaves with instructions - which, of course, they have no minds of their own to disobey - and then sit back and watch all the money roll in. The only inconvenience which a sorcerer has with his undead work-force is that they need to be fed bowls of porridge in order to keep them going; much as the only real inconvenience for a white industrialist or farmer in the past was keeping his own black labourers fed. The fact that, if their witch-owner dies, zombies must wander throughout the land in search of more porridge, whilst undeniably funny at first sight, seems actually to have been originally intended as being some kind of a comment upon the likely degrading effects upon a person of unemployment [36].

Allegories, however, whilst they may originally have been intended as being fiction, can come to be genuinely believed in; you only have to look at the history of a subject such as alchemy to see that process in action. Somewhere along the line, though, it seems that belief in zombies and belief in tokoloshes have begun to converge with one another, at least for some people. As a result, we get outrageous claims such as those of Dr Imrani being made, and a situation arises in which rumours about a secret tokoloshe-zombie farm being in operation in the Drakensburg mountains of South Africa during the 1920s are taken seriously even by such high-status figures as Credo Mutwa [37]. In a later chapter, we shall even examine a bizarre case from as recently as 2002 in which children from a Zimbabwean school began wandering around and acting like zombies after coming to believe that they had been possessed by rogue tokoloshes, which had escaped from a life of slave-labour on local farms, showing that such beliefs are still given widespread credence by some even today. The tokoloshe, in its most popular form, is said to be small, obedient and entirely under the control of its witch-owner; so were zombies, and so, metaphorically, were black labourers. In a certain sense, in southern African folklore, all three figures have simply now become complementary aspects of one another. This is all just yet another example of how beliefs about the tokoloshe can shift around in the eyes of the population in order to reflect changing social conditions over time.

A depiction of naked European witches willingly participating in mass orgies with the Devil in goat-form at their Sabbat; witches have been imagined as being sexually deviant in many cultures throughout time, it seems, and not just in modern-day Africa.

# Chapter Two

## Sexual Politics: Tokoloshe-Rape and Molestation

In 1993, a South African man named Tshepo Maile was faced with an embarrassing problem; he had become impotent. Tshepo's wife, no doubt protesting that she had "certain needs", then promptly threatened him with divorce. Marriage-guidance counsellors probably not being available to the Mailes, they decided to go and see a local inyanga for advice and help instead. He knew exactly what was wrong with Tshepo; his mother was annoyed with him for failing to support her financially, the witch-doctor said, and, as such, the annoyed old woman had begun sending out a tokoloshe to him at night in order to molest all the life out of his penis whilst he was asleep, so that he would then be unable to satisfy his wife afterwards. Harmony was restored to the Maile household, however, when Tshepo went to see his mother and agreed to build her a new house if she would call her tokoloshe off from him. We are not told whether or not this solution actually worked, however [1].

How should we read this story? Well, we could just laugh and call the Maile family gullible fools. However, a more sophisticated analysis might allow us to understand and interpret the tokoloshe being invoked as an explanation for impotency here largely in order to allow poor Tshepo to save some face in the matter. If he had become impotent for whatever reason, then perhaps he might simply have preferred to agree to blame a tokoloshe for the fact in order to help him thereby avoid humiliation and preserve some sense of his own manhood?

Perhaps so; but, of course, Tshepo could hardly have hoped to be able to plausibly maintain such a claim within a society where belief in nocturnal tokoloshe-rape was not already widespread - and, as already mentioned, it is indeed widespread in nations such as South Africa, Zimbabwe, Lesotho and Botswana. The tokoloshe, as we saw in the introduction to this book, has a truly fearsome piece of weaponry hanging down there between his legs, and he is not afraid to use it upon whomsoever he sees fit, whether their bed has been raised up onto some bricks or not. But why does the tokoloshe do this? Does he rape of his own free will, or is he compelled to do so by the witches and warlocks who control him? Apparently it is a bit of both, although the notion that they are under the control of someone evil whilst molesting people is seemingly the most prevalent one.

Tokoloshes, we will remember, were often said to act as their witch-owners' sex-slaves, providing these women with much satisfaction as they did so. One anthropological explanation sometimes put forward in order to try and explain the common belief in this idea has to do with women's traditionally lower place in much southern African society. Women generally having been subordinate to men in most communities for centuries, it has been theorised that some of them will have harboured a sense of resentment against their husbands, and that this was picked up on by the men-folk. Realising that their wives had some level of hostility towards them, it has been postulated that these husbands then began thinking hard about how it might be that their wives could potentially try to take their revenge upon them. Seeing as the most obvious difference between men and women comes in their differing genitalia, it is alleged that resentful men began imagining that certain of the more obstreperous women around them had begun to fulfil their unnatural needs, and deprive men of their natural ones at the same time, by taking demon-lovers to bed with them instead of their real, lawful human ones. In this way, it becomes possible to interpret the imagined gigantic penis of the tokoloshe as being a kind of social symbol, which men can then use to justify their domination over their wives with. The idea was that men actually secretly felt guilty and insecure about their wives' lack of equality with them, and so began slandering them as being witch-whores with unnatural sexual desires who had to be kept down due to their innate female lack of morality, in order to preserve the social order [2]. That, at least, is one theory which has been advanced, although it smacks quite strongly of amateur Freudianism to me.

**Bad Sex**
Nonetheless, it is undeniable that witches are habitually depicted and imagined as having aberrant sexual desires in contemporary African folklore - as, indeed, they commonly were in old European myth and legend. For example, during a witch-scare in the town of Rooiboklaagte in South Africa's Mpumalanga Province in 1994, it was alleged publicly by a local diviner that there were a group of sorceresses secretly casting evil spells across the area, one of whom, supposedly, enjoyed tying an animal-horn around her waist so that she could go out and rape other women with it at night [3]. Significantly, this alleged witch was also said to keep a tokoloshe in her house as her familiar. Lesbianism, of course, is a real taboo in many parts of contemporary Africa, and such an accusation being made against a witch would be enough to instantly identify her in the public mind as being a 'pervert'.

The fact that she kept a tokoloshe would probably have been interpreted by many as being simply another aspect of this perversion. Not only would the tokoloshe have slept with her, but, we will recall, there is also some sense in which the tokoloshe is actually the witch's double, or perhaps simply the witch herself in animal-disguise. Seeing as she would undoubtedly have been viewed as sending this familiar of hers out on nocturnal raping-expeditions, it can thus be seen how, in some cases, the tokoloshe which rapes people in the

OPPOSITE: A detail from Henry Fuseli's famous painting 'The Nightmare', nowadays often interpreted as depicting an instance of sleep-paralysis, with a hairy, ogre-like demon pressing down upon the helpless sleeper's chest. Might this kind of phenomenon be the Western version of tokoloshe-rape?

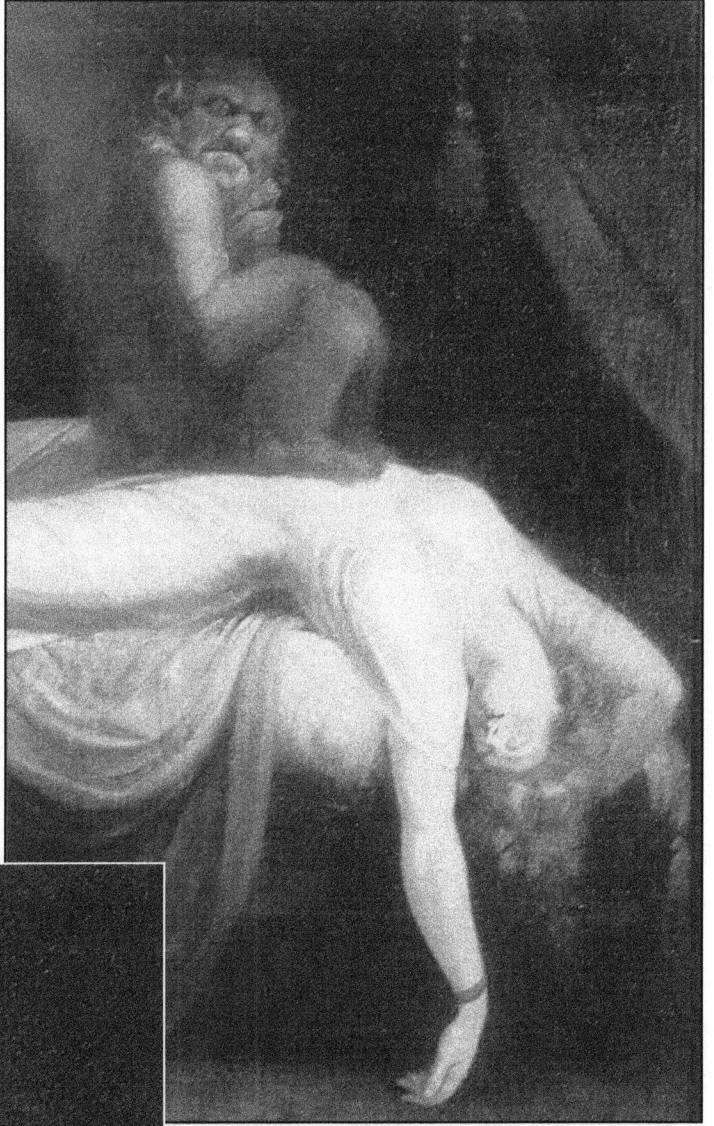

night, be its victims male or female, is actually the witch engaging in the act of rape herself in a different, camouflaged form. Furthermore, of course, we have to consider the confusing nature of the gender of the tokoloshe-witch who is said to be performing these acts. If she's normally a woman by day, but becomes a well-endowed male tokoloshe to rape women by night, then she will in some weird sense be engaging in acts of lesbianism with her victims; and on the other hand, of course, if a witch rapes a man in the form of a male tokoloshe, then she is essentially engaging in an act of forced homosexuality, too, which is perhaps an even more taboo subject than lesbianism is in modern African society. Actually, then, by wider implication, we can see how the figure of the tokoloshe-rapist is actually in a way some kind of supernaturalised symbol of the very concept of illicit or perverted sexual desire itself - and particularly, apparently, of perverted female sexual desire. Tokoloshe-sex is highly unnatural, then, and to either seek it out or enjoy it is a kind of obvious moral depravity.

Because this tokoloshe-sex is unnatural, though, it is also imagined as having numerous unpleasant consequences for those who engage in it. Sometimes the effects of tokoloshe-rape are blamed for women having miscarriages or giving birth to disabled children, for example, as we shall see later - and, seeing as African attitudes towards disability are sadly sometimes less than enlightened, this can be seen as being a kind of unnatural 'perversion' of the female reproductive system itself, yet another inversion of the norms of motherhood to put alongside all those images of tokoloshes suckling at witches' teats. On the other hand, tokoloshes can also be blamed for a woman having an affair or demonstrating what are considered to be excessive signs of sexual desire by the men around her. This is because, according to this view, tokoloshe-rape feels so good, due both to the size of the spirit's genitals, and their magical sex-powers, that the demon's victims walk around in a state of heightened sensual and erotic excitement for days afterwards, being unable to keep their hands off any man who comes near them, no matter who they are.

If excessive sexual desire is viewed as being one kind of unnatural perversion of the feminine ideal, however, then the concept of frigidity is its opposing counterpart - and, as such, it should perhaps be no surprise that tokoloshes are supposed sometimes to be responsible for this quality in a woman, too. After all, one other common rumour about tokoloshe-rape is that it is so unpleasant that it puts women who experience it off sex for life. Yet another explanation for women's frigidity after undergoing such an ordeal, however, combines the worst of both worlds, saying instead that the experience of having intercourse with a tokoloshe is so good that, afterwards, women simply have no interest in the normal-sized penises of human males and so lose all their natural desires, saving themselves instead for their new supernatural lovers (something which is also said to be true of women who have experienced the tongue of the impundulu bird searching between their legs) [4].

Clearly, however, as in the case with which we opened this chapter, all of these ideas could very easily be interpreted as being simply supernaturalised explanations for entirely natural processes and human states of mind. Sometimes, the experience of being interfered with by a tokoloshe could actually fulfil some kind of psycho-sexual function for a person, such as with the couple investigated by Vemon Nicholas Pillay, a student at the University of Zululand, who had been unable to consummate their relationship even after a full year of marriage. The woman, it seemed, would feel an invisible body pressing down on her chest and breathing heavily whenever she and her husband were about to have sex with one another, and she often woke up to find something unseen sleeping between them in bed at night. This kind of case could easily be viewed as simply being some kind of demonic personification of the woman's subconscious fear of intercourse and of losing her virginity, rather than as an actual tokoloshe attack, as such [5].

On the other hand, of course, if her husband accepted this explanation for their lack of bedroom action, then you could also say that he is engaging in belief in this kind of fiction largely as a means of coping with his spouse's rejection of him. There is a sense in which it would probably be more comforting to think that your wife's being bothered by a tokoloshe than that she doesn't fancy doing it with you much, after all. The case of the man who was married to a teacher whose tokoloshe-lover kept on slapping him around in bed at night, which we examined in the previous chapter could also, perhaps, be viewed in such terms. It appears that the man and his wife later got divorced, and maybe claiming that it was a tokoloshe which was responsible for this fact, and not his own failings in the bedroom or elsewhere, would have enabled him to save face in wider society [6].

**Vampiric VD**
Amazingly, tokoloshes have also sometimes been blamed for the high rates of AIDS-infection in southern African society, too. In 1999, for example, Boniface Mankone, the former head of ZINATHA, Zimbabwe's official 'trade union' for sangomas and witch-doctors, gave his opinion that tokoloshes, like vampires, drank blood from their victims - which, in countries like South Africa and Zimbabwe, where, according to 2007 figures, well over 15% of the population have HIV or AIDS [7], is not perhaps the most health-conscious of things for them to do. According to Mankone, if you conjure up a tokoloshe, or pay a witch to create one for you, then "one of your relatives will die within a year. With AIDS claiming so many lives now, people often say this is the tokoloshes claiming their payment."[8] Even some official Zimbabwean health-workers were once quoted in the national press as saying that it was likely that tokoloshes probably spread HIV and AIDS on to women during their nocturnal raping-sprees, thereby seemingly giving the idea actual medical backing! [9]

This strange belief was famously referred to in what might well be the most notorious of all the *Daily Sun's* numerous sensationalist headlines about tokoloshes, namely that organ's incredible cover-story for March 1st 2006, reading, in large capitals, 'GAY TOKOLOSHE GAVE ME AIDS!'. Beneath a further dramatic sub-heading ('Couple's 10-year nightmare with evil sex terror!') was detailed the harrowing narrative of an anonymous couple from the South African township of Vosloorus in Gauteng Province, both of whom, they said, were being raped on a nightly basis by a gender-bending tokoloshe. Apparently, it entered into the couple's bedroom each evening and, to the wife, pretended to be her husband, and to the husband pretended to be his wife, before then ruthlessly raping them. They could not actually see the tokoloshe, said the couple, but they could feel it climbing up on top of them and having its way with them both, presumably mixing and matching its genitals as appropriate whilst it did so (although perhaps, seeing as the *Daily Sun* claimed that the demon was gay, it was in fact sodomising the man in this instance?).

One night, however, the situation began to get even worse, as the tokoloshe, before raping the wife, openly told her that it was going to infect her with AIDS. Seemingly, this prediction then came true; the woman developed mysterious sores and lost a lot of weight, so went to see a doctor who confirmed that she had HIV. Since this diagnosis had been given, the poor woman had begun suffering relentless nightmares, constantly dreaming about things like coffins, and no sangomas or churchmen that the couple had called in to exorcise the tokoloshe had proved able to help. Strangely, though, given that the tokoloshe allegedly had AIDS, the husband refused to go and get tested for HIV himself. He didn't need to, he told the reporter who covered his story - after all, he said, somewhat over-confidently perhaps, "I know that I am clean and I do not have any affairs" and, in any case, whenever he did have sex with his wife, he now always ensured that they both "condomise", as he put it, using slightly odd English [10]. For many men in Africa, it seems, admitting that you might have AIDS yourself is a massive social taboo; much better, apparently, to simply say that your wife has it, and that she caught it from a tokoloshe rather than from yourself or another male lover.

Again, then, the idea of blaming tokoloshes for giving you AIDS seems like a good enough way for people to try and shift blame for what is in fact an entirely human problem away onto supernatural beings - 'don't blame me for having unprotected sex or using prostitutes and sharing needles, it's all the tokoloshe's fault' seems to be the kind of reasoning at work here. But there is, once again, actually slightly more to this idea than meets the eye. One traditional belief in South Africa, for example, states that if you are being bothered by visits from a tokoloshe during the night, then it is possible to satisfy him if you are a male by simply leaving out a bowl of blood for him. But, if you are a female, then you would be better off just allowing him to sleep with you, in the hope that he will then leave you alone after he has got what he wanted [11].

Implicit within this belief, perhaps, is yet another strain of anti-feminine prejudice; after all, if a sick man gives a tokoloshe AIDS by letting him drink his blood, then a female helps to spread the disease by the even more immoral method of engaging in sexual relations with the monster, thereby either giving it to him, or being infected herself, should the tokoloshe already be a carrier. Blaming tokoloshes for AIDS-deaths could thus be interpreted as being yet another supernaturalised commentary upon the alleged ills of female (but not necessarily male) promiscuity, then. If you're a man and you catch AIDS from a woman, then it's not your fault, it's her fault for going around with dirty tokoloshes, appears to be the basic moral to be drawn here. AIDS-infection carrying something of a stigma to it, these myths allow men,

# TERROR of the gay tokoloshe!

By ALEX NKOSI

THERE are three bodies in the marital bed – a man, his wife and a gay tokoloshe.

The tokoloshe only has eyes for the man. He rapes him all night, every night, leaving nothing for the wife to enjoy.

Isaac Malope and Constance Mazibuko are asking for help.
Photo by Alex Nkosi

This has been going on for 15 years and now Isaac Malope (51) and his wife Constance Mazibuko (43), from Allemansdrift C, near Siyabuswa in Mpumalanga, are afraid to go to sleep.

Isaac said: "Every night he comes between me and my wife and rapes me over and over. When he leaves, I no longer have energy for my wife and even if I try to get an erection, nothing happens.

"The only time I manage to get an erection is if I fast for seven days and ask God for it. But it only lasts for a day and then it is back to hell. I have been to many different sangomas but they have all failed to solve the problem."

He admitted spending at least R200 000 on sangomas and healers already. Some of the money came from a group of sympathetic friends. The couple even travelled to Nigeria in June last year to consult a well-known prophet there, but that did not help either.

"I am appealing to anyone who can help save my marriage," Isaac said.

Constance said: "I know it's not his fault and as his wife I have to support him."

Anyone who can help Isaac should call *Daily Sun* in Tshwane on 012 424 6251.

in particular, who are carrying the disease to portray themselves as being simply the victims of malicious witch-women once more, rather than drug-users, incurable philanderers or promiscuous homosexuals. It also allows the families of people who have died of AIDS to do so, too, thereby preserving their sense of honour in the face of the wider community. It is to the benefit of many people, then, to claim that tokoloshes spread AIDS.

**I Have a Dream ...**
Another, slightly reductive, way of explaining the idea of tokoloshe-rape, however, would be to dismiss it all as being no more than a kind of supernaturalised explanation for people having wet-dreams in the night. Certainly, this is a familiar motif to be found in relation to various supernatural rapists from other cultures. The demon-queen Lilith, for instance - the chief bogey of ancient Jewish lore - was meant to come to men in the night, give them erections and secretly copulate with them, stealing their semen in order to make her pregnant and thereby able to give birth to more evil demons to plague mankind with. Thus, when a Jewish man had a wet-dream during the night, he would just say that Lilith had been to see him, milking him dry [12]. Parallel myths appear to have sprung up in many other cultures in order to explain this particular nocturnal phenomenon, too. The early-modern English account of a Goodwin Wharton, who, upon finding himself too limp and tired to have sex with a certain Mrs Parish, was "able to surmise that the Fairy Queen had been with him in his sleep [i.e. his dreams], and sucked out the very marrow from his bones in her voraciousness", as recorded for us by the historian Keith Thomas, for example, is evidence that such ideas can take root anywhere [13]. Perhaps some contemporary tales of alien beings subjecting humans to humiliating physical examinations before then taking sperm samples from them in order to facilitate inter-planetary breeding programmes whilst their victims actually lie fast asleep in their beds are another, more modern-clothed example of the form.

Indeed, during the height of the European witch and demon-mania, there was much scholarly debate about whether or not incubi and succubi were actually physical beings at all, or whether, whilst still real, they actually came to their victims in their dreams rather than through the bedroom door as such. According to the Christian writer Gnaccius, for example, in his *Compendium Maleficarum*, it was perfectly possible for a succubus to enter into the mind of a sleeping man, give him a wet dream, and then collect up some of the sperm he had expelled to take back to the Devil for him to create more baby demons with [14]. In such a theory, a wet dream is still a wet dream, but one which is also simultaneously inherently demonic in its nature.

Another way of explaining away nocturnal sexual encounters with tokoloshes, though, would be just to say that it was all down to that well-known medical phenomenon of 'sleep paralysis'. This phenomenon affects many people during the REM (Rapid Eye Movement) stage of sleep, which is when people do the majority of their dreaming. During this state, the brain releases a chemical inhibitor which paralyses our muscles, to prevent us from acting out our dreams. However, if we wake up whilst this chemical inhibitor is still in operation, we will find our bodies rigid and unable to move. I experienced this phenomenon myself a few times as a teenager, and I can tell you for sure that it is a fairly terrifying experience. Even more terror, however, can be occasioned for some sufferers if they also begin to suffer from what are termed 'hypnopompic hallucinations' before the state of paralysis wears off (something which, I am glad to say, did not happen to me). The hypnopompic state is another stage of sleep, experienced by all of us when we first wake up in the morning, and are not quite sure whether we are still asleep or not. During this state, what we might term 'waking dreams' can occur - which, for whatever reason, often seem to involve experiences of assault, sometimes sexual in nature, by hideous supernatural creatures.

In the West, these creatures, as shown by the folklorist David Hufford in his now-classic study of the phenomenon, *The Terror That Comes in the Night*, seem traditionally to have been viewed as being either incubi or succubi, or horrible witch-like figures generally termed 'old hags' by psychologists, although nowadays, perhaps, you might be just as likely to encounter a small grey alien with big black eyes. In short, you probably see during states of sleep paralysis whatever it is that your culture makes you expect to see; and, for people in southern Africa, what they would expect to see attacking them if they woke up paralysed in the middle of the night would be a sex-hungry tokoloshe.

Sometimes, these frightening cases of sleep paralysis and/or hypnopompic hallucination even appear to involve visions of entities which sound, at first sight, not entirely unlike tokoloshes, even though they are spoken of as occurring not in Africa, but in the modern West. For example, a *Fortean Times* reader named Brenda Ray, from a place as resolutely unexotic as Derby, wrote in to the famous 'Journal of Strange Phenomena' in 2008 in order to tell them about her experience of sleep paralysis. This occurred in 2004, when she woke up in the middle of the night - in a bedroom which was allegedly haunted - thinking that one of her cats had jumped up onto her bed. However, it was not her cat; it was far too heavy to be that, realised Brenda, as she pushed it off down to the floor. After she had done so, her assailant began scratching at her bedclothes and the wooden bed-frame, and even digging its claws into her hands. Getting a look at the creature, Brenda described it as having long claws and "resembling a small bear with a long nose and very thick curly fur" - or, alternatively, as being

"an anteater with an afro", or a malevolent version of Wally Fawkes' popular newspaper cartoon character, Flook. Whatever it was, Brenda described herself as having been paralysed at some point during this encounter, and said that the thing disappeared as soon as she put the light on. Looking down at her right hand, however, she found that there were indeed several large scratches on it, and that several of her fingernails were broken; she was unsure as to whether this was because of the funky anteater-bear's assault being real, or simply because she had done herself some damage in her sleep whilst riddling around during the night [15].

**Wally Fawkes' popular cartoon character 'Flook'; one woman from Derby claims to have awoken one night and been assaulted by a creature which strongly resembled him on a bad day ... Could it have been a tokoloshe on tour, perhaps?**

Another, equally terrifying, account of sleep-paralysis involving a tokoloshe-like entity was sent in to *Fortean Times* in 2006 by a man named Jerry Glover, who wished to tell them about an experience he had undergone one night when he was 16. Jerry awoke in his bed, it seems, paralysed in his arms and legs, and with a severe tightness in his chest. Looking up, Jerry saw what was causing this state of affairs; there was, seemingly, "some kind of animal, like a monkey in shape, brown and hairy" sitting on top of his torso and causing the pressure. It sat there growling and making a "mouth-clearing sound" before leaning in closer to Jerry's face, allowing him to see that it had "a malevolent face with red eyes, somewhat monkey-like, only more demonic", and was semi-transparent. It actually then began speaking to the stricken boy, mocking him and telling him how pathetic and powerless he was in comparison to it, in a "rasping, inhuman voice that was horrible to hear". Eventually, as Jerry forced himself to begin breathing properly, and gained a little control of his limbs, the horrific figure began slowly melting away, taking about a minute or so to vanish from sight. By the time that Jerry was able to get up and turn his bedroom light on, the thing had gone completely.

However, just as with Brenda Ray, Jerry Glover was unsure whether or not the creature - which a South African would surely have taken as being a tokoloshe, due to its evil monkey-like appearance - was literally real or not. He said that he was certain it was not a normal dream, but did wonder whether it was something simply from his own subconscious, or, more disturbingly, a thing from another reality. Interestingly, again like in Brenda Ray's case, the bedroom where this attack took place had previously been the scene of odd, ostensibly paranormal activity; in this case, an inexplicable ticking or rapping noise, as if from a poltergeist, perhaps, had been heard by Jerry and several of his friends coming from a corner of the room late at night [16]. Yet another issue of *Fortean Times*, meanwhile, featured two written accounts from people who claimed to have been assaulted in the night by a hairy creature resembling a squirrel-monkey but with a single claw upon the end of each arm instead of hands. These, also, were not necessarily interpreted by the people who underwent them as being essentially dream-based experiences [17].

Even modern Westerners, then, can view attacks of what sceptics might term sleep paralysis as being possibly down to assault by genuine paranormal entities, and not just modern Africans. The picture is confused for us further, however, by the occasional apparent correlation between poltergeist-like activity and cases of sleep-paralysis. This is fairly atypical, but does, as in some of the instances cited above, apparently happen. For example, one South African informant online makes the claim that, whilst a child, she and her brother used to be able to hear strange disembodied sounds, "like a train but softer", echoing around inside their bedroom at night, which they put down to ghosts. Phenomena in this particular haunted household used to centre around the black maids' room, however, outside which the family dogs would constantly stand guard, bark and growl. Inside, meanwhile, several female black servants underwent disturbing experiences typical of sleep-paralysis episodes; namely, they were held down onto their beds by some invisible force during the night, being unable to move or breathe whilst the assault lasted. Seemingly, they blamed a tokoloshe for these events - and, without exception, quit soon after experiencing them. Eight or so maids were affected by this phenomenon in total, none of whom had known each other or heard of the room's uncanny reputation previously [18]. If this is true, then it does appear that these particular instances of tokoloshe-related sleep-paralysis had some level of objective reality to them - but caused by what?

**Dream Lovers**
So, confusingly, whilst it might be possible to try and dismiss things like nocturnal tokoloshe-rape as being down simply to particularly extreme wet-dreams, or certain erotically-charged states of sleep-paralysis, if the history of European demonology is anything to go by, this does not necessarily mean that there will not be some people who still think it is a real phenomenon, even if it could be shown that it does take place within states of altered, sleep-based consciousness.

For example, in 1993 Andries Mashile, a 23-year-old bank-worker from the South African settlement of Acornhoek in Limpopo Province, began having erotic dreams about things such as a female baboon with gigantic breasts coming into his bedroom and running around the place calling out his name. It seems that, frequently, such reveries would cause him to ejaculate. Worried, he approached a healer associated with a local Apostolic Church (a kind of Pentecostal denomination, very popular in southern Africa), who told him that his dreams were actually real. The parents of some local girl, he said, wanted to marry off their daughter to Andries because he had a stable job, and were sending her out to rape him at night in his sleep in the form of a tokoloshe in order to make him love her. Immediately, he realised that the girl involved must have been his 19-year-old neighbour, Elizabeth Maatsie, who appears to have been somewhat mentally disturbed. She would never speak to Andries when she saw him, apparently, but would simply stare intently at him like a zombie. Furthermore, she was well-known locally as being 'easy'; she had several lovers, had had an abortion, and was once found stark naked in another man's yard. An easy target, perhaps, for Andries to be able to displace the responsibility for his weird and disturbing dreams upon, especially seeing as Elizabeth's mother was already reputed by many to be a witch anyway [19].

When some women from Edinburgh Village near the city of Bushbuckridge in South Africa's Limpopo Province recently claimed that they were being subjected to nocturnal rapes by tokoloshes, meanwhile, the 'wet dream' hypothesis was raised as being a way to explain matters by some educated observers from a distance, which does not alter the fact that, to the women actually involved, the experiences were very real and very frightening. Apparently, the females in question were feeling invisible attackers lying down on them in the middle of the night and then engaging in non-consensual intercourse with them. One woman, Hleziphi Ngwenya, told a public meeting of her fellow villagers the following, apparently causing hoots of laughter to break out amongst them: "I don't sleep at night because I keep on feeling as if a man is having sex with me, causing me to reach a climax, and I become very tired." Ngwenya claimed to experience this feeling at least once a week. Seemingly, the presence of a woman's husband sleeping next to her made no difference to the ferocity of the attacks of the tokoloshe, a Julia Khumalo stating that "My husband was fast asleep next to me one night but I had a sexy feeling and it felt like a penis was penetrating me."

According to Marion Stevens, however, a senior researcher at the Centre for Health Policy at Wits University in Johannesburg, it was all simply down to the women involved having what

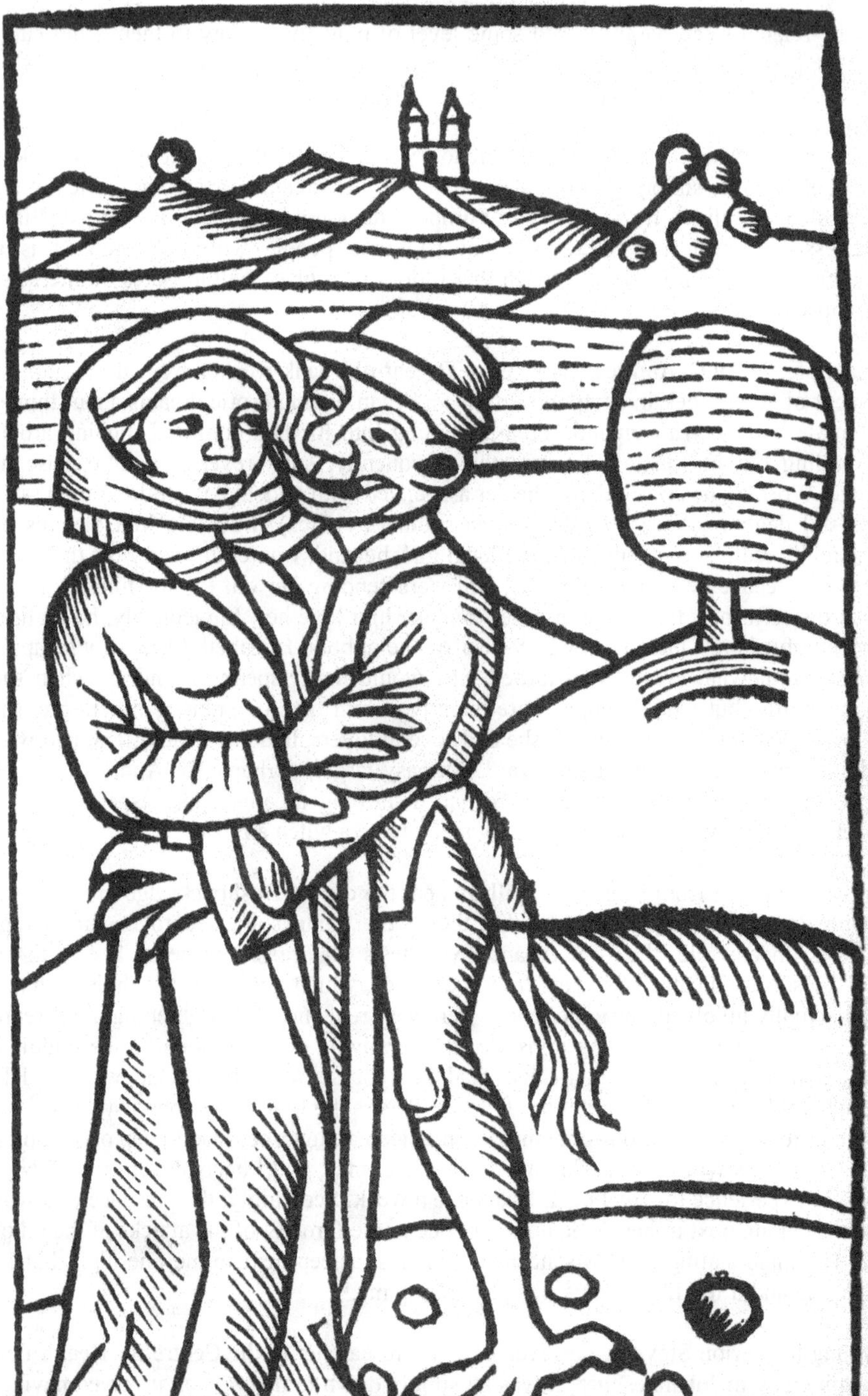

she termed "vivid sexual dreams". The explanation of a doctor at the local hospital was similarly dismissive of the women's experiences. He told one alleged rape victim, Pinky Gumede, that she simply had a growth of some kind on her cervix, gave her some pills and told her to go away.

Interestingly, even the local sangoma had conflicting opinions about whether or not a tokoloshe was responsible for these events, saying that a kind of enchantment known as mtshotshaphansi might have been to blame, instead. This is a kind of sex-magic wherein a sorcerer casts a spell which allows him to have sex with women he desires from a distance away, presumably thereby raping them using his astral body or some such thing. Interestingly, however, an alternative name for mtshotshaphansi is mubobobo, which is also an alternative name for a tokoloshe; the original headline for this story, meanwhile, was 'Long-Distance Tokoloshe Rape', which confuses the issue further, implying apparently that the magician used a tokoloshe to assault the women in such a way that he was able to experience the pleasurable sensation of raping them too [20]. There is some kind of real confusion between two competing concepts here, which perhaps bears more analysis.

For example, the term mtshotshaphansi does not always seem to refer to acts of astral rape being performed by a sorcerer. Apparently, the term basically means 'to go under', and can also be used as a name for a certain special power which tokoloshes allegedly have; namely, the ability to extend their penises magically to whatever length they like and then to send them burrowing underground until they burst up through the bedroom floor of a sleeping woman, whom the tokoloshes then rape from some distance away, perhaps even from the comfort of their own homes whilst putting their feet up and having a nice cup of tea [21]. Whilst tokoloshes are using this amazing power, it seems that their penises begin to acquire certain elastic qualities to them, and they also have the ability to use them as 'feelers' or 'periscopes' before they enter into a household, in order to check that the coast is clear. They can even use their magically-extended penises in order to push aside gates and open doors with, thereby facilitating the tokoloshe's entrance into its victim's home, should he want the rest of his body to get a little closer to the illicit action [22].

In one sense, of course, this bizarre idea of mtshotshaphansi is just yet another way in which African males can calumniate witches, frigid or over-sexed wives, and any other females of whom they wish to show their disapproval, simply by depicting their alleged demon-lovers' genitals as being weird and massively aberrant. Once again, this idea has certain parallels with some ideas from European demonology of the past, wherein incubi were sometimes imagined as having horrible penises which could bifurcate into two separate members, allowing them to penetrate their victims both vaginally and anally at the same time. In some versions of this myth, one of the demon's two penises would even magically and elastically extend itself, just

**OPPOSITE: A witch with her demon-lover or incubus as depicted in a 1489 woodcut from Germany; witches have always been imagined as having perverted sexual relations with animal-like demons and other supernatural creatures, apparently.**

like a tokoloshe's, until it reached up into the woman's face, whereupon he would begin to rape her in the mouth, too [23]. The penis of Satan himself, meanwhile, was generally supposed during the European witch-panic to be unpleasant and scaly, like a fish's skin in its nature, and to be filled with horrible freezing-cold semen, whenever he deigned to stick it inside one of his witch-followers. Such ideas, obviously, appear once more to be intended largely to portray witches as having unnatural desires, and to be implacably opposed to all concepts of respectable human normality.

**Wizard Japes**
However, the initially confusing idea of the word mtshotshaphansi being used to refer to both the practice of astral rape from a distance by a sorcerer, and to the ability of the tokoloshe to extend its penis, is also comprehensible in terms of the witch/wizard's often-claimed duality with his or her hairy little familiar. Put simply, there is much dispute about whether, when a witch sends out a tokoloshe to rape someone, she is getting a demon to do her dirty work for her, or is raping people herself in the form of the tokoloshe in order to gain perverted sexual satisfaction from this act, as we saw earlier. As one of Isak Niehaus' informants put it bluntly, "If a witch sends the tokoloshe to have sex with his neighbour's wife the witch will not enjoy it. If he wants to fuck his neighbour's wife at night he himself has to change into a familiar - the tokoloshe. [24] " Probably, then, this is why the term mubobobo can sometimes be used to refer simply to a tokoloshe - the word being an alternative Zimbabwean name for one - or, alternatively, to a particularly weird form of witchcraft-crime.

Put simply, mubobobo in this latter sense is the practice of 'magical masturbation', and it is an offence which, perhaps by definition, seems largely to be committed by male sorcerers. It simply involves a male witch or wizard looking at a woman he has taken a fancy to and then secretly masturbating in her presence without her knowledge of the fact. During this act, it seems that a kind of 'astral penis', corresponding to the man's actual real physical member, is projected inside his victim's vagina at the same time, physically raping her.

Amazingly, this crime has been the subject of several court cases in recent years, particularly in Zimbabwe. In October 2010, for instance, a 30-year-old man named Mtami Mtami, from that country's second city of Bulawayo, was charged by police with committing several offences of rape against women using his 'ghost-penis'. Interestingly, Mtami was not a wizard himself, but had visited a witch-doctor and 'hired' some mubobobo-powers from him temporarily for a certain fee. The first person Mtami tried out his magic on was a 22-year-old woman who was sweeping out her yard. Foolishly, Mtami had forgotten that you are meant to hide yourself whilst performing mubobobo, however, and simply walked up to her quite openly, pulled his penis out of his trousers and began wanking it off frantically in front of her - which, quite naturally, led to her fleeing and alerting her neighbours.

Like all good criminals, though, Mtami soon learned from his initial failure. Spotting a 29-year-old woman who was stood at her sink washing plates, he crept inside her kitchen and then just stood behind her silently, surreptitiously pleasuring himself. However, whilst she had no idea that the criminal was there, the unnamed housewife, in her own words, "started having some feelings" in her vagina, and turned around to catch him in the act. This time, it was

Mtami's turn to flee. Upon committing his third offence, though, Mtami was finally brought to justice. Seeing a 19-year-old girl sitting on the floor outside her home, he went and stood behind her and began committing mubobobo again. Feeling an uncanny presence between her legs, the teenager turned around to catch him at it and alerted some passers-by who then apprehended Mtami and took him down to the police station, where he was hopefully then given a cell to himself [25].

This case is hardly a one-off. In May 2011, another Zimbabwean criminal, the appropriately named Jealous Dube, 23, (allegedly pictured below in a Romanian newspaper) was arrested after being caught standing outside the window of a 23-year-old woman who was having a bath in her flat in the city of Gweru in Midlands Province, with his pants down. Apparently, the bathing woman first became aware that something odd was going on when she began "feeling strange" in her genitals. Then, she heard whimpering noises coming from outside her window, and looked out to see Dube stood there, committing mubobobo. He tried to run away once he had been spotted, but was impeded in doing so by his trousers becoming tangled up around his ankles, causing him to fall over like some hideous X-rated Mr Bean. He was then "manhandled" - the report's original wording - by a mob of angry neighbours down to the nearest police station, where he confessed to astrally raping women in their baths in the city on a regular basis [26].

Acts of mtshotshaphansi which do not involve elastic tokoloshe-penises opening doors and so forth also sound quite similar to mubobobo crimes in many ways too, though. Amusingly, for example, in modern South Africa, this particular act of sorcery appears to have moved with

the times, and male wizards are now able to commit the crime via remote-control. Apparently, the modern mtshotshaphansi-master is able to manufacture a bizarre kind of electronic remote, not unlike those devices which you can now use to lock or unlock your car with, but which is powered not by a battery but by a body-part from a tokoloshe being placed inside it - presumably a severed portion of the beast's giant penis.

All a man has to do is to hide this device inside his pocket and then approach the woman of his dreams before surreptitiously flicking the switch on it, which will cause his own penis to instantly become erect like a tokoloshe's, whilst simultaneously placing the woman into a kind of hypnotised but sexually-receptive state, in which she will willingly allow the wizard's astral penis to enter into her own body from a distance. The only problem with this contraption, however - which certainly beats such tawdry Western counterparts as those x-ray specs which always used to be advertised at the back of dodgy 1950s American comic-books - is that the warlock who is using it is unable to control his ecstatic facial expressions whilst having magical sex by proxy. This can easily lead to a person with facial tics, or who is staring at a woman just a little too intently, being accused of being a wizard-rapist and then unjustly beaten up, all of which certainly gives a whole new layer of meaning to that age-old question "Are you looking at my wife? [27]"

People genuinely do believe in the nefarious powers of this ridiculous device. For example, there was once a case in which a male South African schoolteacher was accused of owning a mtshotshaphansi-remote after he approached one of his female colleagues and started telling her that he thought she was not much cop in bed, even though the two of them had never actually slept with one another. Then, he summoned several schoolgirls to the library and forced them to stand there for a period of time for no apparent reason whilst he just stared at them. Apparently, these girls later claimed that this act had caused them all to become wet between their legs, which led to the school's headmaster calling the man into his office and accusing him angrily of being a wizard. He threatened to sack him, as the rumours going around about him were causing chaos in the classroom; every time he even so much as looked at a female pupil or member of staff, they took to frantically stabbing at thin air in front of their groins with pens and pencils in order to ward off his invisible flying ghost-penis, which was hardly good for school morale [28].

Again, though, there is a bit more to this story than at first meets the eye. It turns out that this teacher was married, but that his wife worked away in another town and did not visit him very often, something which caused some surprise and created much gossip locally. He readily accepted this unusual arrangement, and people wanted to know why. Perhaps the rumours that he practised mtshotshaphansi were, initially at least, simply some kind of coded way to gossip about the man, then. Maybe the locals suspected that he was actually some kind of sexual deviant, or even impotent and unable to satisfy his wife, leading to her not wanting to stay with him. In African witchcraft traditions, such persons - the impotent, the single, the unmarried, the sexually-frustrated - are sometimes conceived of as being highly dangerous.

Rejected lovers can also procure tokoloshes and send them out to persecute people too, however, whether via a process of shared astral rape or not. For example, there was a really strange case which occurred in the South African town of Grabouw in Western Cape Province in 1981, in which a 38-year-old woman named Maggie Hendricks began to suffer from the attentions of what might sound to Western ears like a poltergeist, but which everyone involved at the time was certain was actually a tokoloshe. At first, the ghostly phenomena involved things such as the rattling of chains being heard, apparitions materialising, and the sound of some unidentified animal running across Mrs Hendricks' house at night. Then, it seems that the unfortunate woman began finding earthworms and slime - supposedly from frogs - in her food when she sat down to eat it.

This was followed by her beginning to suffer from an "itchy irritation" in her throat, something which only seemed to be a prelude to her beginning to vomit up large numbers of disgusting and painful items, such as needles, hair-balls, pieces of glass, earthworms, tadpoles and even upon one occasion, allegedly, a large frog. A policeman called out to investigate claims to have witnessed Mrs Hendricks spewing up several sharp knife-blades from her mouth right in front of him, without even bleeding. Eventually, she even had to give up work as the tokoloshe, which seems to have been generally invisible in its nature, had taken to continually shredding up her clothes and shoes. The main theory about the haunting in the neighbourhood, it seems, was that the demon had been sent out to attack Maggie by a potential lover whom she had recently rebuffed; a notion which was perhaps backed up by the fact that the tokoloshe had begun shouting things like "I love you and I want you!" at her out of thin air [29].

Perhaps the most surprising thing about this most surprising case, however, is that the tokoloshe didn't actually rape her. Perhaps the jilted lover who was meant to have sent it out against Maggie didn't have enough power to be able to experience the sexual act through the body of the tokoloshe itself via a process of mubobobo and just settled for gaining revenge upon Mrs Hendricks in a different way instead. Or maybe the story simply reflects the fact that the terms tokoloshe, mubobobo and mtshotshaphansi have become hopelessly confused with one another in the minds of many of those who use them.

**Enough to Make You Wet Your Knickers**
Occasionally, there have been minor collective panics over the idea of sexual assaults being perpetrated by tokoloshes, particularly in Zimbabwe, it seems. Firstly, in 2009 there was a widespread scare in the Magwegwe suburb of the nation's second city of Bulawayo when several women began waking up in the mornings denuded of their knickers; one woman found them hanging on her door handle, even though she said that she had gone to bed wearing them. Seven adult women, and one 15-year-old girl, all complained of experiencing what they described as being "heavy" sexual encounters during the night, waking up in the morning tired, knickerless and drawn, and with unspecified but unmistakable "signs that they had been raped during the night" between their legs. This was despite the fact that the women's husbands were all away from home at the time of the assaults, working in South Africa - a fact which might possibly admit of some kind of psychological explanation, as we shall soon see. As far as the outraged local community was concerned, however, this was all very obviously down to the actions of a tokoloshe. The local residents' association decided that the tokoloshe must have been owned by a nearby witch or wizard, but that it had recently got out of its

owner's control and begun going on the rampage after dark of its own volition. As such, they hired a local 'prophet' to get to the bottom of the case and find out who owned the tokoloshe, as well as reporting the case to the local police force.

Whilst some of the details of this case might seem comic to us, the women involved in this epidemic of supernatural rape were certainly left genuinely traumatised by matters. One victim who was interviewed by a newspaper reporter, for instance, burst into tears and refused to give her name, saying that "I really wanted to keep it to myself because if my husband got to know about this he might divorce me. Who would want to marry a woman who has been raped by tokoloshes?" Apparently, she said that her experiences had left her needing psychiatric counselling [30].

In this anguished statement, we can see a world of significance. Strangely, there seems to be a real correlation which has sprung up in recent years between migrant labour patterns and tokoloshe-rapes. Apparently, whenever a wife divorces her husband because she has lost all interest in him due to his working away from her all the time, one option open to the rejected man is to blame the fact upon her having taken a tokoloshe as a lover, a sexual partner with whom he could not possibly ever hope to compete [31]. Once again, this could very easily be taken as being yet another means of a humiliated male trying to save face through the conveniently-available figure of a supernatural creature; 'it's not that she doesn't like me anymore or that she's found someone else', a divorced husband could complain, 'it's just that she's been bewitched'.

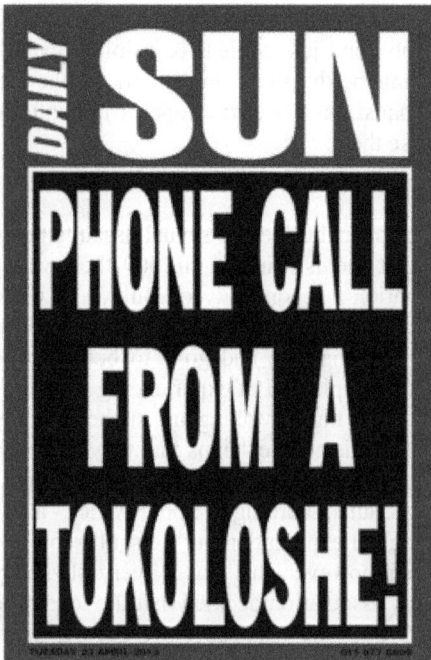

It has already been noted how the spread of the tokoloshe out into wider South African mythology only started to occur after Xhosa and Zulu labourers had been forced to begin migrating around the country by the apartheid government. When men are away, and women left at home 'holding the fort', as it were, it is perhaps only natural that suspicions of infidelity should eventually begin to arise upon behalf of both partners in a marriage. Indeed, human nature being what it is, many of these suspicions were often justified; obviously, some wives and husbands did take new lovers and begin conducting extramarital affairs away from the prying eyes of their spouses. It seems that, in such an environment, absent migrant workers frequently began accusing men who were still employed locally in the towns and villages where their wives had stayed behind to look after the family homes and children, of sending out tokoloshes to rape their defenceless womenfolk. [32]

Once again, this could be simply a good way for

the jilted husbands to bring down the opprobrium of the local community upon men whom they suspect of being their love-rivals, getting them publicly condemned as being wizards, or yet another means for them to be able to save face in public once people had found out that their wives had been cheating on them. It is also a way, of course, for men to promote the duty of their wives to uphold the traditional values of marriage, in which the woman is always faithful to the man. Accusations of men sleeping with tokoloshes whilst they are working away from their wives, however, seem to be much less common, a fact which surely speaks, yet again, of the gender-imbalance which is still prevalent in much of modern-day southern African society. The voice of that woman in Zimbabwe who was so worried about being divorced by her husband because she had been 'soiled' by tokoloshes, as it were, seems likely to be the voice of somebody who is very much the junior partner in her marriage, and who knows it.

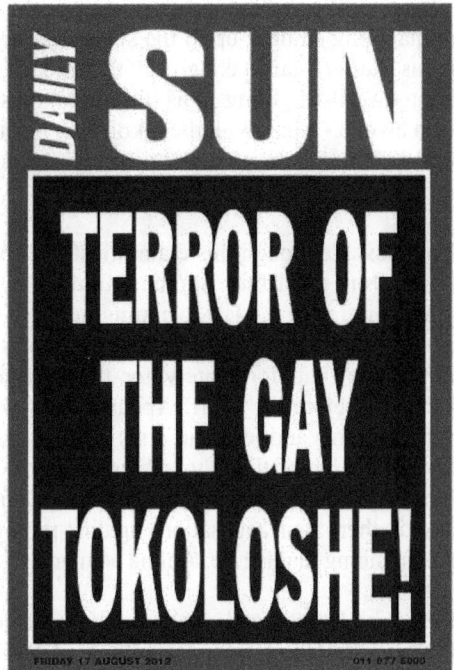

**DAILY SUN**

**TERROR OF THE GAY TOKOLOSHE!**

FRIDAY 17 AUGUST 2012                    011 877 6000

## Unhappy Families

Our second modern Zimbabwean case of collective hysteria also comes from 2009, meanwhile, and speaks of a different kind of family tensions being present. Female members of the same family from Hwange, a town in Matabeleland North Province, claimed to be undergoing some very strange experiences in the night. Apparently, time after time, they had been waking up "tired and wet in the nether regions". Only one thing could possibly account for this fact, of course. According to one woman, Tapia Mwembe, she could feel the invisible tokoloshe having his way with her after dark, leaving her, in the original report's words, "always weak, and unable to satisfy her husband". Maria Ndlovu reported something similar, saying that an "invisible person" was having sex with her at night. Another female member of the same family, Lambiwe Ncube, claimed that she had started having sex with the tokoloshe after her husband had died. After this man's death, Ncube's grandfather had very kindly promised to find her something that would "take care of my sexual needs", in her words. After he had said this, the tokoloshe had begun paying her its nightly visits. From this testimony, it was determined by male family members that the women's 74-year-old grandfather, White Nengwa Ngoma, was a sorcerer and that he had conjured up the tokoloshe to take care of Ncube's needs, the plan perhaps having since got a little out of hand - either that or he was magically transforming into the tokoloshe and then raping them all in that guise himself.

Ngoma's grandsons accordingly decided at this point to take matters into their own hands and hired a local so-called 'prophet', Solani Sibanda, to exorcise the tokoloshe. He wasted no time in marching straight up to the suspected warlock's bedroom and, seeing the tokoloshe hiding in his master's lair, taking it by the throat. So powerful was the creature, though, that Sibanda fainted whilst fighting it, as did the tokoloshe. Cold water was then poured onto the prophet, who awoke - along with the tokoloshe. Fortunately, however, Sibanda was able to grab hold of it and shove it into some hot ashes where it burned to death - or, at least, this is one version of the story. Another holds that the tokoloshe was instead captured and taken to court!

Unbelievable though this claim must be, a very special court case does indeed appear to have arisen from the affair. Ngoma, offended by having his name blackened in this way, took his grandchildren to the law, claiming harassment, and accusing them of making false accusations of witchcraft against him. Since 2006, this has been an offence punishable by jail in Zimbabwe; but, fortunately for the accused, they were able to produce the tokoloshe and parade it before the court! Apparently, it was a kind of dwarf-like creature with downwards-curving horns and legs and arms without palms, and wore some beads upon its person. Given the production of this astonishing piece of evidence, Ngoma's grandchildren were spared any time in prison, even though they were given a restraining order and told to stop harassing their grandfather, their accusations against the old man being judged to be "not without merit" by the presiding magistrate, Aeline Munamati[33].

I must be honest, and say that I have no idea what to make of this last piece of the report. Perhaps the 'court' was some kind of village 'kangaroo' one, and they were all just fooled somehow. Was the tokoloshe actually a dwarf or some kind of small animal in disguise here, or was this final part of the report simply invented or based upon rumour? It seems to be something of a mystery.

However, this part of the story notwithstanding, the rest of it does fit in well with certain other sociological explanations for people making accusations of tokoloshe-rape or mubobobo against alleged wizards. It seems that elderly people, who are either impotent or whose wives have died, are considered to be particularly likely to keep tokoloshes to molest women with. Often, the old men who are accused of doing such things are actually members of the same family as the alleged rape-victim, frequently through marriage - in one case, for instance, a father-in-law was alleged to have raped and impregnated his daughter-in-law using a tokoloshe, rather than with his real, everyday physical body, which is presumably what had actually happened[34]. Perhaps this notion could best be viewed in cases such as this as in reality being some kind of useful psychological means of a person 'distancing' themselves somehow from the unpleasant reality of forced incest.

Married women who stayed at home during the era of forced migrant labour were often compelled by economic circumstance to go on living under the same roof as their parents-in-law, a situation in which various family tensions could very easily - and perhaps inevitably - begin to build up. Indeed, economic circumstance still forces many modern-day African families to adopt similarly overcrowded living arrangements. It is not quite clear whether, in the Zimbabwean case we have just looked at, the various granddaughters were living with one another, or with the old man himself, but it certainly seems possible that this was indeed the case. There could have been any number of pre-existing family tensions involved in this case which we, not being directly involved, just don't know about. Either way, the making of false accusations such as these against your in-laws is certainly one way for a frustrated young woman to try and get rid of them.

Again, it is worth noting that one stereotypical image of a witch during the European witch-panic was also that of an elderly person, perhaps friendless and unmarried, or whose spouse had died, leading them also to become socially and sexually-frustrated. Indeed, no matter what aspect of the tokoloshe-myth we choose to pick up on, it seems that it has not been without its equivalent parallels elsewhere in the world, at some point in time. For example, mass panics over supernatural rapists have also occurred in recent years in both Kenya and Indonesia. In 2008, it was reported that the Kenyan port city of Mombasa was under assault from invisible Islamic spirits named djinn; apparently, they were grabbing people from off the street and then dragging them away beneath bridges, where they then took great delight in raping and forcibly sodomising them. Supposedly, several witnesses had seen the ghosts' victims having their clothes stripped off from them by unseen hands [35]. The recent Indonesian scare, meanwhile, which occurred in 2004, involved a being known as the Kolor Hijau - or 'green underpants monster' - a demon described as being "about 5.25ft tall, bald, with a flat face, a nose like a pig's snout, pointy ears, a paunch and hairy skin", and naked except for its green undies, which was feared to be going around breaking into women's bedrooms at night and then indecently assaulting them [36].

In the modern West, likewise, whilst the incubi and succubi of old might have largely disappeared, tales of people being anally-probed or having their semen extracted from them by aliens in their bedrooms at night seem to be more than adequate replacements for their Medieval counterparts. This, for example, is the description of perhaps the most famous of all American 'abductees', Whitley Streiber, of his being anally raped by a giant alien dildo-cum-shit-sampler in his bed one evening: "The next thing I knew I was being shown an enormous and extremely ugly object, gray and scaly, with a sort of network of wires at the end. It was at least a foot long, narrow and triangular in structure. They [the aliens] inserted this thing into my rectum. It seemed to swarm into me as if it had a life of its own. Apparently its purpose was to take samples, possibly of faecal matter, but at the time I had the impression I was being raped, and for the first time I felt anger [37]."

In short, then, mankind has always imagined, for whatever reason, that supernatural beings have crept into his sleeping-chamber and then committed various unpleasant sex-offences upon him. As such, perhaps we should not be overly surprised by the tales involving tokoloshe-rape which are currently pouring out of southern Africa. Whilst they might seem initially absurd at first sight, as we have seen, they generally have comprehensible social reasons behind them existing in the first place and, furthermore, are surely no more nor less insane in their nature than is the idea that little grey aliens might fly across the vast depths of interstellar space and then hop out from their UFOs into an American person's bedroom only in order to then stick a big, fat needle up their bum and steal their dung with it. Indeed, if anything, this latter belief is arguably far sillier!

SATURDAY
**Sun**
*Vol. 2 No. 113*
www.sunnewsonline.com
*Nigeria's King of the Tabloids* March 12, 2005 N80

Tonight
an estimated
**N4,000,000.00**
JACKPOT is at stake!
Watch the Live Draw
on NTA at 6.00 pm.
N50
Levels go change O!

# AMAZING

## Woman delivers goat...

### After 25-year pregnancy
– PAGES 41 & 42

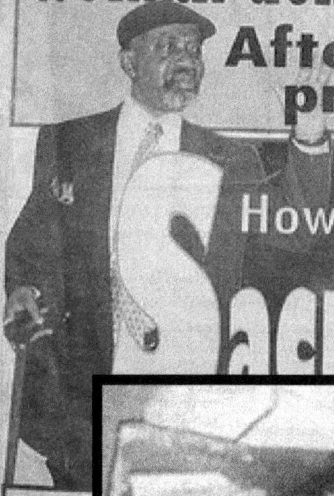

## How Ngige was Sacrificed

# SHUT UP!

Politicians tackle Bode rge over lty claim
– PAGE 5

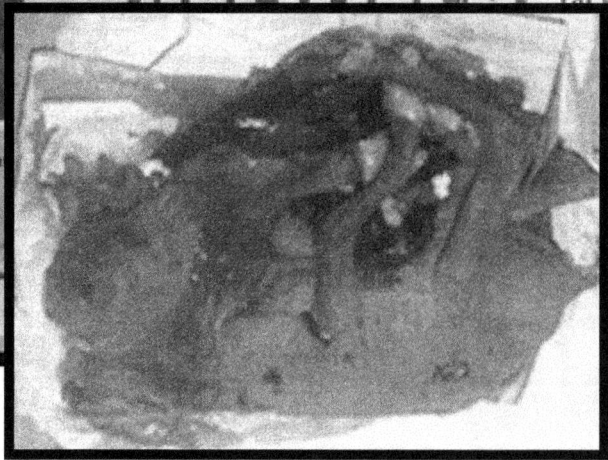

Profit

cards needed.
with pride

# Chapter Three

## Phantom Pregnancies:
## Tokoloshes and Miscarriage, Infertility and Disability

*T*he association of tokoloshes with infertility is an interesting one and a topic which is, once again, loaded with issues relating to matters of female sexuality and morality. Whilst the occasional case of male impotence may be blamed upon a tokoloshe, as we saw earlier - in some traditions, he is alleged to go around injecting men with a syringe of some kind in the night in order to prevent them from being able to get it up [1] - the vast majority of his victims in this regard are women. For example, one possible way of 'explaining' why it is that a certain woman may never have got pregnant would be to claim that a tokoloshe had eaten the foetuses of any children which might have been developing unseen inside her womb before they had even had the chance to be born [2].

Miscarriages can also be blamed upon the malicious interference of tokoloshes with the natural reproductive order of things - and sometimes even by the women who are unlucky enough to suffer them. For example, Isak Niehaus tells us that in 1967 a South African woman named Maggie Segodi married a man called Ripho Moropane and moved into a house with him and his in-laws. She was soon pregnant, but after eight months she suffered a miscarriage. This unfortunate event does not seem to have been considered supernatural in its nature by anybody, and Maggie was quickly pregnant again. This time, all went well and she gave birth to a healthy baby girl. However, she then suffered three further miscarriages in a row, giving birth to what were deemed superstitiously to be "horrible things" by those around her.

Ripho, it seems, was a migrant labourer, and frequently had to go away and work in or near Johannesburg, perhaps in the mines. Whilst he was away, Maggie became convinced that she was being bothered at night by her father-in-law sending out a tokoloshe to rape her with. She said that it was this being which had been impregnating her with 'monsters', not her husband, and that it was thus not her fault that she was repeatedly miscarrying. The old man, it seemed, was a likely candidate to be a tokoloshe-owner as he was somewhat quiet and withdrawn and

---

**OPPOSITE: The delights of the African press ... a characteristically absurd headline from Nigeria's *Saturday Sun*, and a photograph of the dead 'goat' allegedly given birth to by Hadiza Alimi in 2005.**

---

acted eccentrically by wearing an overcoat and hat at all times, even in the height of the South African summer. Sometimes, when she was being raped at night by the tokoloshe, Maggie said that she could see her father-in-law in her bedroom too, and when she asked him in the morning why he was doing this kind of thing to her, he apparently neglected to reply. Disturbed by her accounts, in 1975 Maggie's siblings came and took her away, bringing her back home to her own parents' house. There an inyanga treated her, exorcising the tokoloshe from out of her body, and she soon ended up divorcing Ripho and finding herself a new husband instead. With this man she got pregnant again and, happily, had a second healthy child this time instead of another dead one. [3]

Here, once more, we can perhaps see how the idea of tokoloshe-rape has been used to 'save face' by a person. In traditional South African society, the accepted role of the woman is to give birth to children and be a mother. However, due to some biological quirk, Maggie Segodi clearly had trouble in doing so. Therefore, by passing off blame for this onto an outside party, namely an evil wizard and his pet tokoloshe, it appears that Maggie had found a socially-acceptable way in which to fend off opprobrium and thus 'reclaim her femininity', as it were. Furthermore, there is apparently a belief current in South Africa that, if a woman has difficulties conceiving or delivering a child, simply confessing to having had willing sex with a tokoloshe will automatically cause the problem to end; something which often leads to women 'confessing' to such crimes, even when they know perfectly well that they have not really committed them [4]. Maggie could honestly have believed what she was saying here, then, or else could simply have invented the claim for her own benefit. Either way, the ultimate effect upon her life and standing in the local community would have been much the same.

As we implied earlier, infertility upon behalf of a woman can often be interpreted as being a kind of punishment for her engaging in acts of what might be deemed to be 'immoral sex' - such as sex with a tokoloshe. If the woman instigates it or enjoys it, then that would of course be enough to condemn the act in the eyes of many, but even if she hates it and is simply the victim of a malicious mubobobo wizard, the act being committed by the magical criminal himself is still clearly an immoral one, as it would be based upon perverted desires within the wizard or witch's own mind in the first place. As such, it is perhaps only to be expected that those females who sleep with tokoloshes will be forced to suffer such unpleasant consequences - at least for those who believe in this kind of thing.

Baboons in general, and not just tokoloshes in the shape of them, have long been considered to be threats to the health of unborn children in certain parts of South Africa, too, so perhaps the idea of tokoloshes causing miscarriages and infertility picks up on this tradition, as well. Apparently, if a pregnant woman walked upon the same ground that a baboon had just passed over, or ate food that one had previously touched, then it was thought in traditional folk-belief that the foetus inside her would contract an imaginary illness known as bagwera ba bana ('peers of children'), and begin suffering from convulsions whilst still in the womb [5]. Baboons, as we shall see in a later chapter, are considered to be symbols of unrestrained sexual desire and promiscuity in much of southern Africa so, once again, this particular belief appears to pick up on a kind of coded warning about the dangers of illicit carnal desires.

## Period Pains

The female reproductive system, it seems, has always been considered to be a source of potential supernatural danger, right from the earliest days of mankind. Many ancient tribes, for example, once quarantined their menstruating women, fearing that some form of 'occult infection' could be caught from them somehow. The famed late Victorian/early Edwardian anthropological writer Sir JG Frazer gives a good account of several such primitive menstruation-related taboos in his master-work *The Golden Bough*: "According to [the Roman writer] Pliny," says Frazer,

> "...the touch of a menstruous woman turned wine to vinegar, blighted
> crops, killed seedlings, blasted gardens, brought down the fruit from

trees, dimmed mirrors, blunted razors, rusted iron and brass ... killed bees ... caused mares to miscarry and so forth. Similarly, in various parts of Europe it is still believed that if a woman in her courses enters a brewery the beer will turn sour; if she touches beer, wine, vinegar, or milk, it will go bad; if she makes jam, it will not keep; if she mounts a mare, it will miscarry; if she touches buds, they will wither; if she climbs a cherry tree, it will die. In Brunswick, people think that if a menstruous woman assists at the killing of a pig, the pork will putrefy. In the Greek island of Calymnos a woman at such times may not go to the well to draw water, nor cross a running stream, nor enter the sea. Her presence in a boat is said to raise storms. [6]"

In 2011, a Zimbabwean farmer was surprised to find that one of his cows had apparently given birth to a piglet; he blamed black magic, although in actuality it seems that it was just a deformed so-called 'bulldog calf' – an entirely natural occurrence. Concepts of what might be termed 'inverted fertility' associated with witchcraft are widespread throughout much of southern Africa today, however, explaining the black farmer's belief

Such potentially malignant forces as feminine desire and the fluids associated with a woman's reproductive system have often been imagined as having the ability to cause negative supernatural events, then, particularly in relation to issues of fertility and making things 'go bad'. It seems that certain elements of these old beliefs linger on in some parts of Africa even today, especially regarding the issue of miscarriages and the still-birth of unusually-formed babies. For example, in March 2005 it was reported in the Nigerian press that a woman named Hadiza Alimi, from the village of Kotan Jen in Taraba State of that country, had given birth to a dead goat after, supposedly, having undergone a 25-year pregnancy. Looking at pictures of this 'goat', it seems obvious that it was just a malformed human foetus of some kind, but this did not mean that poor Miss Alimi did not have to fend off numerous accusations that she had engaged in sexual relations with a farm-animal prior to her becoming pregnant. According to a midwife named Jummai Emmanuel Mai, who administered both medical and traditional spiritual treatments to the woman in order to aid her finally giving birth, however, the strange foetus was actually a result of witches or wizards taking advantage of the fact that Alimi had foolishly and lasciviously not said her prayers before having sex, something which had led to the fruit of her womb going so spectacularly rotten in this way [7].

Obviously, Nigeria is a long way north from the realm of the tokoloshe, but similar beliefs are still spoken of further south in sub-Saharan Africa, too. In 2009, for instance, a very strange-looking goat was born in the Zimbabwean village of Lower Gweru, in Midlands Province. Whilst its body was obviously that of a goat, the animal appeared to have the distended head of a human being. Looking at pictures of the beast, you can certainly see why people felt that it was something very odd; its head actually bears a strong resemblance to that of a dead and pink-skinned Homer Simpson! Certainly, the local Government Minister was adamant as to what had caused this outrage, saying that it was "evident" that "evil powers" - presumably witches or demons - had caused a human being to lose control and have sex with a goat, leading the animal-human hybrid to be sired [8].

Once again, we can see how the idea of what we might term 'inverted fertility' -

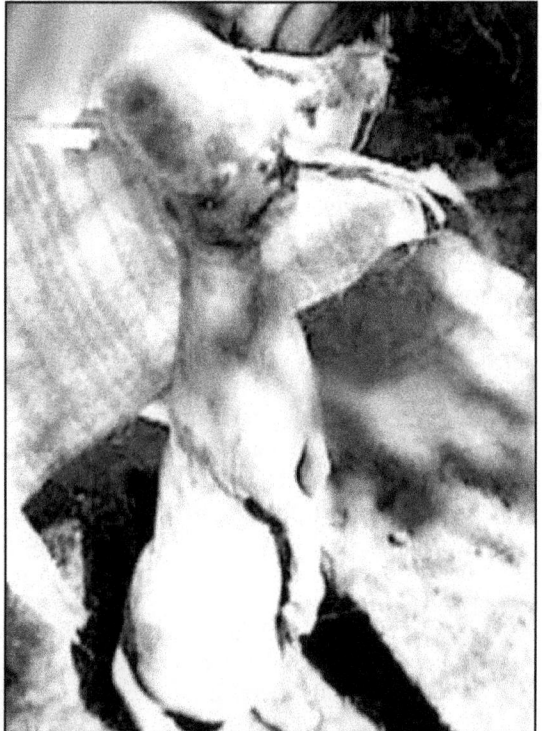

**The 'half-man, half-goat' resembling a deformed Homer Simpson which was born in Lower Gweru, Zimbabwe, in 2009; local opinion had it that the birth was a result either of witchcraft or of bestiality.**

i.e. a female animal giving birth to an alleged 'monster' instead of a normal, healthy offspring - was blamed by local residents upon a toxic combination of witchcraft and aberrant, uncontrolled sexual desire, albeit in this case presumably upon behalf of a male rather than a female, as such (unless the goat herself instigated matters, I suppose ...). Sometimes, it appears that tokoloshes have specifically been blamed for perpetrating such abnormal zoological outrages, though; one source online, for example, makes the claim that tokoloshes can rape dogs and thereby produce many more small hairy demon-babies by getting these bitches pregnant. The birth of a one-eyed puppy in the South African city of Witbank in Mpumalanga Province, for example, was once apparently blamed upon the unfortunate animal having a tokoloshe for a father [9].

So-called 'prodigious births' have always been considered to be coded comments by the cosmos upon the supposed immoral acts of the child's parents, right across the world. For example, in 1642 it was said that a pregnant Englishwoman in Northamptonshire had irreligiously announced to the world that she would rather her child had no head than for it to be baptised with the sign of the cross. When it supposedly was then born without having any head on its shoulders, this was immediately interpreted by contemporary moralists as having been an instant punishment from God for her having made such a foolish and blasphemous statement [10]. In 1517, meanwhile, it was reported that a woman living near Fontainebleau in France had given birth to an infant with the face of a frog. It was hypothesised at the time that this was because she had consulted a wise-woman about finding a cure for a fever from which she was suffering, and had been told to clutch a frog in her hand, so that the illness would then pass from her body and out into the amphibian. However, whilst she had been holding this emblem of witchcraft, her husband had come in desiring to sleep with her, and the act of having sex whilst holding onto such an evil thing had been punished by God's wrath accordingly [11]. At other times, of course, the appearance of so-called 'monstrous births' has been interpreted not as being a punishment from God upon individual sinners, but upon the misdeeds of wider society as a whole; they were reported on with particular enthusiasm in England, for instance, during the turbulent years of the Civil War.

However, it is not always the case that the birth of malformed foetuses and so forth has been interpreted as being a kind of moral slur upon the child's father or mother, either in Medieval Europe, modern-day Africa or elsewhere. Sometimes, in cultures where disability is looked upon less than positively, for example, parents have not sought to lay any blame upon themselves or wider society for their offspring's nature, and tried instead to claim that they have been the unwilling and innocent victims of evil supernatural forces which are beyond their control. In such cultures, it has sometimes proved easy and convenient for parents to pass off disabled or sickly babies as not actually being their own offspring at all but, rather, as 'substitutes' or 'changelings', which have been placed there by creatures like fairies, their own healthy infants having been taken off to live in fairyland and replaced with weak elven lookalikes instead.

This agreed social fiction then permitted the parents of such children to disown or neglect them, allowing them to die or be maltreated without seeming to be as heartless in the matter as they perhaps actually were. It must be remembered that times were harder in Europe in the

**A witch, in the role of a doting mother, feeds her hungry little demon-familiars, in this English pamphlet of 1579; yet another example of inverted fertility and motherhood being associated with witchcraft.**

past, and the idea of having another supposedly 'useless' mouth to feed would not have exactly been relished by the poorest households in the land. Again, such an idea also allowed the parents to save face; if it was possible to accuse people of immorality because of the kinds of children they gave birth to, then saying that fairies were actually responsible for it all, and not them and their sinning ways, was a viable method to avoid being accused of having committed acts of immorality by nosy neighbours. Presumably, sometimes the parents involved actually believed their own reasoning, and at other times were simply pretending to do so for their own ends, but either way equivalent fables still have currency in modern Africa, where tales of so-called 'tokoloshe-babies' are given surprisingly wide credence. It is believed, more commonly than might be expected, that tokoloshes can impregnate women causing them to give birth to only half-human children, even today. The consequences of this fact for those actually entirely-human, yet simply disabled, infants can sometimes be predictably unpleasant and heartbreaking.

**Changing Places**
At their simplest level, negative attitudes towards disability can be expressed in name-calling. In England, for example, it was once common for someone to describe either a person who was genuinely mentally-disabled, or who was simply acting foolishly, as a 'changeling' [12]. When this occurred, it did not necessarily imply that the mocker thought that the target of their

abuse was an actual changeling, however - they were just using the word in the way that certain people even nowadays might attempt to bully or belittle someone for doing something silly by regrettably calling them a 'spaz' or a 'mong' or suchlike. The word 'tokoloshe' is also able to be used in contemporary Africa either as a term of abuse for a disabled person, or in order to chide somebody about being foolish, without the person using the phrase intending it to be taken literally.

Sometimes, though, the consequences of the modern African changeling-belief can be more serious than just name-calling, unpleasant though this must no doubt be; on occasion, it seems that such convictions can actually help break up relationships. In 2008, for example, a desperate plea for aid appeared on the *Yahoo! Answers* forum, purporting to come from a man called Vlakvark Chabala, a Botswanan living in rural South Africa. His problem was that, having arranged to marry his third wife, and having already paid her father a dowry of two oxen, 12 sheep and a hi-fi system, he found to his shock that the woman was already pregnant, in spite of her claiming to be a virgin. It is quite obvious what must actually have happened in this case of course, but the girl's father refused to acknowledge that she must have had an affair, claimed that she simply must have been raped in the night by a tokoloshe and that, as such, the arranged marriage still stood. After all, it had to; he had already sold off the oxen and sheep from the dowry in order to pay off some old gambling debts and buy himself a new set of false teeth with. As such, Chabala found himself in quite a quandary; he was not keen to have to bring up and look after a tokoloshe child himself as, he had heard, they were rather "high maintenance". What should he do?

Plenty of people lined up to give him advice online, and more were supportive of the man than sceptical. Someone calling himself 'Bob Mugabe' (presumably not that one), for instance, seemed full of practical tips. First of all he told Chabala that, if his new wife had actually seen the tokoloshe, then he should dump her immediately. This is because, he explained, if anybody should be so unfortunate as to catch sight of the creature, then they had better keep it a secret - otherwise the tokoloshe will come back and seek his revenge, a belief alluded to earlier. Therefore, he advised the man simply to run away and abandon his bride-to-be. The sheep and cattle are not that expensive, he said, "but I understand about the hi-fi." However, as he then went on to write, "if you think of money now, it is not that much, but a tokoloshe child who is not yours for twelve years, that is a lot of money. [13]"

Of course, the perennial problem with such postings is that they could very easily be fakes or spoofs, perhaps created by racist persons who wish to try and portray all black Africans as being inherently simple, stupid and childishly gullible. Maybe this was one such posting. Nonetheless, the belief that tokoloshes might be able to sire non-human children upon the women they supposedly rape in their beds at night is a current and genuine one, as there are still occasional court reports of people being charged with murder for killing babies which they believed to be tokoloshes, which appear in the southern African press. In 2001, for example, a self-styled medicine-man from the township of Umlazi in South Africa's KwaZulu-Natal Province, Sipho 'Ronald' Khumalo, was hauled up before the High Court in the city of Durban and accused of murdering a baby. His defence, however, was that the baby was not a human being at all but a tokoloshe-child, something only someone in possession of his special magical powers could possibly be expected to see. Whether human or not, however, Khumalo was certainly thorough in the crime he perpetrated against the infant. According to the baby's mother, with whom Khumalo lived, he force-fed it a cocktail of herbs and paraffin before punching and slapping it with a machete until it finally died, testimony which was backed up by a doctor's post-mortem medical report upon the victim. The presiding white judge, Jan Hugo, gave his opinion that Khumalo knew perfectly well that it was a human baby he was killing, however, and said his claim that it was a tokoloshe-baby was simply an excuse. We shall examine this case, and several others like it, in much more detail in the next chapter [14].

This particular baby does not appear to have been disabled, however. Indeed, we should not make the mistake of presuming that absolutely all children who are mistreated in the name of being tokoloshes are actually disabled; some of them might just be unwanted for whatever reason. As the folklorist Jeremy Harte once put it in a discussion of his own about changeling-babies from the European tradition:

> "The goblin stranger of the stories is old-looking, ravenously hungry, and not very responsive to love and affection - much like an ordinary new-born, in short, when the idealising gaze of parenthood is lacking or at a low ebb. There is something of the demon about every baby, especially at two in the morning. Babies become changelings when they are seen as unlovable. [15]"

Perhaps Sipho Khumalo simply didn't love the baby with whom he was living, then - after all, it was not his, so maybe he just couldn't be bothered with the hassle of looking after it all the time.

Frequently, though, it does seem to be specifically disabled children in southern Africa who are subjected to abuse by adults and family-members, apparently acting under the presumption that they are half-human, half-tokoloshe hybrids. For example, in 2005 it was reported that an unnamed South African couple had had their child removed from their custody on suspicion of her being a victim of child-abuse. The little girl had numerous marks, cuts and scratches on her body. Her parents' explanation for this fact was that she had been assaulted by a tokoloshe. According to them, the child had been subject to the attentions of a tokoloshe since birth, something which had caused her to howl like a dog, pull and scratch her ears, bite herself and have an unusually large appetite, indicating that she was presumably thought of here either as being a changeling, or as being possessed by a tokoloshe-spirit.

Given these circumstances, it seems that the child was obviously mentally-disabled, and that, perhaps, she had inflicted these injuries upon herself rather than being kicked and cut by her parents as such, but it is interesting that her mother and father appeared to believe it more likely that she was possessed by a tokoloshe than that she was ill (unless, of course, this was just an excuse for their neglect of her). Taboos against mental illness are still strong across much of Africa, and perhaps the attribution of such states to the actions of tokoloshes is some kind of way to make it easier for people to cope with it all. Nonetheless, there was still a court case surrounding this incident, and the child ended up being put into foster-care by the authorities [16].

## The Baby-Killers

Abuse of alleged changeling-children can sometimes be presented, of course, as being simply a means of driving the evil spirits out of them, or as being intended to diagnose magically whether they actually are demons in human form or not. Again, this is something which has had its European parallels throughout history. Methods for diagnosing whether or not a disabled or ill baby really was a changeling from the European past were as diverse and unpleasant as putting it on a heated shovel or bathing it in a poisonous solution of liquidised fox-glove leaves (Wales), dumping it from its cradle and sweeping it out of the door, possibly either onto a dung-heap or into a grave (England), or leaving it out on the beach until the tide came in to sweep it away (the Hebrides). As one folklorist comments upon this matter, of course, "Often, these methods of revealing the true nature of the changeling were little more than socially countenanced forms of infanticide. [17]" To test whether or not a baby was a changeling, it appears, you usually had to kill it; but, in doing so, you were also in some sense publicly ridding yourself of any alleged 'guilt' for having given birth to it in the first place whilst simultaneously acting in a way which absolved yourself from committing murder, per se. After all, it was not actually a human baby that you were killing under such circumstances, was it?

Sometimes, this kind of treatment was even meted out to adults. As recently as 1895 in Ballyvadlea, County Tipperary, in Ireland, for instance, a 26-year-old woman, Bridget Cleary, (right) was famously burned and tortured to death by her husband Michael and other members of her family for supposedly being a 'changeling-woman'. After falling ill, and beginning to show signs of delirium, Bridget was forced - by being branded with a red-hot poker - to drink a potion of milk laced with herbs (probably poisonous fox-glove) in order to chase the fairy out of her. She was then soaked in urine and held over a slow-burning fire whilst the people gathered around her tried to make her confess that she was not really Bridget at all but actually a pixie in disguise. Eventually, she was covered in oil from a lamp and thrown onto the hearth-side fire to burn to death, her charred body being then wrapped up in a sheet and dumped in a nearby bog. At the later trial, where Michael Cleary made claim to holding very similar beliefs to those of Sipho Khumalo more than a hundred years later, he was sentenced to 20 years' imprisonment [18].

By virtue of this quick comparison, then, we can instantly see how it would be simplistic merely to label the contemporary belief of some southern Africans in tokoloshe-babies as being just 'primitive' or 'backward'. After all, similar beliefs have prevailed elsewhere around the world, even up to the beginning of the modern, mechanised era. People such as Michael Cleary and Sipho Khumalo (presuming that the latter was not just using his tokoloshe tale as an excuse, of course) were not simply idiots; they were merely reacting to the current folk-beliefs then prevailing in the world around them. If these notions were not sanctioned by plenty of the people with whom they lived, then they presumably would never even have thought of acting as they so tragically did. Regrettably, then, modern Africans who mistreat disabled children as tokoloshes are probably simply reflecting the attitudes which the wider society around them holds about disability; attitudes which are often not terribly positive or compassionate in their nature. Not everyone can deal with the idea of having disability in their family, it appears; and for those who can't, the multi-purpose figure of the tokoloshe is ready and waiting to fulfil yet another social role for them.

**The English witch Joan Prentice, apparently depicted being about to breast-feed her ferret-familiar, in a pamphlet from 1589.**

# Chapter Four

## The Spirit of the Law: Tokoloshes in Court

What would you do if you woke up in the middle of the night to find yourself being sodomised by an old man with the head of a hippopotamus? I suppose that some people might simply lie back and try to enjoy the ride, but it is surely the case that the vast majority of us would attempt to put up some kind of a struggle and fight back. Maybe, during such a conflict, we might even find ourselves lashing out at our weird assailant in such a way that he ends up lying down dead on the floor. Fair enough, in my view; this would be a perfectly understandable course of action for the victim of any such outrage to take. But if you did happen to kill a supernatural hippo-rapist in such a fashion, would you then expect to be prosecuted in a court of law for the fact? Perhaps not, but according to a South African magistrate named Michael Osborne, just such a case once popped up in his own courtroom and had to be taken seriously by all concerned.

The bizarre tale emerged when a sangoma was found dead in his home, having been bludgeoned to death with the mallet he used to use to crush and mix his herbs and traditional remedies with. The only clue - albeit a big one - as to who had committed this crime came in the form of a note which had been left next to his body by the man's son. In it, the son confessed to having killed the old man. Whilst he had since disappeared, he said in his note that he was not running away in order to escape custody, but had simply set out to travel to his brother's home in Swaziland to tell him about what had happened in his own words, and to settle the matter with him according to traditional native custom. Once he had done this, he said, he promised to come back and face the music.

The man was true to his word; a month later, he showed up back in town (precisely which town is not mentioned, and neither is the date, sadly) and turned himself in to the police. He admitted to his crime, but said that there were extenuating circumstances. His story was as follows: he was a college student, and had been assigned the task of reading George Orwell's novel *Animal Farm*, something which he was staying up late at night to do by lamp-light. However, whilst he was reading, he said that he kept on being attacked by a bizarre creature which was somehow entering into his room in spite of the door being locked. It had the normal body of a black man, but the head of a hippo, he said, and the figure frightened him so much that he was unable to move, scream or even breathe in its presence, something which the monster took advantage of to enable it to sexually molest and rape him. Frequently, its assaults would cause him to pass out, as had occurred upon the fatal evening in question.

This time, the hippo-man grabbed the boy around the throat and he soon blacked-out; when he awoke, he found that the thing was undressing him, eager to satisfy its unnatural desires upon his unconscious young body. As it bent him over and began to sodomise him, however, the boy suddenly found that he could move around at last and began fumbling about in the dark for something to attack the demon with. Eventually, he came across some object which seemed heavy and hard - the herb-mallet - and, turning around quickly, began hitting the hippo-man on the head with it repeatedly until it fell to the floor. Fetching a lamp, he found that, somehow, he was now in his father's bedroom and not his own, and that the hippo-man lying on the floor bleeding was not a demon at all, but his naked father, who had evidently been using his magical powers to transform himself into a sex-demon and then have his way with his own son at night in this guise. The boy tried to feel for a pulse on the body, but it soon became obvious that he was dead, so the inadvertent murderer wrote out his polite note for the police and then ran away to Swaziland.

In court, the boy stuck to his story despite intense cross-examination. There seemed to be no real motive for the killing, other than the one which the defendant himself had provided. The family's neighbours testified that the two men had had a good relationship, and said that they were unaware of any pre-existing quarrels between the pair. As a result, Magistrate Osborne was minded to take his claims seriously; obviously, he did not believe that the dead man was actually a hippo-monster himself, but he was more than prepared to accept that his son thought that he was. His two black lay-assessors, however, did not agree.

They believed in witchcraft, they said, but thought that the boy was simply using his unlikely story as an excuse for having killed his father in a dispute about money. Osborne tried to explain to the two officials that they could not simply just claim that this was the case and then find him guilty without there being any evidence whatsoever that the two men had actually quarrelled over cash, however. Nonetheless, the two men were adamant and, according to the rules of the court, could overrule Osborne on matters of fact in the case - even if these 'facts' had apparently simply been invented by themselves upon the spot, off the top of their heads.

Fortunately, though, as the presiding magistrate, Osborne was able to overrule them on a point of law, something which under South African regulations he had sole authority over. He pointed out that, whether the boy's belief that his dad was a hippo-man was believable or not, he was apparently still acting in self-defence. Seeing as this was seemingly the case, it was irrelevant whether the person he was defending himself against was a monster or a human being, and whether the fight had been over money or hippo-rape; he was still entitled to kill his assailant if he or it was attacking him. As such, Osborne took matters into his own hands and acquitted the defendant upon his own authority [1].

**I'm a Reasonable Man ...**
Such a case must seem extraordinary to a Western reader; indeed, it probably seems extraordinary to most South Africans, too! However, it is not entirely without parallel, in

**A courtroom scene from the 1999 film 'A Reasonable Man', in which a black youth is accused of killing a small child in the mistaken belief that he was a tokoloshe.**

a number of different respects. It might not have specifically involved tokoloshes by name as such, but the nefarious activities of the horny hippo-man are surely broadly analogous with the notorious bedroom assaults of these evil witch-familiars. Perhaps the most interesting aspect of the case from a legal perspective, however, rests not in the weirder details of the defendant's story, but in the willingness of the magistrate in charge to accept the boy's account as being an extenuating circumstance when considering both sentencing and the matter of his guilt or otherwise. If you tried to make similar claims as an excuse for killing your own father in a Western courtroom, the only sense in which this could be considered to have been extenuating circumstances would be if your lawyers were pleading insanity upon your behalf. However, it seems that Michael Osborne did not at any point consider the killer in the dock to have been insane; rather, he simply accepted that, whilst the boy's story was quite obviously not literally true in its nature, he did honestly believe that it was at the time, whilst he was defending himself from his father's alleged sexual assault.

How you wish to interpret this apparent belief upon the boy's behalf is, of course, up to you - did he simply 'see' his dad with a hippo's head up there on his shoulders when he was being raped in order to try and block out the horrible reality of forced homosexual incest which he was undergoing, for instance, something which the pre-existing beliefs in South African society about things like tokoloshe-rape and mubobobo might have allowed him to do in some way? - but the fact that the magistrate was sympathetic to it in the first place might seem initially remarkable to us. However, in fact Michael Osborne was simply picking up here on a widely-recognised aspect of South African law, something which is often known as the 'cultural defence' option.

The definition of this term is fairly easy to understand; it simply refers to the legal right of any defendant to try and claim that, when committing a crime, they were only acting in accordance with their traditional belief-systems, something which should be taken into account as having been an extenuating circumstance during their sentencing.

For example, in the case discussed above, even if the boy had been found guilty of murder, the fact that he genuinely thought that he was fending off assault from a sex-demon when he killed his father might have led to the defendant being given a lighter sentence than if he had killed the old man simply because he hated him or wanted to steal his money. In effect, then, the cultural defence option is a kind of 'magical self-defence' clause.

Is this idea always recognised in courtrooms as being an acceptable defence, though? Perhaps not; the concept's applicability appears to be something of a moot point, as its acceptance has not actually been formalised onto the statute books. However, in South African law, for a person to be able to be convicted of a crime like murder, it does have to be shown that the accused knew that what they were doing was illegal at the time when they committed the act.

However, as it is obviously not illegal to kill tokoloshes or hippo-men according to South African law upon the grounds that such beings do not have any literal physical existence to them, the defendant can argue that they were not in fact aware, in their own subjective mind, that what they were doing was illegal at the time of the crime. Only if they can be shown to be aware that they were killing a human being, and not a supernatural creature as such, can the accused be found guilty of murder, then - or, at least, this is the theory sometimes advanced by defence lawyers. Seeing as the South African courts do not, in principle, accept the reality of witchcraft, the degree of seriousness with which this defence is taken seems to be dependent upon the whims of the presiding officials [2].

A court case involving a tokoloshe was central to the development of this interesting aspect of South African law, however. Known to legal scholars as the case of R v Mbombela, this took place in 1933, and involved an adolescent male, aged somewhere between 18 and 20 years old, who was accused and found guilty of murdering his nine-year-old cousin. The accused, named Mbombela, lived in a rural area and was described in court as having been of "rather below average intelligence", something which, I suppose, could actually have been used to help either the defence or the prosecution to make their case, had they chosen to do so.

Either way, on the day in question some children were gathered outside a hut in their village which they thought was empty when they suddenly spotted a pair of small feet inside it. Frightened, they called Mbombela over. He saw the feet too and, presumably influenced by the children's disquiet, became scared that what they were confronting was not a mere human being hiding away inside the hut, but a tokoloshe. The local tradition surrounding the tokoloshe in Mbombela's village was that to look one in the eye would bring instant death; therefore, he ran off and got a hatchet which he then took with him as he ran inside the darkened interior of the hut, hacking away at the small humanoid figure he found inside there, endeavouring not to look at its face whilst he did so. When the 'tokoloshe' was dead, however, he dragged it out of the gloomy structure and discovered that it was actually his little cousin that he had chopped up, and not a demon at all.

Taken to court, Mbombela's defence rested upon the fact that he did not know, at the time he was committing the crime, that his victim was a human being - which, as we have seen, could be construed under South African law as meaning that he was not actually guilty of murder at all. However, this defence was dismissed, the youth was found guilty of murder, and then sentenced to death for what he had done. His lawyers took the case to appeal, though, where his defence was once more not deemed to be sufficient to enable him to be found 'not guilty'.

Even if Mbombela had thought that he was killing a tokoloshe at the time of the killing, it was determined, according to the law, "the mistake [the belief that it was a tokoloshe] pertaining to the object [the little boy] had to be reasonable". The accepted yardstick for allowing such a defence to pass was that "a reasonable man in the same circumstances" had to be able to make the same mistake. Seeing as this was the era of white rule, however, we can presume that the definition of 'a reasonable man' effectively meant 'a white man who doesn't believe in witchcraft or tokoloshes', who obviously would not have made such a mistake under similar conditions. As such, Mbombela was still found guilty - but of a different and lesser offence, 'culpable homicide', which did not carry the death penalty, presumably in recognition of the extenuating circumstances surrounding the affair [3]. ('Culpable homicide' is the rough equivalent of our term 'manslaughter' - i.e. a crime wherein the killer does not intend to commit a murder, but takes a person's life by mistake or due to unpardonable negligence)

In subsequent trials, this verdict seems to have been taken as having set a legal precedent to be followed; in one 1990 witchcraft-related trial, for instance, it was determined that "Objectively speaking, the reasonable man does not believe in witchcraft [*]. However, a subjective belief in witchcraft may be a factor which may, depending upon the circumstances, have a material bearing upon the accused's blameworthiness ... as such it may be a relevant mitigating factor to be taken into account in the determination of an appropriate sentence.[4]" That phrase 'depending upon the circumstances' appears to be key. The presence of subjective elements such as this in the law is how lawyers make their money, after all. As such, some South African court cases involving crimes related to tokoloshes have been highly controversial.

---

* It will be noted that this is actually in itself a *subjective* statement, of course!

## Khumalo the Killer

The most common tokoloshe-related crime which comes up before South African courts, of course, involves the murder of children by persons who claim that they thought that their victims were not human babies and infants at all but, rather, half-breed tokoloshe-changelings. The belief that your baby is a tokoloshe in disguise is probably not one which would be considered likely to be held by the South African legal system's usual definition of what constitutes a 'reasonable man', however, so it seems to be rare (but not unknown) that anybody charged with infanticide who pleads 'not guilty' whilst playing the cultural defence card gets off scot-free.

Indeed, frequently attempts by defendants to claim protection under this idea are simply not believed by the court. This was certainly the case during perhaps the most notorious tokoloshe-murder trial of recent times, that of Sipho 'Ronald' Khumalo, which we examined very briefly in the previous chapter. Khumalo, we will recall, appeared in the dock at the High Court in Durban in 2001, accused of force-feeding a three-month-old baby a deadly cocktail of herbs and paraffin (an "enemy of tokoloshes", he claimed) before finishing it off by punching and slapping it around with a machete for eight hours until it died, allegedly because he, as a man in possession of supposed magical powers, could see that it was actually a tokoloshe in disguised human form.

The baby, it seemed, was not actually his, but belonged to his girlfriend, Henrietta Jabu Gcabashe. 56-year-old Khumalo, in his position as a self-styled 'wise-man', appears to have been approached by Gcabashe seeking treatment for some illness. Whilst consulting him, she mentioned that she had encountered some difficulty in giving birth to her youngest child, Zama, and that, as such, her (presumably previous?) boyfriend had accused it of actually being a tokoloshe. Khumalo, sensing an opportunity of some kind, looked at Zama, whom the woman had brought along with her, and confirmed that she was indeed a dangerous goblin, before then inviting Henrietta, the tokoloshe-baby and her three other children, to come and live at his house with him. Here, he professed to have witnessed the baby repeatedly changing its gender in the middle of the night, apparently a sure sign that it was a tokoloshe; but also something which, conveniently, only he had the power to see. These bizarre living arrangements had been going on for three months prior to the tiny victim being murdered in October 1999.

In court, it was never successfully established quite why Khumalo had done all this, although perhaps it could be speculated that he had just taken a fancy to the woman, and was exploiting her superstitious and gullible nature in order to get her to come and live with him. He appears to have informed the child's mother that, as an inyanga, he was immune to the creature's evil influence, and so perhaps she naively agreed to share a home with him in order to get some protection from it?

In any case, Khumalo, who it turned out had a string of previous convictions for such pleasant crimes as murder, robbery and vehicle-theft to his name, told the police who eventually came out to arrest him that he had not killed the tokoloshe outright at all. After all, as a holy man, he had the power to resurrect the tokoloshe - which he said was immortal anyway - from the dead in the form of a healthy little boy, so how could that be murder? He did warn his arresting officers, however, not to refrigerate the dead baby's body, as that would interfere with his ability to later resuscitate it, something which might seem at first sight to have been a rather pathetic ploy upon his behalf to try and disrupt the autopsy by allowing the corpse to rot so that there would be less evidence of its injuries - which included a split liver and swollen feet - to convict him on. However, once in court, it turned out that this was not in fact the case. Rather, Khumalo claimed that, as he had supposedly been intending to bring the baby back to life at some point in the future but had been thwarted in this aim by the foolish officers refrigerating the body against his specific instructions, it was actually the police who had killed the child, wasn't it, and not him at all?

It also seemed that Khumalo had attempted to stop his girlfriend going to the police in the first place by telling her that he intended to resurrect Zama after three days had passed, something which she evidently did not believe. However, he had apparently tried to prove this 'fact' to her by pointing out that the skin had fallen off the baby after it had died - which is perhaps hardly surprising given that Khumalo had been slapping it with a machete and pouring paraffin all over it all night long. He said that, once it was resurrected, he could banish the tokoloshe away from its body to the bush or into a pool of water, so she didn't need to worry. She was worried, however, and prepared to take her child's mutilated corpse down to the police station. Before she could do so, though, Khumalo thoughtfully wrote out an informative note to the police warning them against the dangers of putting a tokoloshe in a fridge, and stuck it to the dead child's head so that they would not make this foolish mistake. He also at one point tried to persuade Henrietta not to take the body down to the station because, after three days, the tokoloshe would automatically resurrect itself in the mortuary anyway, whereupon it would presumably then be eager to seek revenge.

The presiding judge, Jan Hugo, was confused by the number of ridiculous and utterly incoherent inconsistencies in Khumalo's story, however, and asked him to elaborate further. How, exactly, was he intending to bring a baby back from the dead? Khumalo said that, regrettably, he could not explain his method, as it was a sacred secret; "I am not allowed to explain these things," he said, gnomically, then adding that there was no point in the judge asking him "all these prolonged questions" which would only get them nowhere. Instead, he offered to demonstrate his magical powers to the court if Hugo agreed that he could do so. Perhaps unsurprisingly, the judge neglected to give his permission for this to take place.

Furthermore, whilst in the dock Khumalo managed to buy himself some time by denying that he had any criminal record at all, as had been claimed by the prosecution, which meant that there had to be a delay of a few weeks whilst this was all properly checked out. However, he did rather give the game away at one point by claiming that his powers as a magician were so well-known that even the inmates in Westville Prison - where he had apparently once done time - were aware of them! Subsequently, it turned out that Khumalo was indeed a hardened criminal, having committed his first offence in 1976, when he had assaulted a man with an iron rod, and having later been given ten years in jail in 1986 for stabbing a man in a bar. Obviously, then, Khumalo was of intensely bad character and appeared to be set upon demonstrating himself to be a proven liar in public, with the unsurprising result that Judge

Hugo did not believe a word of his insane story.

Whilst admitting that the ultimate motive for Khumalo killing little Zama was unknown, Hugo rightly called his crime "disgusting and brutal", finally sentencing him to life imprisonment with no right of appeal. Khumalo's attempt to exploit the idea of the cultural defence was, meanwhile, dismissed by Judge Hugo with the withering words "The accused has no right to kill people just because he thinks they are not human and that he has superhuman powers." [5]

Amazingly, this was not actually the end of Khumalo's long story, though; once taken to Westville Prison, awaiting final sentencing, it seemed that Khumalo disappeared from his cell, supposedly by making use of his magical powers to do so. When he did not turn up in court at the appointed time, it was presumed that he had either got free somehow or, curiously, was hiding away inside the prison itself somewhere. However, it later transpired that Khumalo had simply been brought to court late by bungling security van drivers, and had not managed to spirit himself away at all. Nonetheless, the fact that some people were apparently willing to believe that he had magically done so, even after the ridiculous debacle of his absurd appearance in court, shows just how ingrained belief in witchcraft and sorcery can be amongst certain sections of South African society [6].

**Suffer the Little Children**
Not everybody from the black South African community believes child-killers when they claim that they only committed their crimes because they were under the impression that their victims were tokoloshes, however. For example when, in 2007, a five-year-old boy named Sanele Mncwabe was abducted on his way home from church in the small city of Pinetown, near Durban in KwaZulu-Natal Province, before being murdered and mutilated by a man who claimed that he thought the lad was a tokoloshe, the victim's relatives did not believe a word of it. Muzikayise Simon Mbeje, it seems, was a former lover of the dead child's mother, Ntombikhona Mncwabe, but she had broken up with him about seven years beforehand. Seeing as Ntombikhona began showing signs of pregnancy - from a new lover - shortly after she had jilted Mbeje, however, it appears that her former boyfriend had begun to brood upon the idea that the child, Sanele, was in fact his.

As such, Ntombikhona was not of the opinion that Mbeje thought that the boy was a tokoloshe at all, and said that he had simply killed her son as an act of revenge upon her. When Mbeje ended up in court, the dead boy's family turned up en masse, and Sanele's uncle, S'busiso, spat upon the accused in order to register his own contempt for him; indeed, after the killing had first been discovered, it seems that Mbeje had had to be taken to the nearest police station for his own safety, seeing as the rest of the community were apparently ready to kill him. It appeared evident to the dead child's family and neighbours that Mbeje was just playing the cultural defence card in order to try and get his sentence reduced, then, but nonetheless the killer still found a psychologist named Irma Labuschagne who was willing to stand up for his version of events in court. "He could have seen the child as evil because he saw it as the root cause of his [relationship] problem. His mind could have projected a [vision of a] tokoloshe when he killed him," she told the courtroom, perhaps somewhat dubiously.

Ntombikhona, however, was having none of this. The idea that her former lover had just suddenly suffered some kind of mental aberration which made him think that Sanele was a tokoloshe was not tenable, she said, as he had been making attempts to entice the little boy to his home for the past week before he had killed him, showing that the crime must have been planned in advance. Furthermore, it seems that the way in which Sanele was killed was inconsistent with the idea that Mbeje had simply thought that he was suddenly being confronted by a monster, as he had not just stabbed and bashed the boy's head against the wall in self-defence, but had also tortured and mutilated him by smashing his teeth out and cutting off his tongue and ear.

Indeed, this latter detail was interpreted by the dead child's mother as meaning that Mbeje had been planning to make a magical potion or ointment known as muti from the child - a process which, notoriously, sometimes involves chopping off certain body parts from still-living children in order to infuse the substance with their life-power somehow. It was Ntombikhona's view, then, that the murder was entirely premeditated, and not an act of self-defence against an alleged tokoloshe at all, something with which the police officers who investigated the case agreed. According to a PC Lungile Jama, for example, in his view "Even if for a moment he thought he saw a tokoloshe, somewhere along the line he had to realise that it was his [alleged] son he was defending himself from ... he will pay accordingly for this.[7]" Presumably, the murderer did indeed do so; but I cannot find any details of his ultimate sentencing anywhere, so this notion will have to remain as supposition for now. I can't imagine that the court would have let him off with it, though.

It does seem to be the case, however, that some modern child-killers have had their sentences commuted and been convicted of culpable homicide rather than murder because judges and juries have apparently accepted that they had acted out of no actual malice, but purely in error. For example, in 2004 a 48-year-old man named Monwabisi Nkathu from Port Elizabeth in South Africa's Eastern Cape Province was brought to the dock after what does genuinely seem to have been a tragic case of mistaken identity led to a two-year-old boy named Masixole Sotenjwa being stabbed to death. It seems that Nkathu's girlfriend, Nosipho Mbakela, had found Masixole wandering around in the street, either lost or abandoned, one day, and had taken him to the local police station. The police said that they would look into it, but asked if Nosipho would look after the toddler in the meantime. She agreed, and took the kid home to her boyfriend's house, where Nkathu was sleeping. When he awoke and saw the two-year-old boy walking around in his house, however, he knew nothing of what had just gone on. As far as he was concerned, there should have been no small child inside his house at all and, this being the case, he panicked at the sight of the tiny waddling being, presuming that it must have been a tokoloshe which had come to get him in his sleep. As such, sadly, he stabbed the baby 16 times with a knife, killing it (it is not said where Nosipho was whilst this tragic event took place, but presumably she must have been out of the room). The court accepted, however, that this was a genuine mistake upon Nkathu's behalf, and sentenced him to seven years in jail for culpable homicide, rather than finding him guilty of wilful murder [8].

Sometimes, meanwhile, defendants have even gone free from court without any prison sentence being handed down at all for committing tokoloshe-related killings. In 2001, for example, a case was heard at Pietermaritzburg Regional Court in KwaZulu-Natal Province, in which it was told how a 35-year-old man named Phathisa Gabuza had repeatedly stabbed both his mother and sister with a sharpened handle of some kind as, apparently, he thought that he was fighting off a band of "small hairy creatures" - tokoloshes - which were attacking him. During this assault, the man's mother was killed, although his sister somehow managed to survive. In court, however, a psychiatrist named Jonathan Dunn appeared for the defence, stating that it was his opinion that Gabuza had undergone some kind of psychotic episode, saying that he lived in a "different world" and that he had genuinely been suffering from hallucinations when he committed his crime. Furthermore, seeing as how it could be demonstrated that Gabuza had not been in any way abusive towards his family-members beforehand, and had no reason to have quarrelled with them, Dr Dunn argued that his act of violence was an isolated incident and quite out of character. As such, the presiding magistrate, Andre Voogt, rather generously said that he would give Gabuza "the benefit of the doubt" and let him off with the killing, as it was his view that, at the time when the crime was being committed, he had not actually realised that he was committing a crime. Fair enough ... but shouldn't Gabuza have been placed in a mental institution instead, then? [9]

It seems that there will always be certain psychologists - generally white - who are willing to come to the aid of changeling-murderers in court. Even during the Sanele Mncwabe case, a Durban psychologist named Rita Suliman was prepared to defend his killer Muzikayise Simon Mbeje by saying that:

> "There's a disorder where someone hallucinates and sees something that's not there. In the traditional sense, a person may need a certain ritual and may feel so guilty about it that they start imagining things." [10]

At other times, though, the excuse of temporary insanity seems to be replaced with that of permanent derangement. Occasionally, it even appears that tokoloshe-killers who are already known to be mentally-disturbed are not charged with murder in the first place, merely culpable homicide, on account of their pre-existing mental conditions. This occurred during a recent South African case in which a prisoner named Mziwothando Dike repeatedly smashed the head of his cell-mate, a 13-year-old orphan named Msimeleli Mazuleni, against the prison wall until the boy was dead in May 1997, supposedly in the belief that he was a tokoloshe. Here, even the prosecution were not of the mind that the killing was entirely Dike's fault; it was obvious to the prison authorities that he was dangerously insane, according to the prosecuting lawyer Xoliswa Soyizwapi, but they kept on delaying sending him off for assessment to a mental hospital, meaning that they were probably as culpable in the matter as the killer was, really. After all, locking a vulnerable 13-year-old boy up next to a known psychopath was hardly the most responsible thing for the authorities to have done, was it? [11]

**Excuses, Excuses ...**
Not all cases involving tokoloshes which come to court centre around the senseless murder of young children, however. Other crimes, too, sometimes involve the hairy little beasts in some way. In February 2011, for instance, a public petition was handed in to Pietermaritzburg Magistrates Court in the South African Province of KwaZulu-Natal accusing a local traditional

healer, Mduduzi Manqele, of training up tokoloshes to steal dockets and evidence from the court; "We fear, once released, his evil creatures will tamper with the investigations", the petition said. It seems that Manqele and an accomplice, Roger Thusi, were up in court on charges of murder after the disembodied head of an 18-year-old girl, Loyisa Jokweni, was found stored away in a freezer in the home of Thusi's girlfriend, supposedly with a frozen snake coiled around it. According to Thusi, he had gone to see Manqele and been advised by him that, if he beheaded the girl and then froze her head, he would get rich quick. However, it appears that the police only had Thusi's word for it that Manqele had told him to commit the hideous crime and, there being no real evidence against him, the sangoma was released on bail. It was this which led the outraged public - some of whom had already burned down the homes of both Manqele and Thusi - to hand in their petition about matters, as they feared that, once freed, Manqele would be easily able to use spells and the tokoloshes under his control in order to influence the outcome of the trial [12].

Civil cases involving tokoloshes, too, sometimes come up before perplexed southern African magistrates, it appears; in January 2012, for instance, a 62-year-old Zimbabwean man named Zachariah Nyakudya took his sons Isaac and Moses to the Harare Civil Court in that country's capital, complaining that they were slandering him by implying that he kept tokoloshes in his house. They were constantly accusing him of being a witch, he said - making such accusations falsely now being a crime in Zimbabwe - and playing the goblin-related song 'Chikwambo', by the popular Zimbabwean singer Alick Macheso, at full-blast whenever he came near them. Furthermore, they were disturbing him by bringing around a constant stream of traditional healers to his house and getting them to perform annoying exorcisms there. According to his sons, Mr Nyakudya had bewitched their sister using evil spirits, but the old man denied this and had had enough of such accusations, saying that he now wanted action to be taken against them. The presiding magistrate agreed with him in this request, apparently, and promptly issued his sons with something called a Reciprocal Peace Order, officially requiring them to stop persecuting him [13].

More common than accounts of cases like these, however, are tales of murderers and rapists coming up before the courts who claim, quite simply, that 'a tokoloshe told me to do it', such as Daniel Molewa, a serial rapist who in 2004 told a court in the administrative capital of South Africa, Pretoria, that he was not truly responsible for his horrific criminal actions. Instead, a tokoloshe was to blame, he insisted - though whether by this statement he intended to imply that he had been temporarily 'possessed' by one or egged on to perform his crimes by such an entity is not mentioned in the relevant news report. Either way, the court clearly didn't believe him, sentencing him to six life-terms and an additional 24 years [14]. During another case, a defendant in a murder trial was quoted as issuing the following anguished statement: "It was not my wish to murder, but there was the tokoloshe. The tokoloshe nipped me and said 'Kill', and I killed.[15]" It is impossible, it seems, to disobey a tokoloshe when he tells you to perform acts such as these - compared to puny human powers of reasoning, his will is simply too strong to resist.

Because of statements such as this being made in the dock, it has perhaps justly been said that "As an extenuating circumstance, the tokoloshe is to African courts what failed memory ('everything went blank') is to puzzled jurors elsewhere.[16]" It is often unclear in such instances, however, as to whether the defendants were genuinely mentally ill and therefore sincere in their assertions that tokoloshes were to blame for their crimes or whether they were simply lying in order to gain sympathy and reductions in their sentences, but it is worth pointing out, of course, that we occasionally hear of directly parallel cases to these in the West; except that, in the US or Europe, murderers and rapists who play this card claim that it was Satan, demons or space-aliens who ordered them to commit their misdeeds, not tokoloshes. No doubt if somebody like Daniel Molewa had lived in France, say, or Canada, he would have done the same.

Another strange ploy which is sometimes used by accused criminals is to claim that tokoloshes are engaging in bouts of what essentially amounts to 'witness intimidation' with them. For example, the genuinely bizarre case of a man named Sibusiso John Gcabashe, which came to a South African courtroom in 2012, featured many odd claims relating to tokoloshes. Gcabashe caused a sensation on 28th January of that year when he turned up at the family home of a dead Zulu folk-singer named Khulekani 'Mgqumeni' Khumalo in the municipality of Nquthu in KwaZulu-Natal Province, claiming to be the deceased celebrity returned from beyond the grave. According to the imposter, he had been kidnapped by a witch-doctor and forced to live in a cave full of zombies (which, it seems from later statements Gcabashe made, were in fact tokoloshe-zombies) in the Johannesburg suburb of Driefontein where he was made to eat a diet of mud and to play songs to his undead jailers to keep them entertained.

Amazingly, several members of Khumalo's family, including two of his former wives and his paternal grandparents, fell for this ridiculous pretence, and accepted him as being the genuine article. Khumalo had actually died in 2009, however, apparently after drinking some kind of poisonous potion which had been given to him by a rogue sangoma. Seeing as Khumalo was something of a superstar in South Africa, though, once word about this unlikely event got round, thousands of people gathered to hear the supposedly reanimated singer make an official announcement about his return from death, an event which grew so rowdy that police ended up having to use water cannon and truncheons on the crowd in order to keep them under control. Using a loudspeaker, Gcabashe informed the crowd that he had never actually been dead at all, but had simply been subject to a process of something called ukuthwetshulwa, or 'spirit-capture', and explained the reason that he looked nothing like Khumalo was simply down to the twin facts that he had lost a lot of weight, and that his captors had been trying to make him into a tokoloshe-zombie, too. According to him, for instance, the evil witch-doctor who had kidnapped him had shaved off his famous dreadlocks purely in order to make it easier for him to then be able to drive a nail through his head and thus transform him into a zombie.

Suspiciously, the imposter then refused point-blank to sing, saying that his voice had changed

OPPOSITE: *"I see tokoloshes who tell me not to come clean. They threaten that my eyes will burst if I change my statement"* – Sibusiso John Gcabashe, in court for fraudulently claiming to be a dead South African folk singer and making out that he had been kidnapped by zombies who kept him inside a cave for several years, makes the kind of claim which would simply be laughed out of a Western courtroom.

during his captivity, so he wouldn't sound like he used to. The fact that he had a gold tooth, which the real Khumalo did not, offered further grounds for suspicion about the man's assertions. He then tried to anticipate being exposed as a fraud by making the outrageous claim that his criminal captor had changed his name to Gcabashe by deed-poll and had even organised some fake ID documents for him. However, it appears that the police took a different view of the reasons for his papers having this name on them, and promptly arrested him for fraud; presumably, seeing as Khumalo had died intestate and his record company had held onto his royalties instead of paying them out to his family, Gcabashe had simply been intending to try and pull off the world's weirdest ever 'get rich quick' scheme.

Fingerprint and DNA tests predictably established that the man was indeed not Khumalo, and Gcabashe appeared before a packed courtroom in May 2012, where he began making several extremely bizarre claims. For example, when asked why he now had a big wound on his head, he expressed the view that it was because he had magical powers and had been stabbed by a fellow inmate at Dundee Prison, where he was now being held, after the other man had witnessed him transforming into a snake. Seemingly, Gcabashe had by now realised that his whole story about really being Khumalo did not stand up, and, under questioning, appears to have implied that he made it all up, but then added that he could not openly admit this, as otherwise seven tokoloshes whom he had recently begun seeing would come and kill him. "I see tokoloshes who tell me not to come clean," he told a shocked courtroom, adding that "They threaten that my eyes will burst if I change my statement." The presiding magistrate did not seem to believe Gcabashe, however, and asked him how he could understand the

tokoloshes' language; a question which he was strangely unable to answer. Indeed, it seemed to be being implied in court that Gcabashe was just a chancer who was merely pretending to be mentally ill in order to win sympathy and so come away with a lighter sentence. Whether he succeeded in this endeavour I do not know (the trial was still ongoing at the time of writing), but I sincerely doubt that he did, personally [17].

### Crime and Punishment

By no means can playing the old 'a tokoloshe made me do it, honest, officer' card always lead to a successful outcome for a defendant in court, then. In 1956, for example, a young Zulu witch-doctor named Elifasi Msomi was executed via hanging after being found guilty of committing 15 murders in an attempt to pacify the blood-lust of a tokoloshe who had promised to help him in his trade if he would kill enough people as a kind of sacrifice to him. Apparently, Msomi was not doing too well in his calling, and went to see another, older - and supposedly wiser - witch-doctor for advice. In his hut, Msomi found the old witch-doctor in conference with a tokoloshe who had temporarily shape-shifted into the form of the man's son. The older sangoma told Msomi that he would be able to become a great wise-man himself, too, if only he would go out into the countryside with the tokoloshe and kill it 15 victims, something which apparently would help the old man in his trade too, somehow. First, said the experienced sangoma, the tokoloshe would desire the blood of a young girl.

After this, it seems that Msomi set out to commit his crimes with his tokoloshe leading the way, the demon being invisible to everyone bar Msomi himself, and telling him what to do. It took 18 months of trekking through the bush in the old Natal Province, apparently, before the tokoloshe finally found a girl who looked to his liking. Accordingly, Msomi killed her, chopped her up and put some of her blood into a bottle for his evil master to later partake of at his leisure.

Msomi was soon captured, however, and put in prison, awaiting trial. Thanks to the power of his tokoloshe, though - or so he said - the criminal quickly managed to escape his cell, and spent the next 14 months wandering around the country killing another 14 people with weapons such as knives, clubs and axes. Finally, once the agreed-upon fifteenth victim had been ritually slaughtered, the tokoloshe released Msomi from his bond. "You have rendered good service; now we will wash in the river and part," the spirit allegedly told him.

However, once the tokoloshe had left him, Msomi's luck began to fail, and he was arrested for an act of petty theft before being recognised by police as the wanted serial-killer. He then freely admitted to his crimes, and even helped the police locate the skulls of his victims. In jail, it seemed that his tokoloshe-master had come back to comfort him, though. When in his cell at night, Msomi would keep on huddling up in order to make room on his bed of rags for some invisible visitor. "It's a friend," he explained to his prison guards, "just a friend." Fearing that the tokoloshe might help the killer to escape once more, the local Zulu chieftains asked permission of the white authorities to stand guard around the gallows themselves whilst Msomi was being hanged after he had been sentenced to death in court, in order to keep a look out for the entity coming to his rescue. Permission being granted for this sensible precaution to be allowed, the blood-drinking tokoloshe did not turn up to save his evil worshipper, and justice was finally done [18].

It is not all blood and murder, though. Occasionally, even financial crimes such as fraud are blamed upon tokoloshes. In March 2011, for instance, a woman named Ndakupinda Chibharo, from the district of Bikita in Zimbabwe's Masvingo Province, admitted to defrauding thousands of dollars from two women in a smuggling scam, but said that she had been forced into it by a goblin. It transpired that she had bought a chikwambo - according to some definitions a specific type of money-spinning tokoloshe, as we shall see later - from a traditional healer in order to make her rich, but that this goblin had then gone rogue and begun stealing money from her instead. Evidently, she expected this claim to be believed, and to be shown lenience by the policemen who had arrested her because of it. According to Chibharo, the chikwambo - described by her as being a "seed" of some kind - had been faithful and helpful to her at first and had brought lots of money to her business. However, at some point she had begun returning home to find that the goblin had taken to stealing money from her stash instead, leaving her in much financial distress. She implied that this might have been because she had at one point temporarily misplaced her tokoloshe, perhaps angering it with her negligence. Therefore, she said, she had no option but to defraud others in order to pay off the sangoma from whom she had bought the tokoloshe in order to get him to take it back off her [19].

Another macabre excuse for one's crimes, meanwhile, is to claim that the bodies of the people you have killed for use in making muti potions are not human remains at all but are, rather, those of tokoloshes. In 2010, for example, South African police in KwaZulu-Natal Province arrested two men for being in possession of human body parts. The first man was caught in possession of two severed human hands, and he soon led police to his accomplice, a sangoma who was found to have a very strange corpse stored away in a large bucket. Its head looked like that of an elderly man, but its body appeared to be that of a child. Presumably it was actually the carcass of a young boy whose head had been mutilated or deformed in some way, and which was intended for use in muti ceremonies; but this did not prevent the rogue sangoma from claiming that it was not a human being at all, but a dead tokoloshe which he had caught and killed out in the bush. The arresting officers, apparently, did not accept his word upon the matter, in spite of his vehement protests [20].

Occasionally, in addition, shocking crimes can even be covered up by claiming in court that traumatised victims have simply fallen foul of a tokoloshe. In 2007, for instance, a case came to court in the city of Pretoria in South Africa's Gauteng Province in which it was heard how a young girl had become disturbed, suffering from nightmares and acting in an irrationally aggressive manner towards her father. Her father had a simple theory to account for this being the case, though; a tokoloshe was interfering with her sexually in the night, something which his wife apparently accepted by way of explanation. They both asked people to pray for the child, who was ten when the disturbances began, but eventually the truth came out. Testifying against her husband in the dock, his wife pointed at him and said that there really was a tokoloshe in the house molesting their daughter, after all - and that "it was him". It transpired that the unpleasant abuser had simply been creeping into the girl's room at night and then raping her, again and again, over a period of six years, and then blithely passing it all off as being the handiwork of a paranormal entity. He had just been exploiting pre-existing beliefs about the tokoloshe which are held amongst many black South Africans in order to help him get away with it for so long [21].

Overall, then, whilst many of the cases discussed in this chapter might seem at first sight to be ridiculous to Western eyes - none of the criminals would be acquitted or have their sentences reduced if they appeared in courts in Britain, America or France, after all, unless they could bring themselves to plead insanity - this is hardly the point. In the minds of many of the people involved in these incidents, the tokoloshe is conceived of as being a real entity; and, as such, it is only by looking at them through the unfamiliar eyes of members of a different culture that we can ever hope to come to understand these sad affairs properly. The notion of a cultural defence option might seem to us as if it is merely a convenient way of allowing criminals to, quite literally, get away with murder - but this would not be the viewpoint of the average black South African or Zimbabwean, perhaps. For the courts themselves, meanwhile, whose laws and outlook are still largely based upon legal traditions handed down to these countries by the British during the days of Empire, there is a difficult line to tread; to try and understand and respect traditional black beliefs about the reality of witchcraft and tokoloshes without in any way actually endorsing them at the same time. Needless to say, this is an extremely hard thing to do. Perhaps it is no wonder, then, that the courts do not always appear to get their judgements in such cases absolutely right.

# Chapter Five

## A 'Common' Superstition?:
## Attitudes of Authority Towards the Tokoloshe

D o black people in South Africa, Lesotho and Zimbabwe really put their beds up on bricks in order to escape the unwanted nocturnal attentions of the tokoloshe, as we implied previously in this book's introduction? And, if so, then why? Surely the beasts could simply climb up on top of the beds to rape people, or else extend their penises via the magic of mtshotshaphansi to do so? Perhaps there is more to this allegedly widespread superstition than meets the eye, then ...

Whilst this practice is certainly often said to be common, especially amongst the poor black servant-class of countries like South Africa, it might well in fact have a rather more prosaic explanation to it. Well into the twentieth century, most native blacks slept on mats on the floors of their homes, beds being a luxury generally reserved for their white masters. When beds - or glorified mattresses, perhaps - started to be provided for them, though, many servants really did begin lifting them up off the ground using bricks. However, it appears likely that the real reason for them doing so was so that they could then use the area of free floor-space which was thus created beneath their beds for storage, the rooms they were allocated by their employers generally being rather small. In addition, of course, the higher a bed is, the less likely it is that spiders, snakes, lizards or mice will crawl in under the covers with you after you have gone to sleep, too. Furthermore, raising your bed up off the floor was a good way to avoid being gassed by low-lying carbon monoxide fumes once fire-braziers started to be used for indoor heating purposes in native servants' rooms during the twentieth century; it has therefore been speculated in some quarters that any 'tokoloshe' which came in the night to kill a floor-dweller under such circumstances could thus actually have been a kind of hallucination caused by the fumes, or a 'rationalised' explanation for why people kept on dying of asphyxiation when they didn't sleep in a raised bed at night.

Surprisingly, then, the explanation that beds were raised on bricks simply so that their black occupants would thereby be able to escape the attentions of tokoloshe-rapists and their gigantic penises appears actually to have been created by whites; probably as some kind of mocking gibe about their servants' numerous superstitions. However, this seemingly entirely invented belief appears gradually to have then passed on to being accepted by the black population as a genuine idea, and the whites' joke thus become reality. Nonetheless, whilst some black people no doubt do genuinely put their beds up on bricks in order to put off tokoloshes, it seems highly likely to me that the actual number of persons who do so has been to some degree exaggerated [1].

One popular way of demeaning the less powerful people in any society has long been to accuse them of superstition; because superstition, almost by definition, is meant to be a kind of foolishness. Thus, white people making up comically irrational explanations for why blacks did things which were, in actual fact, entirely rational in their nature, was a kind of way in which they could demonstrate their higher social status in the past. Often, these invented 'superstitions' involved tokoloshes. Quite apart from the yarns being spun about beds being raised up on bricks, for example, it was once a common jibe in South Africa to say that black people's bicycles were made with a little extra seat on the back of them, just in case a tokoloshe wanted to take a ride on it with its black owner, too [2]. No doubt black people did frequently have small seats on the back of their bikes, of course; and presumably they were intended for use by their young children as passengers, rather than being set aside for any passing tokoloshes who might fancy a free ride, though.

Other traditional superstitions relating to tokoloshes are apparently quite genuine in their nature, however. For example, whenever white people went away on holiday to the coast, it was apparently once quite common for their black servants to plead with their masters to bring them back some bottles of sea-water. When asked why, the servants would reply that they wanted to sprinkle it all over the outside walls of the family home to fool the tokoloshe into thinking that, because he would then be able to smell some salt from the water on the walls, he would have to cross over an entire ocean in order to assault the domestic employees in their beds at night [3]. No doubt many whites indulged their staff in this way and did indeed bring back bottles of salt-water for them; but it would also be safe to presume that most of those who did so will have found the whole idea to be quite funny, and viewed the old belief in rather a patronising manner.

Perhaps because of such gibes being made by higher-status whites, it appears that some black people who believe in tokoloshes now wish to disguise the fact when in public. For example, according to one Zulu sangoma, a good, traditional way to scare off tokoloshes would be to wear a piece of snakeskin around your wrist, this substance being repellent to them for some reason. However, this particular sangoma then added that, if you did not wish to draw attention to your belief and look superstitious by going around everywhere with a bit of dead snake hanging off your arm, then simply going so far as to get your wristwatch fitted with a snakeskin strap would suffice [4]. When even sangomas are offering their clients advice such as this, then it is perhaps a sure sign that belief in the tokoloshe has been relegated largely to only the lower-status sectors of society.

**Black Power**
Or has it? Actually, the situation is much, much more ambiguous than this. If you're a black man working for a Western multinational corporation in southern Africa, say, then it's highly unlikely that going around wearing lengths of snakeskin and taking about tokoloshes will endear you to your white (or, increasingly these days, Chinese) superiors and make them

consider you to be a suitable candidate for promotion. However, it is now around twenty to thirty years since the fall of the apartheid regimes in both South Africa and Zimbabwe, and it is thus no longer the case that all high-status people in society are white men; indeed, far from it. The Presidents of both countries are black, and they lead black-majority governments. In addition, the oldest traditional figures of authority in southern African countries - tribal chiefs, inyangas and religious leaders - are predominantly black too, and many of them believe, quite openly, in things like tokoloshes. Sometimes, it is true, representatives of authority only encourage ordinary people to believe in tokoloshes in order to then exploit or intimidate them - as with the 2009 case of Lucas Mamadi, a South African village chief who levied a 10-Rand charge on every household under his control in order to pay for a sangoma whom he alleged had removed a tokoloshe from his home, leading to a local rebellion against him [5] - but most appear to be quite sincere in their beliefs.

One of the most useful sources I used when writing this book, for example, was a thesis submitted in 2006 by a student named Vemon Nicholas Pillay, as part of a requirement for his qualification for a Philosophy degree at the University of Zululand. In it he expresses, quite openly, the following view about tokoloshes: "It is my opinion that these are demonic spirits that have been covenanted with workers of evil for the purpose of creating anti-social behaviour as well as providing financial stability.[6]" Try putting a sentence like that in an essay at a Western university and see what grade you get! Evidently, Mr Pillay must have expected his tutor or course supervisor to have either believed in, or to be sympathetic towards a belief in, tokoloshes, otherwise he presumably would not have seen fit to write such a thing in his work, for fear of being marked down. Thus, there must be at least some respect for the idea of belief in tokoloshes present in some official, high-status southern African institutions.

You can even find support for the belief in tokoloshes amongst certain members of the black southern African political class. One such official, high-status person to have expressed open belief in the tokoloshe, for example, was KK Manyika, the former director of security for the Zimbabwean parliament, who in 1999 claimed that an employee with a grudge against him had sent out several invisible tokoloshes to attack him. He said that he had suffered car crashes, lightning strikes and physical assaults, all at the hands of tokoloshes who had been invoked against him by a man whom he had intended to fire. According to Manyika himself, "I was assaulted by invisible tokoloshes as I walked along a road. They were beating me about the head, shouting things like 'You! You! You are an unfair boss! You want too much money!' They were trying to knock me into the road so I would be run over by a car." Apparently, however, they ultimately failed to do so [7]. If only somebody could be prevailed upon to send out some similar things against Robert Mugabe ...

**Church Controversies**
Interestingly, one high-status source of encouragement for those who believe in tokoloshes comes from certain southern African priests and pastors. However, just because your local parish priest comes out and says that he believes in these things, this should not necessarily be taken as meaning that such ideas actually have any official, institutional backing behind them. In fact, there seems to be some tension present between the attitude of the Catholic Church as an institution towards tokoloshes and the opinions of individual black African priests upon the

matter. For example, in 2005 representatives of the Church in Namibia filed a suit in the Namibian High Court, asking for an order declaring that Gert Petrus, a priest from the suburb of Khomasdal in Windhoek, the capital, be excommunicated and defrocked for participating in witchcraft activities. The trouble began in 2004, when Petrus started to suspect certain of his parishioners of perpetrating witchcraft attacks against him. In order to get help, he enlisted the services of some Zimbabwean witch-doctors who declared that an evil tokoloshe was living in his parish residence. In order to make it visible, some special salt water was thrown over it and the creature caught and then tossed onto a fire to burn. Later, when what Petrus very vaguely called three "objects of witchcraft" were found inside his church, he once again enlisted traditional magical aid in order to nullify their effects.

Word of this all got back to higher authorities in the Archdiocese, and Petrus was thence accused of participating in witchcraft and the proceedings to ensure excommunication began. Petrus pleaded, with some justification, that he was only acting to dispel witchcraft, not to practise it as such, but the Church did not listen. The judge in the case, Arthur Pickering, found that the excommunication was valid, on the grounds that Petrus was deemed to be highly superstitious and believed "almost fanatically" in the existence of tokoloshes [8]. From this, we might be led to conclude that it is official Catholic policy that things like tokoloshes do not exist; but, if so, then why do they still send out exorcists to supposed poltergeist and demon-hauntings in the West? Their position here seems to be somewhat inconsistent upon the matter, to say the least.

Attitudes towards tokoloshes appear to differ between competing Christian denominations,

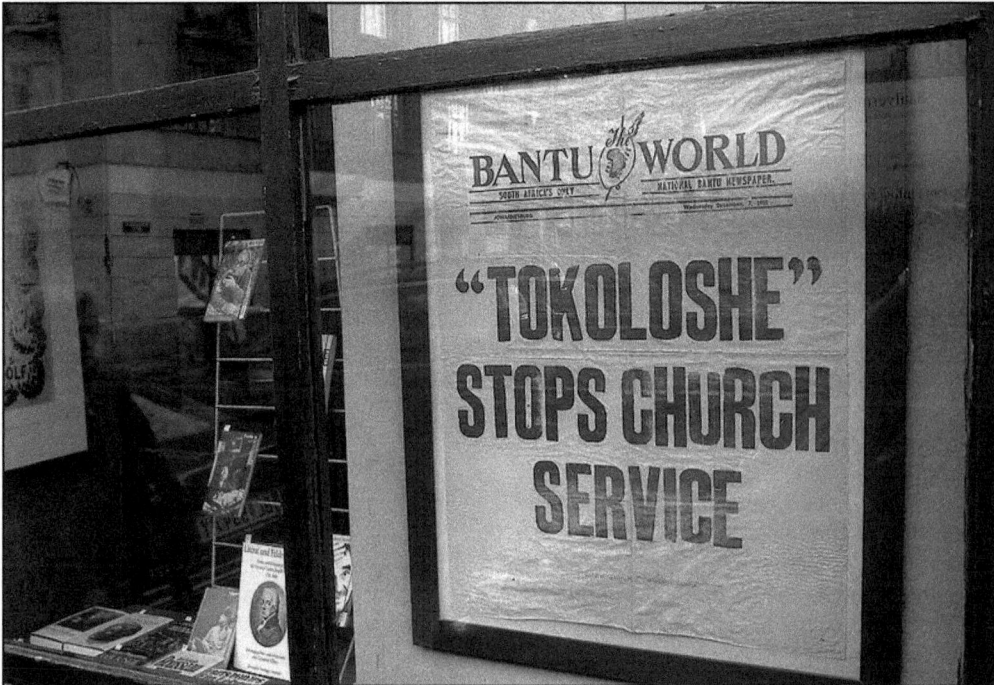

too. A case from 1956, for instance, originally reported in *Time* magazine, in which a tokoloshe invaded a Presbyterian church leading to the local priest performing an exorcism in order to rid the building of evil forces, did not end unhappily with some kind of reprimand for the holy man involved from his superiors. Rather, everything seemed to turn out very much for the best.

Apparently, one quiet afternoon in July of that year the peace of the village of Moroka in South Africa's Gauteng Province was shattered by the place's children running around and squealing en masse, seemingly following something unseen and pouring into the nearby brand-new church. One of the adults grabbed a child and asked what was going on; the reply came back that they were following a tokoloshe - a little old man with hair all over his body, a long white beard and claws instead of any fingers. With the being trapped inside the church, the adults piled in to try and kill it. However, they were at a disadvantage; only the kids could see the spirit. No doubt having fun, the children ran around pointing at thin air, urging their parents to destroy whatever it was their eyes happened to settle down upon. Windows were smashed with stones and hymn-books, and the pulpit torn down and reduced to matchwood as the crowd tried to beat the tokoloshe out of it. Within a matter of minutes, the entire interior of the building was ruined.

The Reverend Shedrick E Majola, who had raised the money to build the church, and had laid its foundations himself, was devastated, especially seeing as everyone in the village was too superstitious to now go back inside the ruined building in case the evil tokoloshe was still hiding in the shadows there. However, in order to demonstrate his holy power over the creature, he gathered his congregation around him at night and wandered through the pitch-black church unharmed, thereby showing that Christ was stronger than the tokoloshe. Gradually, Reverend Majola's congregation began to return, but he could still see their eyes wandering about during his services, keeping a beady look-out around them for the demon [9].

**False Prophets?**
If some Catholic priests find themselves being the subject of official reprimands from higher Church authorities if they believe in tokoloshes, however, then this leaves a convenient gap in the market for marabouts, sangomas and inyangas to exploit. If a person needs help in expelling a tokoloshe infestation, and the local priests either do not believe them or are unwilling to go the way of Father Petrus if they do intervene, then a witch-doctor might be able to perform the task for them just as well, if not better. Supposedly, for example, certain muti-men are said to have the ability to kill tokoloshes and then make some sort of magical prophylactic from grinding up their bodies. Market-stalls and shops devoted to selling muti objects often carry a range of tokoloshe fat which people are meant to smear on their skin as a kind of repellent; the genuine article is said to leave your flesh feeling cold to the touch. Alternatively, substances made from dead tokoloshes can be sprinkled over the rear entrance to a cattle enclosure, if a tokoloshe has been busy stealing the milk from your cows. If the pesky demon touches the magical substance it is rendered visible and paralysed, making it easy for a sangoma then either to kill and make some more magic fat out of it, or to trap the poor creature for life inside a bottle [10].

Alternatively, if no dead tokoloshes are available, a witch-doctor can step in for the Catholic priest directly, and perform a traditional ceremony of exorcism. Sometimes, however, these can go badly wrong. In 2009, for example, a man named Mangisi Chikorobho called out a tsikamutanda - or self-styled 'wise-man' - to come and perform a ceremony of cleansing upon his home in the Zimbabwean village of Lalapanzi, in Midlands Province. Every year for the past six years a child of the family had died there, it seemed, and he feared some kind of a curse was in operation. The tsikamutanda, Alicias Musiiwa Denhere, agreed to participate and diagnosed a tokoloshe infestation. He sat in the kitchen drumming and singing when suddenly he shot up and ran out of the house claiming that he had been injured by an invisible goblin. Then, he put on a show of wrestling with the unseen tokoloshe before throwing it into a fire to burn to death. During this performance, however, it seems that Mr Denhere somehow managed to burn himself too, perhaps by prancing around too closely to the fire. The police were called out and the tsikamutanda rushed to hospital with burns on his right thigh, stomach and genitals! [11]

Whether such exorcists really have any powers or not, however (and the above case, perhaps, suggests that many do not), they can fulfil a very real psychological purpose, and make people feel better about things which have gone wrong in their lives. A personal account of his own encounter with a tokoloshe written by a Zimbabwean journalist named Mduduzi Mathuthu in 2009, for example, gives a good illustration of this fact. In 1991, Mathuthu's grandfather had died at the family farm in the Filabusi region (a district in what is now Matabeleland South Province) and it was suggested by some that the death was not a natural one. As such, an inyanga was called out to diagnose what the problem had been. Immediately, he said that a killer tokoloshe was responsible and began saying some prayers as a prelude to going out and hunting the evil entity down.

As soon as he went outside after this ceremony had taken place, the inyanga shouted "There it is!" and ran into one of the outhouses occupied by the farm-workers. The tokoloshe sped upstairs, passing through closed doors as it did so, according to the holy man (who at this point was the only one able to see it) until it ended up hiding in a wardrobe inside one of the bedrooms. The inyanga then produced what he called his 'holy stick' and began bashing the wardrobe in order to weaken the tokoloshe, before then going inside to capture the creature with his bare hands. What he produced was small - "perhaps the size of a TV remote control" - and, according to Mathuthu, appeared to be breathing. The inyanga then ended its life by pouring holy water all over it, and the family demanded to see what it was. He explained that it was a tokoloshe, and said that it lived, like a vampire, by sucking blood.

Upon closer examination, the 'spirit' proved to be nothing more than some pieces of cloth wrapped around a lump of fat dripping with blood. Nonetheless, it had to be burned, the holy

**OPPOSITE: The poster for the acclaimed 1999 South African film 'A Reasonable Man', in which contrasting attitudes towards belief in tokoloshes between whites and blacks are explored. As a figure of white European authority, Nigel Hawthorne's Judge character is less than sympathetic towards traditional black native beliefs, it seems.**

man pronounced, so a fire was created outside and the figure tossed onto it. Then, the entire family were forced to take part in a cleansing ritual, in which they had to slaughter a goat and then bathe all over in the blood and offal from its stomach so that the tokoloshe would be unable to return. Then, the inyanga picked up the dead goat and took it away for himself, allegedly for his clients' protection, but clearly in actuality as some form of payment [12].

It would be easy to laugh at this story, of course, as the tokoloshe in this instance was clearly just a rather bloody prop. However, this might be to approach the incident in the wrong way. Evidently, this was some kind of socially-sanctioned ritual which was being participated in by the family and, presumably, it left them with some kind of peace. After all, it 'explained' the old man's death somehow, rather than just leaving it open as being the random act of an uncaring and inanimate universe - and, furthermore, all the inyanga took as payment was a single goat to eat. As such, 'fraud' might be the wrong word to use here; the whole escapade was clearly psychologically satisfying to all those involved and, as such, the holy man's legerdemain fulfilled a useful, and apparently widely socially-countenanced, purpose.

Undoubtedly, however, there are many other ersatz 'holy men' who encourage belief in tokoloshes purely so that they can then gain money or other advantages from desperate clients who come to them seeking help; there is, after all, such a thing as a false prophet. A particularly extreme example of this kind of abuse can be found in the story of Jack Mogale, who in February 2011 was finally brought to court in the city of Johannesburg in South Africa's Gauteng Province after a reign of terror lasting three years, during which time he was alleged to have committed no less than 61 acts of kidnapping, rape, murder and robbery. His method of tricking one of his victims into being raped was particularly interesting - and shocking.

Basically, he got hold of an official badge from the ZCC, or Zion Christian Church, a widely-followed organisation in South Africa, put it on and then approached a woman after a chance meeting between themselves, claiming to be a 'prophet'. The woman, who described herself as being "deeply religious", believed him, especially seeing as he seemed somehow to be aware of some problems involving her private life. He said that her relationship issues and a medical difficulty she had with her uterus were the result of a tokoloshe which was living inside her and filling her with what he termed "bad blood". Therefore, he took her away to the veldt (an expanse of flat scrubland, very common in South Africa) near her place of work and told her to lie down on her back and remove her underwear. Once she had done this, Mogale produced some tea leaves and started rubbing them into her vagina in order to expel the tokoloshe. However, he said that the spirit was a strong one and refused to come out. Explaining that the only way for him to be able to exorcise it now would be for him to sleep with her, he began to unzip his trousers. The woman protested that the Bible said that sex before marriage was wrong, but he explained that it was not a sin in this particular instance as he had been sent by God to battle tokoloshes with his penis in this way and that, furthermore, the Holy Father would protect them against any sexually-transmitted diseases they might otherwise contract from one another whilst he was performing the 'ceremony'. Then, the woman simply closed her eyes and braced herself whilst he lay on top of her body and raped her [13].

Belief in the tokoloshe had negative repercussions for another (real) pastor from the Zion Christian Church in April 2011, meanwhile, when a Pastor Joseph Moruti made public allegations against his ex-wife, whom he accused in a newspaper of having spread false and malicious rumours that he had sent out a tokoloshe to abuse her after their divorce. Because of these charges of witchcraft and tokoloshe-use which had been made against him, he said, he had become a social pariah, with people openly accusing him in the street of being evil, and he was now no longer even able to attend church without being abused. A story had been put about by the former Mrs Moruti that other ZCC pastors had exhumed the corpse her husband had allegedly been using as a tokoloshe-zombie and exorcised it, he declared. When these accusations were put to his wife, however, she had a different story; it was all the other way around and Moruti had been making false allegations of witchcraft against her daughter, she said, and had even threatened to kill her with a brick. Whoever was telling the truth here, of course, it is noticeable that, whilst Moruti denied using tokoloshes against his wife, at no point did he attempt to ridicule these rumours by simply saying that these creatures were not real - implying, of course, that he too really believed in them, in spite of his former position of respected authority in local society [14].

**All in the Mind?**
Many figures of traditional authority profess to believe in the reality of the tokoloshe, then - although, of course, it is to the financial benefit of some of them to do so. Other powerful and high-status people, though, really do appear to believe in them quite genuinely. Given the public acceptance of belief in tokoloshes by such diverse people as prophets, priests, university-lecturers and politicians, it is perhaps no surprise that many other, lower-status people go on believing in the beasts too. After all, their elders and betters are effectively providing them with a social sanction to do so. Rather than denigrating belief in tokoloshes, then, many traditional and non-traditional figures with status, wealth and power are actually encouraging the belief to grow, or at least to be maintained. Rather than having to hide your superstitions by doing things like wearing discreet snakeskin watch-straps, then, perhaps the rise to positions of influence by black tokoloshe-believers in post-apartheid South Africa and Zimbabwe has only encouraged people to come out and express their beliefs in such hairy monkey-demons more openly. Certainly, it appears that there is generally little stigma or embarrassment attached to most people who believe in them, unlike that which often surrounds UFO or ghost-believers in the contemporary West.

This is because in most Western countries, of course, traditional religious and other beliefs have now long-since been replaced as being the representatives of the 'official' prevailing world-view by the institutions of materialistic science. Scientists are our new priests, our new arbiters of reality, and they tend not to believe in demons and so forth; and, as such, our culture as a whole simply dismisses these entities glibly as being fictional, whether rightly or wrongly. African representatives of modern science also seem able to find reason to be highly sceptical about belief in tokoloshes, however.

In 2009, for example, an issue of the *South African Medical Journal* carried a letter which was co-authored by Dr Anand Moodley, a neurologist from Greys Hospital in the city of Pietermaritzburg, and a Canadian neuropsychologist from the University of Saskatchewan called Neil Fournier. They claimed that the origin of tokoloshe sightings lay not in the witch-doctor's hut, but in an obscure part of the brain called the indusium griseum. These two thin strips of material have no known function in adults, but act as a kind of embryonic prototype of the adult hippocampus region for a foetus in the womb. Seeing as the adult hippocampus stores a kind of inherent internal map-like representation of the human body, and hallucinations of humanoid forms can apparently be induced by electrical stimulation of the brain's temporal lobes, the report's authors speculated that some kind of inadvertent overstimulation of the indusium griseum could also produce a similar effect in an adult.

However, seeing as this area of the brain was the unborn foetus' version of the hippocampus, it could be presumed to store not a representation of the adult body, but of the foetus'. "The outcome would be visual hallucinations of a small humanoid with a large head, big eyes and a small body", the letter's authors claimed, asking "do we here in Africa have a pre-programmed tokoloshe homunculus [tiny man] waiting to be activated [in our brain] in times of distress, dreamlike states or during a seizure? [15]" In the West, similar theories centring upon the stimulation of the temporal lobes have also been put forward, particularly by the neurologist Professor Michael Persinger, to account for 'bedroom invader' experiences involving more typical Western cultural demons such as aliens, poltergeists and ghostly rapists, showing how even Western and African sceptics can adopt similar methods of explanation for at first sight apparently widely-divergent supernatural events ("a small humanoid with a large head, big eyes and a small body" does, after all, sound like the stereotypical Western description of a so-called 'Grey' alien).

This, it must be said, does seem rather reductive of matters (although the joint authors of the letter did also add that "Beliefs are just what they are and should be left alone"). But it also brings us around full-circle to the issues that we were discussing at the beginning of this chapter; because science, traditionally, was considered to be a 'white' cultural sphere in southern Africa, and something which was seen as being inherently opposed to what was often denigrated as being mere 'native superstition'.

Educational opportunities once being somewhat limited for blacks in these countries, of course, few doctors or scientists were anything other than white, or perhaps sometimes of Asian origin. Thus, explaining tokoloshe sightings as being down to medical issues is in southern Africa essentially a traditionally 'white' way of explaining the phenomenon; whereas explaining them as being down to demonic activity upon behalf of witches is a traditionally 'black' way of doing so. Things are changing now, of course, after the fall of apartheid, and no doubt soon we will have large numbers of native black doctors and scientists making similar claims about the true home of tokoloshes being in the human brain; but, until this point comes to pass, I think it is fair to say that belief in the tokoloshe will continue to be thought of by most as being, essentially, a 'black' thing. Perhaps because of this, complex issues surrounding racial politics have sometimes been explored by proxy through the more neutral figure of the tokoloshe, as we shall see in the next chapter.

# Chapter Six

## A Matter of Black and White: Tokoloshes and Race

D o any white people living in southern Africa believe in tokoloshes? Not usually, it seems, though there are of course exceptions. The white Hollywood star Charlize Theron, (below) for example, a native South African, has in the past spoken openly of her belief in the tokoloshe. Apparently, this belief had its roots in her childhood on a farm outside the small city of Benoni, east of Johannesburg, where her household maid would make sure that the infant Theron would never sleep on the floor but safely up in a high bed at night. Interestingly, however, this was not represented to the child as being a precaution against tokoloshe-rape, her nurse instead claiming that a tokoloshe, if it found her sleeping down there on the floor, would crawl inside her ear and make her become evil [1].

It is unclear as to whether this was a variant local belief about the tokoloshe, or merely an attempt by the maid to spare the little girl's blushes by avoiding talking about sexual matters, but it is a good illustration of how once black-only superstitions can subsequently be passed on to whites and other races, too. The transmission of folklore from low-status maidservants to high-status children who later on act to record and thereby keep the traditions alive is a pattern which has found itself repeated worldwide, in many ages. In his celebrated 1584 book *The Discoverie of Witchcraft*, for example, the Kentish squire Reginald Scot made the following now-famous remark, deriding belief in the kinds of folklore entities that the bedtime tales of uneducated domestic servants would sometimes inculcate in their higher-status young charges: "In our childhood our mothers' maids have so fraied us with bull-beggers, spirits, witches, urchens, elves, hags, fairies, satyrs, pans, sylens, Kit with the cansticke, tritons,

centaurs, dwarfes, giants, imps, calcars, conjurors, nymphs, changling, Incubus, Robin Goodfellow, the spoorne, the mare, the man in the oke, the hell wain, the fier drake, the puckle, Tom Thombe, Hob gobblin, Tom Tumbler, boneless, and such other bugs, that we are afraid of our owne shadowes.[2]" Such sceptical attitudes, you have to say, are only likely to be held more widely and strongly during the present-day by most white people in southern Africa. Therefore, whatever belief in tokoloshes might be implanted in higher-status white children by their black maids and nurses whilst they are young will probably end up in most cases being pushed out of them by disbelieving and mocking adults as they grow older.

Indeed, belief in tokoloshes by a white African person once they are in adulthood can probably be considered as being the rough equivalent of continuing belief in fairies amongst adults of whatever colour in most modern Western countries - i.e. something which is viewed by mainstream society as being highly eccentric at best, and at worst a sign of outright madness. For example, one of the most widely-covered and sensational South African tokoloshe-related trials of recent years took place in 2012 and involved two white siblings, Nicolette and Hardus Lotter, who were accused of murdering their own parents, Magdalena and Johannes Lotter, under the influence of Nicolette's ex-boyfriend, a man of Indian descent named Mathew Naidoo. During this trial, it was quite strongly implied that Nicolette Lotter was somewhat mentally unbalanced, something which was supposedly given away most obviously by the fact that, despite her race, she appeared to believe implicitly in the reality of tokoloshes.

**Dishonour Thy Mother and Thy Father**
The whole affair was a complex and sorry tale, and seems to have begun with Nicolette's belief that, sometime during 2008, her family's black domestic worker, Clementia Msomi, had been trying to bewitch her. Nicolette claimed to have found magical substances, such as pig's fat, dead dried-out frogs and a severed chicken foot, scattered around her family's property in the city of Durban in KwaZulu-Natal Province, something which she blamed upon her servant whom she later accused of being a witch. Once this idea had got itself stuck inside her head, Nicolette then began telling her parents that she was being repeatedly raped in her bed at night by a hair-scalping tokoloshe, which had been sent out against her by the malicious sorceress. Tellingly, however, her mother did not believe a word of this tale, and, accusing her of simply seeking attention, sent her off to see a well-regarded South African psychiatrist named Lourens Schlebusch, who no doubt also did not believe Nicolette's weird claims. Indeed, during their sessions together, it seems that Nicolette dropped her yarns about tokoloshes and witchcraft altogether, instead saying that she had issues with Msomi simply because the maid, in her words, "had an attitude". In court, she later said that she had lied to the psychiatrist about the extent of her belief in witchcraft because she did not want to be deemed mad and sent off to be incarcerated in an asylum.

**OPPOSITE: Nicolette Lotter, a very rare example of a white woman who claims to have been raped by a tokoloshe, appears in the dock in Durban charged with murdering her two parents. As a result of her beliefs, she was portrayed as being somewhat mentally unstable in some quarters of the South African press.**

These meetings with Schlebusch ended quite quickly after only two sessions, however, Lotter apparently feeling that she would rather seek help from church pastors about her problem, thinking that she could only really open up to religious people about her alleged nocturnal ordeals as they were, in her view, "a spiritual matter" which medical doctors could not really be expected to help her out with. Telling her mother that she was now okay, Nicolette began secretly going from church to church in search of exorcists who could aid her, but seemingly drew a blank. Eventually, she ended up at the home of a woman in the Durban suburb of Phoenix, after this lady had promised to pray for her. There, for the first time, she met Mathew Naidoo.

Naidoo, who was friends with this woman, made a very bad initial impression upon Nicolette, seeming as he did to to be "very loud and irritating", but he appears to have made it his mission to latch onto the girl, got hold of her mobile number, and began sending her text-messages. Eventually, Nicolette started feeling bad about ignoring Naidoo seeing as he appeared to be so concerned about her tokoloshe-visitations, and the two became friends. Apparently taking advantage of Lotter's seemingly obsessive religious beliefs, Naidoo then began claiming that he was the "third son of God" to her, and said that he had been sent by the Lord to help her out. All she had to do was sleep with him, he pronounced, and then the demonic rapes would end. Nicolette agreed to this and, she said, the tokoloshe came no more.

Accepting Naidoo as her boyfriend, and even agreeing to a proposal of marriage from him, Nicolette's behaviour soon began to grow steadily stranger. For instance, she took to locking the family's maid Clementia out of the house and screaming at her that she was Satan, and then, once she had been let back in by her parents, following the poor woman around whilst she did her polishing, constantly spraying her, and any surface which she had touched whilst cleaning, with some kind of watery substance in order to counteract her hypothetical evil influence. The disturbed young girl even appears to have made an attempt to poison her maid by making her a doctored meal, supposedly as an apology for her previous behaviour, and she and Naidoo eventually ended up dragging the lady off to church to be forcibly exorcised by a pastor.

Naidoo also began causing problems with Nicolette's parents, stealing her dad's bank card and using it to withdraw money, and sending them both anonymous death threats. He also started sneaking into the Lotter household after dark and sleeping with his new girlfriend, living in her room secretly, without her parents' knowledge. Such was his hold over Nicolette by this point that he even succeeded in persuading her to begin drinking his urine, and had her convinced that her father had secretly been raping her since she was a small child, but that God had subsequently "erased" it from her mind in order to protect her from any memory of the trauma. He also began to work his influence upon her brother Hardus, a socially-isolated and apparently quite depressed young man, who seems to have fallen for Naidoo's bizarre and unbelievable patter as well. Apparently, he told them both that he had brain cancer but that this didn't really matter much because he was immortal, so he could just live with the fact without any real fuss. He also managed to convince Nicolette and Hardus that they were both two of

the twelve mystical 'Knights of God', who, in his view, had been sent down to earth by the Lord in order to save it from evil. According to Naidoo, Nicolette and Hardus each had a special number imprinted on their foreheads which only he could see, adding that, whenever they disobeyed him, the number would decrease by one, illustrating God's displeasure with them.

God, it seemed, had a mission for the Lotter children; in order to save the world, they would have to kill both their parents and then allow Naidoo to live in their house with them after they had inherited it. Originally, Naidoo's idea had been to get hold of some tasers, get the Lotter siblings to stun their parents with them, and then inject air bubbles into their veins in order to give them both heart attacks, making it look as though they had just died from natural causes. However, this proved impractical and, on July 19th 2008, whilst Naidoo was careful to place himself elsewhere and thus give himself an alibi, the Lotter children followed their new instructions. First, Hardus used a stun-gun on his mother, punched her and then sat down on top of her before Nicolette then began stabbing her repeatedly. Then they went after their father, whom they strangled with an electrical cord. Naturally, the pair did not get away with this sickening crime and were arrested soon afterwards, as was Naidoo, whom they both blabbed about to the police.

In court, it was the opinion of the prosecution that all the stuff about witchcraft was mere nonsense, that the Lotters had known what they were doing all along, and that they had both simply plotted together with Naidoo in order to get their hands on their parents' inheritance money and the family home. They both denied this, but the presiding Judge, Shyam Gyanda, professed himself nonplussed as to how a university-educated woman like Nicolette Lotter could believe in what he termed "mumbo-jumbo" like witchcraft and tokoloshes. Other people were also puzzled; white people do not usually believe in tokoloshes, so reasons for this aberrant fact had to be sought.

The South African press seem to have hunted out evidence that Nicolette in particular was mad. For example, one media organisation tracked down the family's maid, Clementia Msomi, for an interview. In the report which followed, it was then claimed that Nicolette Lotter was "a complex, troubled child" who "constantly created turmoil in her family." According to Msomi, Nicolette had been a religious zealot for years, something which "tore the family apart" and had caused her sister, Christelle, to flee the family home and go to live in Cape Town, simply in order to escape her weirdness. She had grown paranoid and obsessed with the occult, it was said, and was always fighting with her mother about one thing or another. Hardus too, Msomi said, was odd, spending hours sat at his computer and talking to nobody. One day, she claimed, he was stood standing at the gate looking distraught when she came to the house to report for work. She asked him what was the matter and he burst out "I am waiting for the people who are coming to kill my mother!" before then turning around, running into his house and then locking himself inside his room. Clearly, then, neither

**OPPOSITE: The fanatically religious Nicolette Lotter reads her Bible and prays during a recess in the court's proceedings; as well she might, given what she did.**

murderer was depicted as being of entirely sound mind to the general public in this report.

This depiction of the people involved as being, essentially, insane continued in the courtroom itself, too. For instance, one person called to testify during the trial was a pastor named Leon van Assenderp, who had been brought in by the police to counsel the Lotter siblings and Naidoo after they had all been arrested. It was his view that all three of them had been possessed by evil spirits whilst committing their crimes; Naidoo, for example, threw himself down onto the floor and began "twisting, twirling and [making] other unusual body movements" when van Assenderp started praying for him. Whilst to the pastor this must have seemed like clear evidence of demonic possession, however, no doubt to most of the other people listening to his testimony in the courtroom it would have sounded like mere insanity.

Nicolette Lotter's psychiatrist, Lourens Schlebusch, made further claims about her and her brother being mentally unstable when he took up the witness stand in court, too. According to him, both siblings had been "reprogrammed" mentally by Naidoo in order to make them obey his every word. He said that Hardus, for example, had very low self-esteem and depression before the whole farrago had even begun, as he was a loner who was constantly mocked at school, being called "sleepy head" and "tortoise" by all his classmates, presumably due to his perceived dullness. "This," the good doctor opined, "made him vulnerable and affected him emotionally because he thought he was not worthy," thus making him good, easy prey for the cunning con-man Mathew Naidoo, who had even instructed Hardus to try and commit suicide after the murders had occurred in order to take the blame for it all upon himself. Schlebusch said that Hardus and Nicolette had been simply "victims" of "religious reprogramming" and "coercive persuasion" which, ultimately, had reached "cult-like dimensions". Thus, in Schlebusch's view, the Lotter children genuinely did believe, due to their pre-existing mental vulnerabilities being exploited, that they really did have to murder their parents in order to prevent the end of the world.

Eventually, of course, all three defendants were found guilty as charged. In Judge Gyanda's opinion, however, whilst Naidoo was clearly more responsible for the crime than the Lotters themselves were, and his brainwashing of them was indeed a mitigating factor to take into consideration, the siblings could not be excluded from having any criminal liability for the killings. As a result, Nicolette got 12 years' imprisonment for each of the murders committed, to be served concurrently, and Hardus 10 years on each count. Naidoo, however, got two full life-sentences, as the evil mastermind behind the whole plot [3]. That, then, appears to be what happens when middle-class white people in southern Africa profess to a belief in witchcraft and tokoloshes; they are depicted (in this case probably quite justifiably) as if they were mentally disturbed. If the Lotters had been black, then they could have pleaded the old 'cultural defence' clause, but, this option not being open to them, the notion of 'madness' had to be invoked by wider society in order to account for the bizarre crime having occurred in the first place.

Popular culture in South Africa constantly acts to reinforce this message. For example, one edition of the widely-read South African comic strip *Madam and Eve* (to be discussed in more detail below) under the heading 'More South African culture explained for international

Some editions of the popular South African cartoon strip *Madam and Eve*, in which tokoloshes are presented as cunning little devils whose appearance is very much in the Western tradition. Typically, they are presented as having a stake in the racial politics of the South African state which is every bit as complex and valid as is that of their human counterparts.

readers', depicts an old white woman ('Mother Anderson') introducing us to our first lesson, 'What exactly is a tokoloshe?' At first, she gives a reasonable answer, saying that, "According to legend, a tokoloshe is a small mythical demon that carries away people while they're asleep." However, in the next frame she is shown sat at a table playing chess with one (the tokoloshe wins), explaining that "What many people don't know, however, is that they're also excellent chess players." In the final frame of this strip, though, the old woman is then shown being dragged away across the floor by her unimpressed daughter and her black maid, the clear implication being that she is delusional and dementia-ridden for claiming to have seen and interacted with a tokoloshe for real, and so just needs to be taken away for a nice lie down, perhaps. White people in Africa who believe in tokoloshes, then, can expect to be frequently laughed at, mocked and condemned by their peers, it seems.

**White Magic**
Most southern African whites, therefore, do not really believe in the tokoloshe - at least, not once they're out of short trousers and school uniform. In the past, though, it was possible for white people to simply go along with black native belief in the reality of tokoloshes in public, in order thereby to add to their reputation and status amongst their black workers and underlings. In particular, it was possible to exploit such native beliefs in order to pretend to be able to exorcise or dispel tokoloshes, preventing them from attacking people. After all, if black people felt that the whites around them had witch-doctor-like powers, then they were more likely to obey them without question.

For example, a white farmer from the Pondoland region of South Africa - a coastal area on the eastern edge of Eastern Cape Province - told the ghost story collector Eric Rosenthal of the first time that he encountered what Rosenthal terms "tokoloshian activity". It occurred in 1906, it seems, when the white farmer was riding out on horseback in search of some stray cattle which had escaped from his property, when he came across four young black herd-boys, all sitting around and staring in the same direction at something unseen, as if hypnotised, with a look of fear and horror written large across their faces. Riding up to them, the farmer asked what they were looking at, whereupon the spell was broken and they all jumped up and ran away home, screaming. The next day, the father of one of the boys came up to the farmer and thanked him for freeing the boys from the evil spell; he said that they had been entranced by the appearance of a tokoloshe out in the bush, who would undoubtedly have done them harm had the farmer not intervened to save them.

Given the ambiguous nature of what had happened in this case, we can presume that the white farmer would probably have actually been of the opinion that what the little black boys had seen was just imagination, but nonetheless he appears to have been happy enough to accept the man's thanks for 'saving' his son. Presumably, this event would only have led to his reputation being enhanced locally as being a 'powerful man'. Indeed, it appears that this reputation persisted for quite some time, as the farmer informed Rosenthal that his second encounter with a tokoloshe had occurred in 1923, almost two decades later, when a male schoolteacher came up and asked him if he could break the spell of a tokoloshe for him. Apparently, this man had been being bothered by poltergeist-like phenomena for the past four weeks, with typical tricks occurring in his home such as objects being moved around and knocked over, and the pictures on his walls continually reversing themselves so that they were facing the wrong way. Recently, however, his bedclothes had been being tugged away from him and stones hurled around the place, events which he saw as being somehow threatening in their nature.

The white farmer, probably influenced by his previous meeting with a (to his mind, at least) entirely imaginary tokoloshe, appeared to be sceptical about this account, though he did not let this fact slip to the black teacher. He simply asked him if he had made any enemies of late; the teacher replied that he had. Recently, it seems, he had punished one of his pupils for misbehaviour, and the boy's father had become most angry about the fact. To the sceptical farmer in this case, the conclusion to draw must have seemed obvious; this angry parent was simply playing tricks upon the teacher. To the teacher himself, however, a different and equally-obvious conclusion most probably would have been drawn; namely, that the irate father was practising witchcraft and thereby sending out a tokoloshe to get revenge against his new enemy. Whatever the true reasons for the poltergeist's appearance were, however, the white farmer had a simple remedy for it. He told the teacher to go out and spread the word in the locality that 'Nomkolokoto' (the local blacks' name for the white man) was going to set up a gun inside the hut in order to shoot the tokoloshe, and that, as such, nobody had better go near it in case they accidentally ended up getting killed instead. The fact that, once he had made this public threat, the poltergeist activity ceased, could have been interpreted in two ways here; for the black teacher, it simply would have meant that the 'white man's magic' was powerful enough to outwit even a tokoloshe. For the farmer himself, though, it would have seemed evident that the threat of there being a gun in the hut must have scared away the angry human parent from approaching it and pretending to be a ghost. Whichever of these was the truth, the white farmer's prestige in the area would surely have been enhanced by the ultimate outcome of this whole escapade far more than it would have been if he had simply openly dismissed the teacher's fears as being 'mere superstition' in the first place[4].

## Paranormal Polling Stations

A very telling attempt which was once apparently made by whites to exploit what they saw as being 'black superstition' about tokoloshes occurred during the famous 1994 elections, which were of course the first in South African history where blacks, Indians and coloureds * were allowed to cast their vote as well as whites. Obviously, many white people were nervous about the idea of Nelson Mandela and his ANC (African National Congress) Party colleagues coming to power, and seemingly attempted to make use of black people's belief in tokoloshes in order to try and skew the outcome of the vote. According to an academic called Anthony Minnaar, who made a contemporary study of how black witchcraft beliefs might affect the polls, there were several strange fears abroad amongst the general black populace at the time. One fear, apparently, was that evil spirits like tokoloshes were hiding inside polling booths,

* In this book, the term 'coloured' is used in a special sense; namely, to refer to southern Africans of mixed race. People who had at least one recent white ancestor – even if their other close relatives had been black, Indian, Malay, Chinese or other – were given the official 'racial designation' of 'coloured' in countries like South Africa, and afforded certain rights one notch above those of the native black population, but several rungs below those of the ruling wholly-white Europeans. This whole concept is explained in much more detail in the chapter concerning poltergeist phenomena.

and were either waiting there to invisibly observe who voted for the ANC, intending to come out to their homes and attack them later, or were temporarily taking over black people's minds when they were marking their crosses on the ballot-sheets, making them vote for white parties instead. Some black people, apparently, went to visit inyangas before casting their vote, hoping to be given magical protection against these demons who were, presumably, working upon behalf of the white men.

Another, related belief, was that tokoloshes liked to hide in corners, and so it was only safe for a black person to cast their vote inside a polling booth which was round, as in such places there would be nowhere for them to lurk. This idea, apparently, became a widespread urban legend during the period leading up to the 1994 elections, as did the rumour that, in the rural areas of South Africa, the ballot-papers themselves had been altered so that a person now had to put a cross inside a circle rather than a square box, because otherwise the voters were terrified that there might be tiny tokoloshes hiding inside the ballot-papers themselves.

However, some commentators have been unsure as to how seriously all of these anecdotes and urban legends should really have been taken. One explanation for the alleged tokoloshe-scare during the 1994 election could indeed be that certain white people, afraid for their future in a post-apartheid society, were spreading around ridiculous gossip which was then genuinely believed in by some black people, in order to try and prevent them from casting their votes. An alternative view, however, taken up for instance by the prominent collector and interpreter of South African urban folklore Arthur Goldstuck, is that such myths were not actually believed in by black people at all but were, rather, simply a kind of "wishful thinking on the part of those whites who would like to believe that blacks are too superstitious to run a country." Then again, of course, it is a fact that in 1990, during nearby Namibia's first multi-racial free elections, all three of the main political parties had called in sangomas and paid them lots of money to bless their own polling stations in order to free them from the malign influence of evil spirits, so maybe some of these alleged beliefs could have been genuine ones after all.[5]

## Devil's Advocates
Another way in which the figure of the tokoloshe can be used to explore issues of racial politics is through fiction. For example, one well-known pop culture outlet for tales of the tokoloshe is the highly popular South African syndicated newspaper cartoon-strip *Madam and Eve*, detailing the relations of a wealthy white household with their black maidservant, in which tokoloshes, represented comically as being nothing more than miniaturised Western-style devils, complete with horns and forked tails, are recurring characters [6]. In the panels of this series, tokoloshes are used to explore and satirise many contemporary racial concerns, both from a black and from a white perspective - although both the author and the illustrator of the series, Stephen Francis and Rico Schacherl, are in fact white men who were born in America and Austria respectively.

One particular running storyline in the comic concerns the tokoloshe-human 'Truth and Reconciliation Committee', in which the little devils and the people who live amongst them attempt to come to terms with their differences and try and work out some kind of framework for living together as equals. In this, of course, they mirror the real-life Truth and Reconciliation Committee which was set up to mediate between blacks and whites during the fall of apartheid, not necessarily entirely successfully. In fact, there seems to be a certain hidden subtext in the related *Madam and Eve* cartoons, in which the tokoloshes could conceivably be considered as standing in for black people in the eyes of whites who have perhaps been made nervous by the fall of apartheid. Once the old race-laws have been removed, it is implied, and tokoloshes (for which you might want to read 'blacks') have been allowed to gain their own place of power in society, they will simply take advantage of this fact in order to take what they want from life; and, in the comic strip as in folklore, it seems, the tokoloshes' main desire is to rape people.

For example, there is one strip wherein the white householder ('Madam') is depicted in full-on idealist mode, with a rather naively hopeful expression on her face, talking about the wonders to come in a post-apartheid world where both tokoloshes and humans can be considered equal. "Let the word go forth," she proclaims, pointing up into the air, "From this day onward, tokoloshes and humans will co-exist together in harmony. And, in a symbolic gesture of trust and faith, I will now remove the bricks from under the beds." Whilst she is spouting off self-righteously like this, however, Madam's black female maidservant ('Eve'), is depicted as looking somewhat bored and unimpressed in the background; having closer knowledge of the ways of tokoloshes than her white mistress does, it seems, she is rather more unmoved by the notion of such a 'rainbow coalition'. Indeed, she is correct to be so; in the final frame of the strip, Madam bends over to remove the bricks from beneath her bed whilst the tokoloshes take the opportunity to stare up her skirt and whisper things like "The big one with the earrings is mine!" and "No way! We flip for her!" to one another. In this strip, perhaps, suppressed and irrational fears about what black men might take the opportunity to do to white women once they have gained full legal equality and political power can be seen to be being expressed and presumably thence parodied in a way which could not really be done openly for fear of causing offence.

Another strip, meanwhile, titled 'The new tokoloshe-human interim agreement', speaks of the old-fashioned fear that a black man in a suit is really little more than a savage native devil in a thinly-westernised disguise. A tokoloshe lawyer is seen seated at a table, whilst Eve - generally depicted as being more 'canny' than her naive white mistress, it seems - reads through the draft constitution that the demonic advocate has written. At first, all seems reasonable, but by the end it becomes clear that they are trying to use devilish cunning in order to get their sexual way again. Eve reads the proposed document out loud, thus: "Okay. Let's see ... the right to food, clothing and shelter. The right to vote in elections. The right to a fair trial ... the right to carry people away at night?!" Once confronted by evidence of the tokoloshes' treachery in this way, their lawyer simply shrugs and says calmly "That's odd. I asked my secretary to take that out ..." Here, again, we can see expressed in coded form a reflection of the pre-1994 fear held by some whites that ANC lawyers and politicians, whilst presenting themselves as simply being professional and educated people who wished to gain equality for their people, were actually secretly employing so-called 'native cunning' in order to create themselves a society in which they could do as they pleased and take revenge upon their former white oppressors - as here, for example, by kidnapping and raping them in the night at will. The formerly widespread white South African idea that society would break down once the blacks got in power is, once again, parodied and satirised here, via the convenient proxy figure of the tokoloshe.

Another issue of racial politics, relating to matters of both overt and covert racism within wider society, meanwhile, is expressed in a further *Madam and Eve* strip headed 'Tokoloshe truth and reconciliation'. Here, a tokoloshe addresses the humans of the household, saying specifically that "It's time to stop the racist name-calling between tokoloshes and humans. Behind our backs you call us 'monsters', 'devils' and 'demons'" - as, no doubt, many white people in South Africa once did to black people, whether in secret or quite openly. The humans look ashamed when confronted by this statement, and Madam apologises. The tokoloshes, however, are in forgiving mood. "That's okay," says one, "We call you 'brick-heads', 'take-aways' and 'blanket-bait'." Madam is shocked by this revelation, but the tokoloshe, seemingly taking pleasure in the tables being turned in this way, simply shrugs and says "Hey, it's good to get these things out in the open." Here, the delight of the tokoloshe/ symbolic black man finally being allowed openly to say what he could only previously think in private is obvious, and a fundamental power-shift in South African society seems to be being confirmed.

No doubt there are many other editions of *Madam and Eve* that could be discussed in relation to such issues, but that will have to do for us now. The ultimate import of the symbolism in such comic strips, however, is really most interesting, as the idea that tokoloshes, just like South African blacks before the fall of apartheid, had a justifiable desire for access to things like free voting and adequate food and shelter, as well as wanting an end to racist name-calling, of course, seems to show how even spiritual creatures are often seen as participating in some way within the contemporary concerns of the human world amongst certain sectors of southern African society.

This might sound like a rather pretentious conclusion to draw from examination of a fictional comic strip, but it seems that there have been some real-life cases wherein tokoloshes have expressed a desire to be given what might be termed their 'non-human rights' too, however. For example, in September 1998 it was reported that a committee of prominent tokoloshes had made a visitation to a South African woman and demanded that they be given equal rights with human beings by the hypocritical ANC government. According to a 42-year-old special needs teacher - and part-time sangoma - Nothemba Bekebhu, of Queenstown in Eastern Cape Province, five tokoloshes had visited her at her home one night complaining that they did not have the same housing rights as black and white people did. "These strange people, with only heads and no facial features, are demanding houses like all other people in the country," she said.

Clearly, in the post-apartheid era, this state of affairs could not be right, and the tokoloshes sat themselves down on the woman's sofa and insisted that their grievances be passed on directly

**OPPOSITE: An uncredited image of the tokoloshe from a Brazilian paranormal website**

to Nelson Mandela himself. Ms Bekebhu obliged, and contacted the President's office by telephone. However, the member of his staff who answered refused to take the matter any further unless he could speak directly to the head of the tokoloshe-tribe, who was sadly not willing to comply with this request, and so the matter was politely dropped.

Bekebhu then called the police and reported her problem, though, as it seemed that the

tokoloshes were refusing to leave her residence until they had been given homes of their own. None of the policemen she called took her seriously, however, and when a local reporter visited the woman's home, he found her distraught and down on the floor, desperately pushing the receiver of her phone beneath the couch so that the police on the other end of the line could hear the tokoloshes talking to one another. There was only silence, though, and it does not appear that the reporter saw the homeless tokoloshes with his own eyes, either. He said that Ms Bekebhu appeared to have been crying, and was burning various muti substances all around her room in an attempt to scare the demons away with the thick smoke. She said that she thought that the tokoloshes had been sent out to get her by her previous domestic servant, whom she had recently sacked[7].

The tokoloshe, as we have already said, is a supernatural figure which is always shifting its form in the popular mind in order to reflect shifting changes in society, belief and politics. In many ways, it is a figure through which fundamental truths and issues about the world surrounding a person can be discussed at one remove, in disguised and thus less controversial form. As such, in societies such as South Africa where race has long been one of the central concerns of everyday life, it is surely no surprise that issues surrounding racial politics have been projected out onto its form almost as often as sexual ones have been. Indeed, it would probably be much more surprising if they had not.

# Chapter Seven

## Ghoul Schools: Tokoloshes and Mass Hysteria Amongst Schoolchildren

The term 'mass hysteria' is an oft-misused and misunderstood one; which is perhaps why many psychologists and medical textbooks now prefer to refer to it under the name of 'Mass Psychogenic Illness', or MPI, a term which has not yet really caught on amongst the general populace. Colloquially in the West we tend to use the term 'hysteria' to describe everything from press overreaction to a prominent news story, to the latest 'craze' that sweeps across teenagers or schoolchildren, but of course in the medical sense it is something far more serious - and strange. So-called 'social panics', whereby large groups of people begin acting in a way which, to people outside of that group, might appear to be bizarre and irrational, have happened throughout history, right across the world.

The current African witch-hunts are one manifestation of such a phenomenon; the European witch-hunts of a few centuries beforehand were another. The weird so-called 'dancing manias' which swept across mainland Europe between the 12th and 17th Centuries, wherein people suddenly began to take part in uncontrollable bouts of rhythmic and convulsive movements, were an example of hysteria on a wide scale, and the famous case of the 'Devils of Loudun', in which numerous nuns in a French convent began to act as if they were possessed during the 1630s, are an example of it on a smaller canvas.

An important point to make about such incidents is that the form they take is without question highly dependent upon the social and historical context within which they occur. To take the case of Loudun, for example, there is no way in which people would be able to act as if they were possessed by demons in a society where there was no concept of such entities available to them. Nowadays in the West, however, belief in the reality of demons is very low; and so, instead of groups of people collapsing and fitting due to demon possession, we get cases of mass hysteria wherein people, perhaps in a factory, school or other workplace setting, collapse and go into spasms claiming to be the victims of a gas-leak, chemical-spillage or mysterious germ - all of which, to modern Westerners, are culturally-acceptable explanations for venting repressed anxieties and acting in this way.

In many parts of Africa, however, belief in witchcraft, demons, ghosts and other supernatural entities is still strong, as we have seen, and so it is considered, subconsciously, by victims of mass hysteria over there to be entirely culturally-acceptable to blame their fits and panics upon these creatures' malign actions - and, in particular, upon the malign actions of tokoloshes. Because of this fact, modern African cases of mass hysteria seem, from a distant perspective, to be much more entertaining and amusing than Western ones are; learning about whole schools and colleges being terrorised by entirely imaginary demons makes for a more satisfying read than an account of fainting majorettes who think that they have smelled chemicals during a band-meeting, for example. However, it must be emphasised that they in fact represent cases of exactly the same psychological disease as effects Westerners, only in different cultural clothing.

The general explanation given for cases of mass hysteria by psychologists and commentators is that they represent the breaking-through into the world of repressed or underlying social or personal stresses upon behalf of the people involved, perhaps allowing the victims thereby to have an outlet for their passions and emotions which could not otherwise be safely expressed within the society in which they happen to find themselves living. For example, some of the scares we shall examine below appear to have had their origins during periods of exam stress, or to be being used to convey the underlying fears of children about taboo topics such as the imminent approach of puberty; obviously, children in the West feel similar fears themselves, and express their anxiety about them in any number of ways too. Western children don't have the option of using the tokoloshe as a means of expressing their hopes and fears about the future, however; but southern African schoolchildren most definitely do.

**Pinky-Pinky Panic**
The pinky-pinky is a recent arrival within the continent's cabinet of supernatural curiosities, belief in the entity being thus far largely confined to South Africa, where it first began to appear - as far as is known from newspaper reports, at least - in the early 1990s. A particular sub-breed of albino tokoloshe, the ghost was meant to be either all-white or all-pink and to live either inside school toilets or in the space between the boys and the girls' cubicles. Imagined as being half-male, half-female (wearing trousers down one side of its body and a dress down the other), and half-human, half-animal (with cat-like features down one side of its face and the mouth and chin of a snake), its main character-trait was that it enjoyed either raping schoolgirls who were wearing pink panties or simply stealing pink underwear from under-age girls- hence it being given the name pinky-pinky. As its main interest was supposed to be girls, only they could see the being, whereas boys going to the toilet would experience its presence through being slapped or scratched on the cheek by invisible claws. Adults, needless to say, could never have the power to set eyes upon the beast.

Viewed generally nowadays as being an exclusively 'black' experience, the pinky-pinky was actually first rumoured to be on the loose at all-white schools in the Johannesburg area in September 1993. However, it seems that more widespread hysteria about the pinky-pinky then broke out across several all-black schools in the administrative capital of Pretoria one year later, in September 1994. White schoolchildren invented this entity, it appears, but it was their black counterparts who then really ran with the idea. Schools were closed, children became hysterical and the press began reporting upon supernatural attacks allegedly taking place in toilets, leading even some adults to start believing in the pinky-pinky's reality.

Probably the most widely-reported pinky-pinky scare occurred at Moretele Primary School in the black township of Mamelodi, just north of the city of Pretoria in Gauteng Province, in 1994. Here, the scare became so bad - or so exciting, perhaps - that every child in the school was soon claiming to have had an encounter of their own with the pinky-pinky. The teachers were sceptical, but their pupils were beyond their control, so they ended up calling out the police. Lieutenant Elias Maswele arrived at the establishment having been told that there was a case of alleged child molestation to investigate - but he had not bargained for what kind. Children frantically gathered round and told him tales of girls being raped and slapped about, and of boys having their socks stolen from them. They told him that the monster was living in the toilets, so Maswele went in and investigated; he could find nothing. The children were unsurprised; pinky-pinky would not appear to adults, they said. They told Maswele to wait outside while they went in and chanted a new song they had invented in order to conjure up the demon, instead. It went like this:

> My name is pinky-pinky,
> I live in a toilet;
> My father is a sangoma
> And my mother is a witch.

Once they had finished, the kids began screaming and poured out of the toilets, the summoning allegedly having worked. Meanwhile, a concerned parent had arrived on the scene and went into the toilets himself armed with a monkey-wrench, intending to kill pinky-pinky. He soon came running out himself too, however, claiming that an invisible being had began touching him in the cubicles. The next day, a mob of angry parents arrived at the school, demanding that the loos be burned down in order to kill the pinky-pinky and cleanse the place of evil.

Outraged by the presence of demonic forces in the school, the irate adults started calling their children out and subjecting them to cross-examination about what exactly they had seen. They soon discovered, however, that every child had experienced something very dissimilar from the rest of their peers; the different children's stories about pinky-pinky simply had no correspondence to one another. Some said that he had elephant-legs; others that he had cow's hoofs; yet others asserted that he had chicken-legs. A few said that the tokoloshe was friendly and would dance for you if you asked it; whilst others claimed that it had threatened to chop their legs off and take them away with it to "mend its child", who presumably had none of its own. It became obvious that the kids were just making it all up, and the mob dispersed, leaving the school toilets intact.

The scare did briefly resurrect itself a few days later when one parent claimed that a pinky-pinky had made her son levitate through the air and then burned his hand by sticking it to a hot geyser, but it later transpired that this was just a pathetic attempt by the woman to cover up the fact that she was physically abusing the boy herself. Pinky-pinky had disappeared from Mamelodi Primary, then, but this did not prevent him from later popping his head up through the toilet-bowl elsewhere, instead [1].

**Wetting Themselves in Terror**

The initial scare broke out in South Africa, of course, but that is not to imply that the concept of the pinky-pinky has not crossed national borders in Africa whatsoever. I have not seen the term itself used in school panics from any other African nations, but there are some reports of tokoloshes supposedly encountered by children in other countries which do sound very much like pinky-pinky scares, albeit without that specific word being used in relation to the curious manifestations. For example, in November 2010 reports began appearing in the Botswanan press about a so-called 'creature school', Boipuso Primary, in the large town of Palapye in the east of that country, where terrifying tokoloshe attacks were supposed to be occurring on a regular basis in the school toilets. A report was made to the regional education office, complaining of a "short hairy man with fiery red eyes" who was harassing pupils when they tried to make use of the conveniences. The main trick this beast liked to play was locking the toilet doors whenever the children went to go inside them, presumably causing them to wet themselves. Persistent reports of this from the children caused adults to go and check up on affairs, only to find the cubicle doors all open and entirely normal.

Given such facts, it seems obvious that there was nothing to the claims, but before long one

**Boipuso Primary School in Botswana, the scene of an outbreak of tokoloshe-related mass hysteria in 2010. The tokoloshe in this instance was supposed to be hiding out inside the school toilets and stopping the children from using them, with no-doubt horrific consequences.**

girl turned up in class with scratches on her face. When asked where she had got them, she professed ignorance, but a rumour started up amongst her classmates that the tokoloshe living in the toilets had done it to her. Panic spread amongst the children, and was soon transmitted to the parents. Evidently believing in the reality of the tokoloshe, it was they who then reported the incidents to the local education office, demanding that the school be closed down before one of their offspring ended up being seriously hurt. Reasoning that there was no actual proof that there was a tokoloshe-infestation in the building, though, the director of the office, Marcos Maedza, refused to do so, eventually coming up with a compromise solution of approaching local churches to pray for the school in order to expel any potential evil influences [2].

The most recent pinky-pinky-type scare from outside South Africa itself, however, occurred in 2012 in Mahlebezulu Primary School in the suburb of Tshabalala in Zimbabwe's second city, Bulawayo. Here, what one teacher called a "stark-naked female goblin" - or chikwambo - was seen sitting on the toilet before attacking schoolgirls who had gone in there to empty their bladders. Supposedly, the result of these assaults was quite serious - one nine-year-old girl, for example, ended up with swollen feet (?) after being attacked, and another was described as being left in a "critical condition". When word got out about there being a goblin in the toilets, the school's teachers rushed into the cubicles to confront it, but could see nothing; as always, it seems, pinky-pinky could only be seen by schoolchildren, not adults. However, the adults on this occasion supposedly did hear the beast; upon returning back to the staffroom and holding a prayer meeting to exorcise the chikwambo, the teachers were startled to then hear it laughing at them in a sarcastic fashion. Word soon got around that the tokoloshe belonged to one of the pupils, who was maliciously bringing it in to school with her. Eventually, some parents hired a local prophet, a Mr Ndlovu, to come out and bless the school, and matters seem to have quietened down [3]. Pinky-pinky it seems, then, is on the move - expect more such cases to pop up from outside South Africa in the future.

Of course, given the ostensibly ridiculous nature of the pinky-pinky's appearance, and its strange paedophilic predilections, this particular social panic appears especially absurd upon first glance. Undeniably, it all sounds quite amusing - but we should not just mock the children for believing in the entity. For one thing, children right across the world seem almost to be genetically predisposed to believe in strange things; indeed, it is perhaps quite natural. This, for example, is a description from one South African woman of how she felt when, as a little girl, she was told of the pinky-pinky living in her school toilets; I think many readers will remember dreading some allegedly haunted or spooky location, or weird creature meant to be living under the bed, in much the same way. "For years I had to sleep with the passage light on. I remember the day clearly. I was in primary school. Everyone was talking about pinky-pinky. I pretended not to care, but every time I walked into the bathroom, the thought of some bathroom monster locking the door and killing me made me feel ill. I would have nightmares, not want to go to school, insist that at least two school friends go to the bathroom with me and, of course, greet the thing as I entered the bathroom. If one of the basins were flooding, we suspected pinky-pinky. If the wind from the well increased, we thought it was angry. It was downright petrifying, until someone explained to me it was a hoax. I slept with that light on for another four months or so.[4]" It seems to me that such fears and rumour-mongering are common to children the world over, and nothing too unusual, really.

Furthermore, the alleged presence of the pinky-pinky in South African schools has been explained, relatively plausibly, by some commentators as being merely some kind of manifestation or expression of local schoolchildren's fears and stresses about a variety of other, real-life matters. The South African collector of urban legends Arthur Goldstuck, for example, was struck by the fact that the creature seemed frequently to appear just at the point that schools began gearing-up for their end-of-year examinations (the South African school year is different from our own; its third term ends in September - when many of the scares occurred - and then the final term, in which the children are examined, lasts from October to December, after which they have their Christmas and summer holidays combined into one). Pressure on the children being high to succeed heading into this final and crucial term, Goldstuck felt that the appearance of pinky-pinky might be a way for them to express their anxieties about their forthcoming exams in a way which was socially acceptable to them. In support of this idea, Goldstuck says that pinky-pinky scares tended to begin with the older kids - those sitting their exams - and then spread their way down through the age groups, and not the other way around [5].

**Fear of Sex**
This seems to be a standard way for people to try and explain cases of mass hysteria amongst African (and indeed Western) schoolchildren, particularly when they are girls, who genuinely do appear to be more susceptible to the condition than their male counterparts are. However, in the case of the pinky-pinky there have been other, more elaborate, reasons put forward to account for the panics than simple exam stress. For example, in that indispensable volume *Ladies and Gents: Public Toilets and Gender*, there is a chapter entitled 'Geographies of Danger: School Toilets in Sub-Saharan Africa', in which an academic named Claudia Mitchell sees great significance in the fact that the pinky-pinky lives, according to some accounts, not in the girls' toilets, but in the space between the girls' and boys' conveniences. Therefore, she essentially deems it to be occupying a so-called 'liminal' space ('liminality' is a concept used by sociologists and folklorists in order to describe something which seems to be 'borderline' in its nature somehow).

As such, Mitchell views the pinky-pinky as being some kind of expression of young girls' fears about going through the borderline state of adolescence, and entering into the adult world as young women. In current South African society, the author seems to view this change as being a dangerous one. She quotes the artist Penny Siopis, who made a series of artworks relating to the pinky-pinky, to the effect that the entity "embodies the fears and anxieties that girls face as their bodies develop and their social standing changes," something which she sees as being a particular concern in South Africa where, she says, "rape and the abuse of women is extremely high[6]".

In a country where, according to one recent study, over 40% of women can expect to be raped within their lifetime [7] (a higher percentage than finish high school), and where one in four male respondents to a 2009 survey admitted quite openly that they had raped someone at some point in their lives [8], this is perhaps a plausible theory. To judge by the experiences of one

African schoolgirl quoted in Mitchell's essay, the casual molestation of women seems to be a kind of behaviour which is ingrained in some African males from a young age. She spoke despairingly of how she hated "All the touching at school - in class, in the corridors, all day every day. Boys touch your bum, your breasts.[9]" One horrific recent news report even carried the results of a survey made of 1,500 schoolboys in the black township of Soweto, in which around 25% of those questioned gave their charming opinion that "gang rape is fun" [10]. To make matters worse, teachers, tutors and other school administrators have even been known to join in with this disgraceful state of affairs, demanding sex and other such favours in return for grades, references and handing over exam certificates. In such a society, simply being a young girl or woman could be viewed very reasonably as being a fairly dangerous thing in itself. The fact that the pinky-pinky chose to attack only girls wearing pink knickers could, perhaps, according to this interpretation then be seen as being some kind of coded warning against the victims flouting their gender or maturing sexuality within such a potentially dangerous social environment - or, at least, that is how I choose to read matters.

The notion that the pinky-pinky attacks girls in the school toilets makes further sense according to this theory as, seeing as they really are liminal points within a school (on the premises, but out of sight of the teachers), they provide a kind of space in which unpleasant things such as rape and bullying really can occur to children in real life [11]. As such, Mitchell views the haunted school toilets in alleged pinky-pinky manifestations as being in some sense emblematic of all those liminal, in-between spaces in the outside world, such as alleys, bushes and stretches of lonely veldt, where there is a substantial chance that these same hysterical schoolgirls might one day come across rapists or other such abusive and dangerous males in their rapidly-approaching adult life [12].

In the catalogue for her 2005 exhibition featuring pinky-pinky paintings, *Passions and Panics*, meanwhile, the artist Penny Siopis seems to view this particular tokoloshe-variant as being an expression not only of South African schoolgirls' fear of the dangers which their gender may well place them in during adulthood, but also of wider social malaises, the catalogue saying that the mass hysteria the demon gave rise to in South Africa as a whole "speaks of the fears and phobias of our post-apartheid moment, and the unspeakable psychic states of anxiety and moral panics in society at large." According to Siopis' own words:

> "As much as pinky-pinky is a perpetrator of violence, it also seems a victim of, and scapegoat for, violent, uncivil actions - a constructed something to blame for social problems. [13] "

In many ways, it would be difficult to come up with a better description of the ultimate psychological source for 'demons', 'evil ghosts' and many other of the imaginary figures at the centre of some mass hysteria outbreaks than that.

Indeed, the fact that pinky-pinky first began to rear its ugly head in 1993 and 1994 is surely highly significant; South Africa's first free and fair elections were held in 1994, as we saw earlier, and there was much anxiety about what would happen to the country once this had occurred. Much as the end of apartheid was looked forward to, certain sectors of the population - i.e. some whites - feared that, under black rule, civilised society might simply collapse; and, given this fact, surely it is not insignificant that the first pinky-pinky scares actually occurred in all-white schools? Within a matter of months, forced segregation in schools would be ended. Did white schoolgirls, kept apart from young black males throughout their childhood education up to this point, secretly fear that they might end up getting raped in the toilets by newly-liberated black boys? Maybe they did, but in the newly-prevailing social climate, they could hardly be expected to say so openly - and so the figure of pinky-pinky appeared on the scene. That, at least, is one way of looking at these events.

**Crying in the Toilets**
So much, then, for the South African pinky-pinky panics. But are there any other cases of mass hysteria surrounding supernatural creatures being sighted in school toilets around the world? I would suggest that there are, but probably upon a more local and barely-reported scale than occurs in southern Africa. The title and subject-matter of Claudia Mitchell's essay may well very easily be mocked, but I think that she is spot-on in identifying school toilets as being liminal zones. Many kids seem to find them spooky, and I think that the legend of the 'haunted school toilet' will be familiar to many readers of this book; certainly, there were rumours to that effect about our school toilet when I was a young boy. I am ashamed to say that I believed them.

The particular form of ghost which is supposed to haunt a Western school toilet can even reflect the more generalised fears of children about certain aspects of their own wider society, just like the pinky-pinky is supposed to reflect South African schoolgirls' fears about rape. In some Kentucky schools, for instance, there used to be a legend current amongst schoolchildren about an old man with a big knife who would sometimes lurk inside the toilets before cutting up any children who should wander inside there and then disposing of their mauled bodies, chunk by chunk, down the nearest sewer. This dread seems entirely irrational, of course, until you consider that these tales first became known amongst Kentucky pupils around the end of the 1940s, not long after a real-life serial killer, William Heirens, had actually been apprehended in Chicago after chopping up a five-year-old girl, Suzanne Degman, and then throwing her pieces of flesh down into a sewer.

Media reports of these horrific but all-too real events seem to have then percolated down through society into the minds of the schoolchildren, before being transformed ultimately into rumours of a ghostly old man hiding in the toilets, ready to get them. The fear was of a real enough thing, then - homicidal adults obviously do exist, if only on a small scale - but found its childish expression in the supernaturalised figure of the violent and murderous ghost in the toilet [14]. This is exactly the same kind of process as apparently occurred in South Africa.

However, belief in paranormal beings is not as widespread in the West as it is in Africa. And the stresses of junior school children in general are probably not as high, so I am unaware of many rumours of this kind about paranormal terrors lurking in school lavatories growing up into full-scale social panics in the West, as happened with pinky-pinky (although there was one exception to this rule, from Texas in 1983, when primary school children came to believe that killer Smurfs were lurking in their toilets, waiting to murder them). Kids running out of toilets and screaming about imaginary ghosts is something that might well occur, on a very, very small scale, in junior and infant schools throughout the Western world all the time, but these annoyances will soon be quelled quite quickly by the actions of irritated and sceptical teachers and most certainly will not find themselves being reported on in the newspapers, even as humorous 'filler' material. There is, however, an interesting parallel case to the pinky-pinky scares from South America where, evidently, enough distress was caused by the bizarre incidents involved to merit its wider reporting in the media.

What happened was as follows. In June 1996, it was widely reported in Nicaragua that a group of children from the Simon Bolivar School in the city of Masaya had been terrified out of their wits after seeing a number of what they termed "elves" climbing out from the toilet bowls in the girls' restroom. A group of five girls ran screaming out of the lavatories, claiming to have witnessed three elves dressed in red hats, suits and shoes, emerging from the bowls before disappearing into thin air. One girl was so terrified that she fainted.

During break, when the incidents occurred, the female students ran out into the playground shouting about what they had just seen. A 10-year-old boy, Darwin Altamiano, said that he didn't believe them, but went inside the toilets to have a look anyway; he saw no elves but claimed to have witnessed the cubicle doors opening and closing by themselves (we will remember, interestingly, that the pinky-pinky was not meant to be visible to boys, either). Another boy who went in, Bismarck Altamiano, claimed to have heard "strange laughter" from these same invisible elves echoing through the air. Reports of the incident caused widespread public interest, and some commentators openly speculated about the nature of these alleged elves, claiming that they were probably living in a kind of earthly limbo, too good for Hell but not good enough for Heaven (a once-common European explanation for the existence of fairies, too) [15].

This, of course, suggests that there was some kind of underlying cultural belief - or perhaps half-belief - in the existence of elves in the area which, presumably, helped to shape the form of the creatures which the children thought they saw. The daily newspaper, *Barricada*, tried to rationalise, and stepped in with the notion that the children had merely been hallucinating due to malnutrition caused by poverty, but this does slightly miss the point about the affair. The schoolgirls saw their elves not simply because they might have been hungry - how many famine victims do you hear of sighting gnomes? - but also because of some kind of prevailing cultural belief in them. If they had happened to have lived in South Africa, they would most likely have seen a pinky-pinky coming out of the toilets to attack them instead. In other southern African nations where belief in the pinky-pinky has not yet become widespread, however, such scares tend to involve plain, common-or-garden tokoloshes, rather than their perverted knicker-loving cousins.

**Hairy Horrors**
In 2010, for example, reports began to appear in the African press about strange goings-on in a Botswanan primary school, accompanied by rather sensationalist headlines along the lines of 'Children Attacked by Hairy Sex Dwarf'. Coming across such headlines, it would be hard for most people not to read on. If they were to do so, then they would come across a most

extraordinary tale. It seems that, beginning in 2009, children at the Kalamare Primary School in Central Province had been being assaulted and molested by what one victim described as being a little long-clawed creature which was "hairy with cat-like features and dressed in colourful clothes". This was soon identified by locals as being a tokoloshe; and it was causing chaos at the school.

Following these supposed attacks by the thing - which were generally described as being sexual in their nature - the schoolgirl victims, all of whom were aged around 12 years old, were found lying on the ground around the school in a comatose state in which they could remain for as long as four hours. The mother of one of the affected girls, Lenyatso Galebetwe, explained to the Botswanan newspaper *The Voice* what is meant to have happened to her daughter:

> "My child will not go back to that school until that evil thing has left. She has had enough! She was the first to be molested and has suffered repeated attacks since then. On the first day [of school] a certain schoolboy ran into my yard crying saying the teachers had sent him to summon me ... When I got there my child was lying in a seemingly lifeless state with her eyes wide open and whitish thick saliva dribbling from the corners of her mouth. It was a pitiful and painful sight."

This will sound, of course, to many ears simply like the girl had suffered some kind of epileptic fit whilst in the classroom; an interpretation which could perhaps be backed up by the fact that Mrs Galebetwe's daughter at no point identified a tokoloshe as being responsible for her convulsions herself. Instead, she professed herself to be unable to say what had caused them. Nonetheless, the girl fits the profile for what students of mass hysteria would call the 'index case'; namely, the person around whom a scare or panic begins, and from whom symptoms soon proceed to pass on to others. In this case, it seems likely that other children, either seeing the sick child fitting or hearing descriptions from other pupils of it, were worried by the symptoms and interpreted them along what were, to them, culturally-acceptable lines - they said it was the work of a tokoloshe.

When other children then began fitting in the same fashion as the Galebetwe child, it appears that this idea was then reinforced for the pupils by the adults and other such figures of authority around them. These, for example, are the words of Kereng Peloentle, a mother whose daughter also started to suffer from convulsions in the school:

> "My child who is 12 and in standard five was attacked last month while in class. I took her to the New Good Shepherd Church where the prophets told me the thing that had attacked my child is a tokoloshe. That's when I decided to withdraw her from school ... She will only go back when that thing has been dealt with. I think only churches, especially the Zion Christian Church, can chase this creature away and give our children a chance to go on with their education."

It seems likely that, once authority-figures like parents and 'prophets' from local churches had begun endorsing the children's belief in the reality of the tokoloshe attacks, they began to

**A close-up view of the wounded legs of some teenage schoolgirls from a boarding school in Rietfontein, Botswana, who had been suffering from nocturnal assaults allegedly perpetrated by pin-wielding evil spirits between 1985 and 1992. Were they tokoloshes?**

spread and affect the pupils more and more. Certainly, accounts of the assaults and what precisely it was that the tokoloshe did to his schoolgirl victims in this case began to become more elaborate and disturbing, fitting in with some of the more widely-known aspects of tokoloshe-lore. Examinations of the girls after their fits, for instance, were soon reported as showing signs that they had been raped by the entity, perhaps reflecting the widespread belief that the tokoloshe is a kind of incubus-figure, as we saw earlier.

According to one woman, who claimed that her little sister had been raped by the tokoloshe, nurses at the local health clinic "told me there was evidence of sexual activity and I asked her if she had a boyfriend. She replied in the negative and they gave her vagina-cleansing tablets." Apparently, these tablets were prescribed by doctors to several other alleged tokoloshe-rape victims from the school as well, thereby presumably enhancing the apparent legitimacy of their claims in the eyes of some. Indeed, it appears that just about the only person who didn't take these claims seriously was the local village chief, Kgosi Kgang - with the result that there was widespread public anger and hostility being expressed towards him for having the temerity to be sceptical about it all [16].

Mass hysteria about tokoloshe-attacks involving some kind of sexual element to them seems to be a periodic feature of life in some African schools. One particularly extreme example of this came from Zimbabwe in 2002, when the headmaster of St Mark's Secondary School in Mhondoro, a village in Mashonaland West Province, was forced to flee for his life after being accused of possessing an army of goblins and tokoloshes which he was using to rape his pupils with. The troubles started about six weeks before the start of the mid-year exams - a perfectly good reason for tension building up of its own accord - when girl-boarders began to complain of being assaulted in their beds at night by invisible beings which were attacking and trying to rape them. About 30 girls claimed to have been affected in this way by tokoloshes, one of whom said that she had been bitten on the arm by a spirit after wrestling with it when it tried to climb into bed with her. Others started to complain of being beaten up by what were termed, vaguely, "invisible objects". The hysteria then spread to boys at the school as well as the girls. One teacher described how a male pupil went into a trance and appeared to become possessed by a tokoloshe in quite disturbing terms:

> "He was demanding meat, threatening that after finishing with the students, the spirits would attack the teachers next. We are living in fear here."

As this statement implies, even the teachers at the school took the rumours of spirit-attacks seriously at the time, thereby giving them further credence in the eyes of their pupils. A number of female teachers were even reported to be considering leaving, penning a written statement for a newspaper in which they made several allegations about being sexually assaulted by the tokoloshes themselves, including the intriguing phrase:

> "Sometimes we get up in the morning to find the bedding mysteriously wet and we suspect foul play."

At the height of the panic, many students joined the school's Anglican Scripture Union group, hoping to combat the demons through prayer and religion. However, it seems that the headmaster - possibly sceptical about matters and no doubt infuriated by the chaos into which his school was descending - acted against this Union in some way. Possibly it was this action upon his behalf which led to accusations of him being the evil wizard behind it all; either way, before long angry parents had begun turning up at the school en masse, withdrawing their children and demanding to see the headmaster in order to confront him about his supposed use of tokoloshes against their offspring. It was at this point that the poor man fled, and the school got temporarily closed down before then reopening again with those few students and teachers who still remained there, under the control of the Deputy Head [17].

**Follow My Leader**
It seems that 2002 was a good year for tokoloshe-hysteria in Zimbabwean schools, as during September of that year an equally-strange outbreak occurred at Moleli High School, an establishment run by the Methodist Church in the rural area of Msengezi, west of Harare, when 24 girls started acting bizarrely. Their hands, legs and shoulders began to shake, and they started to hallucinate and show signs of apparent spirit-possession. Most sensationally,

however, they took to walking around in a somnambulistic state described as being "as if they were zombies". Seeing as one of the variant descriptions of a tokoloshe is that of a zombie created by a witch, as we have already observed, it was perhaps not overly-surprising that these entities were thus blamed by some for causing the outbreak.

Others, however, had different ideas; the girls' rooms where they boarded were, according to some pupils, being haunted by the ghosts of 22 ex-students of the school who had drowned on Lake Chivero, in the south-west of the country, when their boat had overturned in 1995. Poltergeist-like manifestations, including disembodied footsteps and screams, were reported by terrified pupils who were disturbed in their beds at night. It seems that some staff may have believed these explanations themselves, as they were criticised by the Zimbabwean Education Minister, Kwadzanai Nyanungo, who blamed merely "rumours and fear" for cases like these, saying that the ultimate blame for them lay not with the pupils but with the adult members of staff who failed to address and dismiss the tales in a timely manner, adding that a few such cases occurred every year in the country because of these failures.

The then-head of ZINATHA, Zimbabwe's union of sangomas and other traditional healers, Dr Peter Sibanda, disagreed, however, recalling that a similar outbreak of panic at the same school a decade earlier had been caused not by hysteria but by a disgruntled ex-employee who had not been given a pension by the school and so had cast an evil spell against it. After locals had been told to "discipline the man" (meaning beat him up, presumably), he said, the problems had stopped immediately. His explanation for the current panic was that some local farmers must have had some tokoloshes in their possession, presumably in the form of slave-labour zombies, but that these had gotten out of hand because they "lack socialisation" and thus enjoyed going out "to prey on females". He recommended hiring an inyanga to solve the problem, as I suppose he would [18].

These last few cases which we have discussed illustrate clearly one of the key explanations for these outbreaks of mass hysteria, in terms of their severity and scale; namely, the widespread acceptance upon behalf of responsible adults of the reality of what the children are panicking about. If teachers believe that they are being raped and assaulted by tokoloshes too, then clearly this will only reinforce the belief of the children that something weird really is going on.

It is an inescapable fact that adults in southern African countries sometimes come to believe that they are under assault from massed supernatural forces, and not just schoolchildren. In 2010, for instance, a small hospital named Makande Rural Clinic, 60km south-west of the town of Karoi in Zimbabwe's Mashonaland West Province, had to be temporarily closed down for two weeks when the nurses who worked there downed tools after claiming to have come under repeated attack from what they called "goblins". The nurses were busy vaccinating people against malaria when the alleged attacks began, and locals blamed evil goblin-owners who wanted to do ill. Eventually, tsikamutandas were called out to perform exorcisms upon the haunted hospital, but this, apparently, did not prevent the scare from spreading; details are scarce, but it seems that numerous pupils at the nearby Makande Primary School also soon began coming under attack from demons, supposedly upon a daily basis. One of their teachers gave information to the press about this fact, giving his (or her) opinion that the whole area was "prone" to tokoloshes [19].

Seeing as the majority of adults around them - including their teachers - believe in the reality of mass assault by tokoloshes, then, it is not surprising that many southern African children do, too. As such, it is not enough simply to accuse the youths involved of being backwards idiots or simpletons, as some Western commentators have occasionally tried to do.

There are actually some unpleasant racist discussion groups online, for example, whose members like to repost stories such as these on their sites, and then use them as an excuse for mocking black people. For instance, the story about tokoloshe-rapes at Kalamare Primary School was reposted on one such website under the title 'Niglets [a slang term meaning 'baby niggers'] Attacked by Hairy Sex Dwarf', prompting comments such as the ironically illiterate "Another fine example how stupid nigger are" and "niggers are so stupid and primitive". Other posters suggested that Gary Coleman, the black midget actor from the US sitcom *Diff'rent Strokes*, must actually have been responsible for the incidents, and not a tokoloshe at all [20].

Clearly this assumption of racial stupidity on behalf of the black African pupils involved cannot be the truth, however, as cases of mass hysteria involving supernatural creatures do sometimes occur in Western schools, too, where the majority of pupils are presumably white, although we do not really have the space to discuss such incidents in any real detail here. Suffice to say, however, that the 1983 Texas Smurf panic was just as strange and outrageous in its nature as any of the above-detailed cases were. It is wrong to accuse black African schoolchildren of being stupid simply because they sometimes have to endure tokoloshe-panics, then. When they do undergo such bizarre outbreaks, they are, after all, only picking up on the pre-existing beliefs held by adults in the wider community around them. In Medieval Europe, children believed in witches and demons because their parents and religious leaders did so, too; and why, exactly, should modern African schoolchildren not do exactly the same under similar conditions today?

# Chapter Eight

## Goblin for Sale!: Changing Conceptions of the Tokoloshe

*O*f course, belief in the tokoloshe being widespread in southern African societies, it is perfectly possible for con-men to exploit this fact for their own financial gain. A newspaper reporter who walked around the slums and market-places of Zimbabwe's capital Harare in 1999, not too long after that country's catastrophic economic collapse had begun, for example, was without difficulty able to find people who claimed to be able to sell her a tokoloshe. One such person was Lucas Gogoyi, a 'traditional healer', or so he alleged, in his early sixties. He said that he could easily sell her a tokoloshe in the shape of a monkey, a gremlin or an invisible spirit. It didn't matter what item he sold her, apparently, as the tokoloshes he had in stock could effortlessly transform themselves into any object they pleased, the example he gave being a peanut-butter jar.

Seeing as his shop was filled up to the rafters with old jars and containers of various descriptions, this perhaps implies that he was selling on gullible people empty pots and then claiming that they were actually tokoloshes. (The idea that ghosts and demons could be trapped inside bottles and jars by powerful sorcerers and exorcists is one which has been held in many cultures, incidentally - including the Europe of the past. It seems to still be a contemporary belief in modern-day Africa, as well; according to a 1992 interview with a self-styled South African 'ghostologist' called Dr Ismael Ballin printed in a newspaper called *The Star*, for example, Dr Ballin claimed that he was able to lure unwanted ghosts inside bottles by placing yellow flowers and magical powders into them, and then corking them up once the ghosts had gone inside in order to retrieve the pretty blooms. Then, he would throw the imprisoned ghosts into the sea, ridding his clients of their presence forever; obviously, Lucas Gogoyi was exploiting such pre-existing local beliefs in order to sell his own magic bottles. [1]) Gogoyi claimed that his bottled tokoloshes were worth their fee, however, as they could be used to take away money and trade from a business-rival, punish errant spouses and their lovers, cause heart attacks and AIDS and, most likely, do anything else a person asked for. In a society on the verge of collapse due to the disastrous economic and social policies of President Robert Mugabe, no doubt Gogoyi found many takers for his dubious wares amongst the desperate and unwary [2].

As reports of cases of witchcraft began to rise in Zimbabwe throughout the 2000s, as the country hurled on headlong into chaos and oblivion, there was a rash of such pieces of investigative journalism taking place in the market-places of Harare. In 2007, for instance, a report appeared in the Zimbabwean press under the heading 'Zimbabwe: Open Market for Goblins' in which two undercover reporters went to Harare's flea-market and posed as a pair of orphaned siblings who were in great need of money. It was not too long before they came across a man who professed himself able to take them to meet a famous witch-doctor who would happily sell them what he termed a 'goblin' - or chikwambo (also spelled zvikwambo), a specific sub-species of tokoloshe used largely for protective purposes and for attracting riches - in order to satisfy their desires [*]. The next day, a meeting had been arranged, and they went to see the inyanga in his flat. He said it would be easy to solve their problem; all he would need to do would be to sell them on a goblin that, in his own words, "I made last night using medicines from a far away land where gold and silver are in abundance", for the princely sum of 890,000 Zimbabwean dollars (probably not as much as it sounds, given the rampant inflation there).

He then said that, if they wanted the goblin, which he described as "fuming with power", to obey them, the reporters would have to refrain from eating chicken for the rest of their lives, and keep it in a safe place where they could worship it and pay it homage once a year. Still, though, the man tried to get more money out of them, telling them to take the chikwambo home and then come and fetch him there anytime they "felt free" (i.e. had more cash) so that he could "plant" it and make it work properly. The reporters then took the goblin to ZINATHA, the country's official organisation of registered traditional healers, whose deputy secretary examined the creature and told them that they had been conned. The 'goblin' was, in fact, nothing more than a potato dressed up in beads, cloth and some fur from a baboon hide; "This goblin is not genuine", as he put it in his own words [3].

Another such piece of first-hand investigative reporting appeared in a May 2011 edition of a Zimbabwean newspaper called *The Herald*, warning the country's citizens against fraudulent tokoloshe-sellers operating openly in the nation's market-places. The reporter here encountered numerous market-vendors trying to sell him bottles filled with hand-made dolls of one kind or another, labelled with the word 'tokoloshe' on the front, together with a description of how the things were supposed to work and crude advertising slogans such as "the strong one". According to the report, many of the sellers were formerly earning their money in illegal diamond-mining operations but, when Mugabe's government had begun to clamp down on such practices, these same criminals had decided to turn to being con-men instead, importing fake tokoloshes from South Africa and then selling them on to the desperate.

Interestingly, the creatures seemed by now to have shifted in the public mind in Zimbabwe from being living spirits or goblins that had to be worshipped and pacified if they were to do your bidding, and instead into some kind of odd magical substance which had to be diluted and then sprinkled around or bathed in in order for it to work. One market-stall holder, for example, advised *The Herald's* journalist that, if he wanted to gain good luck from his tokoloshe, he would have to dissolve it in his bath-water and then wash himself all over in it. An increase in cheap Nigerian and

---

[*] This is one possible interpretation of what the word 'chikwambo' means, at least; some sources seem to suggest that it is simply the Shona-language word for a tokoloshe in the usual sense, whereas others appear to imply that it is instead a kind of catch-all word for fairies and other supernatural creatures – I did see at least one report in which some alleged Zimbabwean mermaids were referred to as being chikwambos, for instance.

Ghanaian movies showing wizards getting rich quick from using tokoloshes, together with the desperation which frequently comes with mass unemployment, were together blamed by the reporter for the public's increasing receptivity to such scams [4].

**Objects of Desire**

Due perhaps to the increase in tokoloshe-sellers across the country, it does seem that the conception of the beast in Zimbabwe is increasingly changing in some areas from being a hairy supernatural rapist, and into some kind of badly-made doll imbued somehow with magical powers by witches, instead. For example, in February 2011 it was reported that there was widespread shock and panic in Chitungwiza, a satellite town of Harare, after a goblin of some kind was discovered inside a meal-bag on a rubbish dump by children who were looking inside it scavenging for food. The report was accompanied by a photograph of a local man, Rangarirai Mutomba, holding up the tokoloshe triumphantly for the camera; it looks like a large potato with straw and animal hide stuck onto the bottom of it, although the report described it as having "a cone-shaped horn with what looked like human hair attached to it with red, black and white beads". When it was ripped open by Mutomba, who, as a Christian, disapproved of the item, it was found to be full of red powder, presumably intended to be imbued with juju magic. Mutomba claimed that the fact that the tokoloshe's owners had thrown it away indicated that it was dangerous and that they could not handle its power - although an alternative interpretation might be that it simply didn't work and was thus nothing

The alleged 'goblin' (handily picked out for us here by a Zimbabwean newspaper) found on a rubbish dump in Chitungwiza, just outside Harare, in 2011. It appears to be an entirely artificial creation, presumably fashioned in order to bring its creator good luck and riches.

**A hand-made chikwambo, which caused a panic in the Zimbabwean settlement of Mabvuku in April 2012 after being thrown out of a passing taxi-cab. The snake which was inside the object was later killed by an angry crowd.**

more than a piece of worthless rubbish [5].

Another such scare erupted in Zimbabwe in April 2012, when what was described as a "strange-looking creature" was tossed out of a moving 'kombi' (a type of shared taxi, common in southern Africa) as it sped past the Manresa Shopping Centre in Mabvuku, an eastern suburb of Harare. Very quickly, a crowd gathered around the thing - from which a live snake then slithered - and determined that it was nothing less than a chikwambo. As such, the mob killed the snake themselves, and then determined that they would go and ask some local prophets to burn the goblin and exorcise its power. But what was this 'goblin'? As a photograph of the thing makes clear, it was in fact a calabash - a type of hard-ripened melon which, when hollowed out, is used as a water-container or gourd - covered over in some kind of animal-fur, in which the snake had been placed [6].

The idea of snakes being placed within a seemingly inanimate object which is then claimed to be a chikwambo was also involved in a peculiar case from January 2012, in which it was reported that a man from Zimbabwe's second city of Bulawayo, named Malibeni Mhlanga, had got rather more than he bargained for when purchasing five tokoloshes in order to bring him wealth. The inyanga who created them had died, he said, releasing the demons from out of his control, with the result that his wife, Margaret, was being raped by the dastardly beings on a nightly basis. Malibeni had managed to get three of them killed by an exorcist, but the others were still free to roam the neighbourhood creating chaos. According to Margaret, these tokoloshes walked like goats, and caused her to spit blood after they had had their way with her. Malibeni had a similar complaint - every time he went to the toilet, the evil goblins were making him piss blood.

One day, however, after Margaret's bag allegedly began "mysteriously increasing in size" and bulging out of its own accord, the bewitched couple called a prophet in to help out. He opened her bag and discovered two snakes inside it together with what Margaret called a "human-creature-like goblin" which "looked like an owl". However, it seems that this 'owl' was in fact an artificial object of some kind, as the prophet proceeded to rip it apart, finding a photograph of the couple's son inside it, this item presumably being intended to act as a kind of curse. This action seemed to do no real good, however, as the tokoloshes still remained on the loose and were attacking the couple's neighbours; in the report's original words, women in the neighbourhood were "being sexually abused by gnomes at night". Eventually, several residents gathered outside the Mhlanga family home and demanded that they either move or be evicted [7]. Greed for wealth, it seems, can often have unpleasant consequences for those who seek it in much of southern Africa, a moral message which appears to be frequently reinforced in these tales.

### Buyer Beware
The kinds of artificial witchcraft-object which we have been discussing above, however, seem to be as far away as possible from the original South African concept of the tokoloshe as can be; don't they? Not necessarily. In fact, whilst apparently fairly rare, there are a few historical accounts on record of the word 'tokoloshe' being used in South Africa in relation to inanimate objects imbued with muti-power, rather than to living, demonic beings as such. For example, there is an account online from a white man whose father, he said, had a run in with a tokoloshe "many years ago" near to the town of White River in Mpumalanga Province. This tokoloshe, though, was not of the usual kind we hear about from within South Africa; rather, it was "an evil-smelling package of carefully wrapped leaves" which had been placed behind the rear wheel of a tractor by a disgruntled employee, apparently in order to bewitch the vehicle and cause it to turn over with the white farmer inside it, which it did. The black labourers on the farm immediately identified this item as being a tokoloshe, and advised that it be burned right away, so the concept of the tokoloshe as an enchanted object must have had some historical currency amongst certain black South Africans, at least [8].

However, whilst I could not find many accounts like this on record from South Africa, one recent - and very prominent - story from our old friend the *Daily Sun* does feature a vaguely similar motif, concerning, as it does, the activities of a 63-year-old inyanga named Shadrack Mdakana, who claimed to be able to sell people little home-made models of tokoloshes which, when planted in the ground, would come to life and bring their owners wealth. Mdakana, who lived in the Chris Hani squatter's camp in the Eastern Cape Province city of Port Elizabeth, seemed to have a very good grasp of the concept of keeping manufacturing costs down and then selling on his products at an uncorrespondingly high price. After all, his "little men", as the paper described them, were made out of a substance as cheap as porridge (or 'red Lesotho pap', as the dish is known locally) and then sold on for absurdly high prices ranging from 15,000 to 25,000 South African Rand (approximately £1,100 to £1,900 in English money). Looking at the model tokoloshe which Mdakana allowed to be photographed by the reporters, these little beings were not overly-convincing; it looks like a small child's plasticine model of a midget with two round green blobs of vegetation stuck onto it for eyes.

According to Mdakana himself, however, his porridge-men were well worth the investment. "This tokoloshe is deadly," he explained, telling the men from the *Daily Sun* how livestock-farmers from neighbouring Lesotho made good use of his products by employing them as slaves to herd their sheep, goats and cattle for them. As such, he said, his tokoloshes sold like hot cakes; they could be used to bring a man riches, to expand businessmen's empires, or to cause the downfall of your enemies. All you had to do was to buy a doll from him, and then bury it in your yard. He would also give you some muti-substance, which you then had to rub all over your naked body whilst standing upon the 'tokoloshe-grave', presumably at such a time of night that nobody would be able to see you doing it. After a month, alleged Mdakana, the planted tokoloshe would grow up to be the size of a toddler and raise itself up from out of the ground. You would be able to tell that it was him, he said, because the tokoloshe would look strong, have a beard, and only the one eye in the middle of his forehead. He would also come equipped with a "small stone like a marble" which he would keep inside his mouth in order to render himself invisible. This little man would then be your slave; but, nonetheless, you had better watch out. If the being's owner should die, then the demon would break loose and become very violent, warned Mdakana, in an echo of the Malibeni Mhlanga case, cited above. In his own dread-inducing words, once this event should come to pass, the liberated tokoloshe "rapes the kids or pokes the wife of his owner. He will do this until the whole family is dead.[9]" Quite a design flaw!

This amusing report does not really seem to be in line with the traditional South African image of the tokoloshe, however. Perhaps the demon now morphing into a money-making model or object in this country too, is, like in Zimbabwe, a reaction to harsh economic times in the modern world? Or maybe the Zimbabwean concept of the chikwambo is now spreading down south across the border into South Africa and influencing the ever-changing nature of the tokoloshe there, as well? We can, as ever, only speculate.

**OPPOSITE:** According to a 2012 story from South Africa's best-selling tabloid the *'Daily Sun'*, an inyanga named Shadrack Mdakana was offering to sell his clients some 'grow-your-own' tokoloshes made from red Lesotho pap (porridge), for the princely sum of at least 15,000 Rand (over £1,000). Once planted in the ground, he said, the tokoloshe would grow up to become a real, living creature which would act as your life-long slave!

# THIS PAP TOKOLOSHE SELLS LIKE HOT CAKES!

## ... for R15 000 to R25 000!

By MKHUSELI SIZANI

HE's a little man – made of red Lesotho pap.

The man who makes these little men says they are otokoloshe . . .

And they are often very violent.

The price for just one is R15 000 – at least!

The father of the little men is an inyanga from Chris Hani squatter camp in Port Elizabeth, Shadrack "Mkhulu" Mdakana (63).

He told *Daily Sun*: "This tokoloshe is deadly. Stock famers, business people and jealous people make use of it.

"The Lesotho people made this tokoloshe in order to shepherd their sheep, goats and cows because there's a lot of stock theft there.

"This pap tokoloshe sells like hot cakes these days. Business people buy it to expand their businesses and attract more customers. Jealous people also buy it to stop the progress of others and make their lives hell.

"This tokoloshe costs between R15 000 and R25 000!" he said.

"The sellers of this otokoloshe make it with Lesotho pap mixed with evil muthi.

"They make it look like a human figure.

"Then you dig a hole and place it there in your yard.

"When it is partly buried the zangoma will give you muthi to wash yourself. But when you wash yourself you must be naked and stand on top of this 'tokoloshe grave'. . .

"After a month the tokoloshe will grow into a size of a two or three-year-old boy. But when you look at him, he looks like a strong man with one eye on his forehead and a beard!

"In his mouth he always has a small stone like a marble that makes him invisible to people.

"Most of the time he likes to play with kids." he said.

But watch out: the pap tokoloshe is a troublemaker.

"Hell breaks loose when the owner of this tokoloshe is dead – the tokoloshe becomes very violent!

"He rapes the kids or pokes the wife of his owner.

"He will do this until the whole family is dead," Mkhulu said.

Inyanga Shadrack "Mkhulu" Mdakana shows a tokoloshe. INSERT: A R15 000 tokoloshe made of Lesotho pap. *Photos by Mkhuseli Sizani*

**Do the Mamlambo**
Interestingly - or confusingly, perhaps, depending upon your perspective - the transformation of tokoloshes into money-making goblins, idols or potions is not something which is entirely without parallel in the supernatural history of southern Africa. After all, there is yet another kind of witches' familiar which we have not so far mentioned - the mamlambo - whose traditional functions were to provide its wizard-owners with both sex and, significantly, wealth. It appears to me that, in the desperate economic times of Africa today, the tokoloshe has begun merging in some way within the popular mind with this rival (but in many ways complementary) breed of magical familiar, too.

The mamlambo is, in most cases that I could find, female; a few tales of male mamlambos do exist, but these tend to be much rarer, and of comparatively modern invention - the exact opposite of the gender-pattern which we find depicted in tokoloshe-stories, it will be noted. Originally, the mamlambo appears to have been considered to be some kind of water-sprite or river goddess - in some traditions, such as that of the Xhosa people, at any rate, from whose word umamlambo (meaning 'mother of the river'), the modern word was ultimately derived - which is, of course, yet another similarity with our little furry friends. Unlike tokoloshes, however, the true form of a mamlambo is rather more reptilian than simian in its nature; whilst they might appear to a person in the guise of a beautiful woman, their 'true' form, underneath it all, is that of a large and hideous river-snake with shining eyes like old-fashioned car-headlights.

When she does manifest in the form of a woman, though, she sheds this particular skin and becomes altogether more appealing; supposedly, she shifts her form so as to become the embodied sexual ideal of the man who looks upon her. No man can resist her and, once she has got a poor dupe in her clutches, he is hers to do with as she pleases - something which leads, as might be expected, to some fairly unpleasant consequences. In the original legends concerning this succubus-like creature, she is meant to appear to a man whilst he walks alone through the bush with his mind wandering upon daydreams of women and sex. This, it seems, is enough to alert the mamlambo, who quickly jumps upon her unsuspecting prey. It appears to be the case that this was originally conceived of as essentially being the man's fault; there is some sense in which the man's lustful daydreams actually create the succubus in the first place. As the old Xhosa story-teller Dwali Nekompela put it, such a man's head "becomes like a bucket of water on a woman's head. If she puts no leaves on top, the water spills over the edges. So man's thoughts of beautiful women also spill over - if not during the day, then when he sleeps. [10]" In the original myth, once a man's sexual desire has been awakened in this way, his uncontrollable love for a mamlambo then leads him on to do something awful; namely, to kill his own father. No doubt Freud would have a field day [11].

In more contemporary African mythology, however, the mamlambo has been transformed from an independent spiritual femme fatale, and into a witches' and wizards' familiar who can not only be used for sexual purposes, but also in order to gain money via magical means, like a chikwambo. It is supposed to attract financial luck to its owner - into whose double, just like a tokoloshe, it can transform, and vice versa - and to steal the rightful wealth of others in order to satisfy its master or mistress' own needs at the expense of the wider community. However, in order to keep on doing a witch's will in this way, the mamlambo requires to be fed sacrifices of chickens, beef and human blood. Failure to keep it fed means that the mamlambo will slither out at night and kill the witch's relatives in snake-form, whether she likes it or not. Other sources, meanwhile, say that it will require a sacrifice of the wizard's family members no matter how many chickens or bits of beef her owner feeds her. Chikwambos, too, are sometimes spoken of as needing to be fed in order to maintain them in full working order - but, seemingly, never with murdered humans.

Another curious similarity between chikwambos and more modern conceptions of the mamlambo, meanwhile, is that the mamlambo, too, can now apparently be kept inside a bottle by its owner - whereas, originally, it used to step out of whirlwinds of its own accord and could not really be captured in this way. Just as some witches are said to grow tokoloshes and chikwambos up from magical roots, so the mamlambo is often now said to be acquired in the form of a root or twig which is then kept in a bottle (or, sometimes, it appears as a fish-like thing swimming around in a bottle of water which has been specially scooped up for the purpose from a haunted river). This root, however, is already alive; it glows at night and, if you were to try and cut it, it would jump out of your hands and magically evade any harm. Looked after well, though, it will soon grow up into a hairy snake with huge fangs and glowing eyes, which is the true form of the mamlambo. One particularly bizarre method of rendering a mamlambo harmless also involves the idea of the magic twig or root. A powerful inyanga who wishes to exorcise one from a wizard's home will go inside, retrieve the money-bringing root from its jar, and then shove it promptly up a goat's anus. This somewhat unfortunate goat is then thrown into a river or dam to drown, the mamlambo, returned back to its watery realm, accepting the goat as an acceptable sacrifice in place of human blood, and returning beneath the liquid depths to bother mankind no more [12].

### The Female of the Species
The crossover points between tokoloshes, chikwambos and mamlambos, then, are numerous. Indeed, in many ways they all simply seem like little more than varying versions of one another, at least in their more modern forms. If the generally-male tokoloshe, with its gigantic penis, can be seen as being some kind of comment about male sexuality, then the seductive and generally female mamlambo appears to embody certain stereotypical fears about female sexuality, or about the effect that female sexuality can have upon some men. For example, the old idea that the creature will make a man kill his own father once she has slept with him could be interpreted as being some kind of message about a certain type of woman manipulating men through her sex-appeal in order to let her get what she wants, no matter how immoral that desire may in fact be. The fact that the mamlambo brings wealth to its new owner initially also disguises the fact that, once it has its claws dug into a man, it becomes greedy and possessive, dominating and manipulating the person who is meant to be in control of it. Its desire for human blood also makes it, literally, into a 'vampire' or 'bloodsucker' - both of which are, of course, colloquial terms for persons who are greedy for other people's wealth. In other words, then, the mamlambo becomes a kind of Lady Macbeth figure, goading its cowed dupe into doing as it pleases for its own ends; to steal Lady Macbeth's own words for a moment, the initially attractive mamlambo really does 'Look like the innocent flower' but is in fact quite literally 'the serpent under't'. Its association with money could also be

**Male and female mandrake-roots, as imagined during the Renaissance; the idea that humanoid-vegetable creatures could be 'planted' and then 'grown' is not unique to the modern Zimbabwean idea of the money-spinning chikwambo-goblin, then.**

viewed as being some kind of comment upon supposed female avarice, I suppose.

Isak Niehaus, indeed, has the opinion that the imaginative function of the modern mamlambo is to illustrate the dangerous and socially-destructive aspects of an uninhibited desire for wealth at the expense of all else. According to him, "the duality of the witch and the mamlambo is similar to the relationship between the person and his or her [financial] desires [13]" - which is, again, yet a further similarity between these beasts and tokoloshes. The tokoloshe's raping-sprees might well be taken to symbolise the witch or wizard's perverted desire for sex at all costs, whereas the mamlambo appears to represent such evil magicians' perverted desire for wealth at all costs. Apparently, however, the desire for illicit sex is considered by most southern African people to be less destructive in its nature than the desire for wealth is; according to Niehaus, he was told by informants that the general opinion was that the tokoloshe was a less dangerous creature than a mamlambo was, seeing as tokoloshes tended 'only' to rape people, and not generally to demand human sacrifice in return for bringing their wizard wealth [14]. The fact that the sacrifice demanded by the snake is often a family member of the witch also seems to symbolise how some people will do almost anything, and commit almost any atrocity, no matter how taboo, simply in return for some money. Perhaps this is why, nowadays, the mamlambo is frequently described as taking the form of a beautiful white woman, whites often being considered to be inherently greedy in nature by the popular black southern African mind [15].

Indeed, it seems to be a truism that the traditional southern African mentality was in some sense inimical to the idea of an individual accumulating much wealth. According to the old African ideal, the community was much more important than the individual, and the individual could only really gain any sense of his own identity through participation in that group and its way of life; a notion which is, of course, diametrically opposed to the ideas we now tend to have about the importance of individual identity above all else in much of the modern Western world. The old African idea about wealth tended to be that an individual could only hope to accrue it at the expense of the wider community and that therefore, by being rich, you were simply causing other people to suffer by taking what should rightfully be theirs away from them. Such people were frequently denigrated as being witches, an idea expressed rather succinctly by an old Zambian saying: 'To find one beehive full of honey is good luck; to find two is also good luck; to find three is witchcraft' [16]. Witches, being thought to be inherently opposed to all the usual social norms, were of course thought of as being eager to become rich at the expense of their peers, and thus any well-off person could easily be accused of being a sorcerer. It was one way in which to express your social disapproval of a person's financial affairs; and it seems that the modern way of doing this is now to accuse a fortunate person of keeping a mamlambo or a chikwambo.

However, despite the anti-wealth message of these traditional beliefs, it is a fact that people need money to live, and perhaps more so now than ever in modern African societies, where the old barter economies have been inevitably replaced by currency-based ones ever since the days of white colonial rule. The association of the mamlambo with rivers and water could be related to this, as water is both necessary for life, and yet, in terms of things such as floods and drowning, can bring about destruction - just like money, in fact. This kind of idea, of there being some kind of metaphorical association between money and water, is even referred to in the fact that Botswana's currency is called the pula, which means, literally, 'rain'. Snakes, also, are associated with money in metaphorical terms in southern Africa; as their scales, like silver coins, and like the water where the mamlambo has its origin, all shimmer attractively at first sight, and yet can be immensely dangerous if approached carelessly [17]. As such, you could speculate that the mamlambo has, in contemporary Africa, become almost a symbolic figure illustrating the dangers of the new, modern Western economic model which has been imposed on the continent over the past century or so.

People nowadays do have to live in the reality of such a world, however, and so maybe this is why the variant figure of the chikwambo (which could, perhaps, be considered as being a 'commodified' tokoloshe, seeing as it can apparently be bought and sold by anyone) has recently come to prominence in countries like Zimbabwe, where the economy has, as already stated, begun to totally collapse in recent years, and in nations such as South Africa where, even in spite of the fall of apartheid, the gap between the rich few and the dirt-poor many has only grown even wider over the last decade or so.

In some ways, the chikwambo - in the sense in which I am choosing to interpret the word in this chapter, at least - can be seen as being an 'intermediate' figure between the ordinary, sex-hungry tokoloshe, and the more avaricious mamlambo. People will always need money, after all, and worshipping a chikwambo-root is perhaps considered to be a less immoral way for a poor person to attract it than to keep a mamlambo would be. After all, chikwambos do not seem to require people's blood or human sacrifice in order to keep bringing in the coins; or, at least, not in any of the sources which I read. Maybe, then, as the economies and living conditions within certain southern African nations and cities continue to decline and become harsher in nature, even whilst the new black political class who rule over them grow ever wealthier at the expense of their people, the crossover points between tokoloshes and mamlambos will continue to grow, as supernatural entities begin to reflect social anxieties over issues of poverty as much as they do issues surrounding sexuality. The chikwambo, I think, has a great future ahead of it in places like South Africa and Zimbabwe - sadly.

# Chapter Nine

## Hairy Ghosts: Tokoloshes and Poltergeists

*I*s there, however, any actual reliable first-hand evidence of the tokoloshe's existence, or is it all just entirely a myth? Surprisingly, there are some direct accounts of reliably-witnessed tokoloshe manifestations in southern Africa; most of which might at first sound, to Western ears at least, like some form of weird poltergeist-hauntings. Probably the most entertaining and remarkable example of this class of event occurred in January 2000 when a 12-year-old boy, Tsamaiso Sejake, of Motlonyane village near Mafeking, the capital of South Africa's North West Province, saw what he termed as being a "short old man" who appeared suddenly and then slapped him in the face several times. Telling his family of this event, they concluded that he had been assaulted by a tokoloshe and prepared for the worst. They were wise to do so. That very night, poltergeist-type incidents began occurring in their home, with the parents' wardrobe moving itself spontaneously from their bedroom into the kitchen, and various kitchen objects then turning up in the bedroom.

For the next three weeks, further strange pranks were pulled on the family by the tokoloshe, who remained visible only to young Tsamaiso. During the night, bedclothes would find themselves being pulled from people's beds and substances like Vaseline, shampoo and hand lotions were smeared all over them whilst they slept, Tsamaiso himself also being kept awake by the ghost's constant pinching. When the Sejakes went out to the toilet, the chain would find itself being flushed on them before they had finished, causing much annoyance - especially seeing as, whilst members of the family were in there, the door kept on being locked on them from the outside by invisible hands. In addition, the children of the household would frequently wake up only to find themselves having been apparently teleported into the kitchen or even outside of the house, and people were furthermore spat on by the spook.

More typical poltergeist events occurred at the Sejake family home as well, however, such as furniture moving around of its own accord, threatening messages appearing written on the walls and things getting smashed. Bombardments by stones were a particular problem; when Tsamaiso's uncle visited and began praying, a rock was hurled at his head, leaving him with a serious gash there. Whenever any professional holy men, whether Christian or traditional, came to the house to try and perform an exorcism, meanwhile, their prayers were proved similarly useless; as soon as they left, the tokoloshe seemed to take great delight in redoubling its activities and intensifying its bothersome attacks (a classic poltergeist trait).

Strangely, the tokoloshe in this instance appeared to hold a particular hatred towards the children of the household, rather than the adults. Several times, when Mrs Sejake had cooked breakfast for her offspring and called them down to eat, she turned around to find that the pots, plates and bowls had all been mysteriously emptied by the spirit, and even washed up and cleaned - a kind of malignant inversion of the old 'helpful brownie' motif, perhaps. The food being nowhere to be found, the boys had no choice but to go to school on an empty stomach. Still, though, it wasn't all bad news for Tsamaiso, the most persistent focus of the tokoloshe's activities; it wrote in his schoolbooks and then ripped them up into shreds so often that he was given permission to leave them all at school every evening, thereby presumably freeing him up from the necessity of doing any homework (as good an excuse as any, I suppose ...) [1].

Here, we have direct eyewitness accounts and experiences from several named people, and even, with the smashed objects and daubed threats on the walls, some apparently tangible evidence of the tokoloshe's actual existence. Furthermore, this story was originally reported in the South African *Sunday Times* - a reputable newspaper - not a tabloid like the *Daily Sun*, home of such sensationalist and unlikely headlines as 'Tokoloshe Took My Virginity!' and 'Greek Turns Into Tokoloshe!', something which is further suggestive of the story having some kind of possible substance to it. In fact, there are many motifs present in African tokoloshe hauntings which have their direct counterparts within Western poltergeist outbreaks, something which perhaps gives them a certain level of credibility as being potentially real events.

**Poltergeist Parallels**

Tokoloshes, it seems, do many things that poltergeists also like to do. Perhaps most obviously, they enjoy throwing objects around, smashing them and knocking them over, actions which are, of course, perhaps the most stereotypically-described of all Western poltergeist activities.

For example, one of the earliest written descriptions of a tokoloshe that we have states quite clearly that "He molests people of dark deeds by hiding under their beds and upsetting everything when the lights go out", although the white author of this

A 14-year-old domestic servant, Therese Selles, experiences poltergeist / spontaneous PK activity in the home of her employer, the Todeschini family at Cheragas, Algeria, as featured on the cover of the French magazine *La Vie Mysterieuse* in 1911.

sentence, Phyllis Beard, does then add the following caveat to this idea - "Author's query: Natives don't sleep in beds! [2]"

An amusing - if not necessarily of impeccable provenance - contemporary tale about tokoloshes smashing objects up, meanwhile, was posted on an internet message board by an unnamed South African man in 2010. He described how, one night in 1992 whilst he was sleeping at his girlfriend's house, he was woken up by what he termed "the quickest diarrhea [sic] in my life" which, apparently, "happened in a split of a second". Knowing that, as he put it, "It would take me a second to mess up the whole place", the man ran out of the bedroom to go to the outside toilet. However, whilst he was trying to open the door, he began being assaulted by flying detritus from his girlfriend's birthday party which had taken place earlier that night. Bottles, plates, ashtrays and pots started hurling themselves towards him and hit the walls with great force, yet never actually smashed themselves. Despite an invisible force pushing against the door, the desperate man finally managed to open it and ran outside to the toilet, where he remained for about fifteen minutes. When he returned back inside the house, all was quiet, and yet everything in the living room, even things like sofas, tables and the TV, had been overturned and thrown about the place. Apparently, he blamed a tokoloshe for this outrage [3].

By way of furthering our comparison, meanwhile, both tokoloshes and poltergeists allegedly sometimes start fires. In 2002, for instance, five buildings burned down at the Tihalogang Secondary School in the east of Botswana and tokoloshes were blamed, the establishment apparently having been bothered by their invisible tricks for some time beforehand [4]. A case from 2004, likewise, concerning a family from Glenmore in South Africa's KwaZulu-Natal Province, involved the detail that the tokoloshe had set fire to the household's curtains, beds and sofas [5]. Any number of instances of Western spooks allegedly being responsible for starting conflagrations could easily be cited here too, of course, though seeing as this book is supposed primarily to be about southern African manifestations of the paranormal, I shall spare you the bother of reading about them right now.

It is notable, though, that in 2001 the Mutual and Federal insurance company actually made a payout to a white South African woman named Irene Dames, after her home in the city of Port Elizabeth in Eastern Cape Province had been damaged by a series of mysterious fires which were blamed, by both her and several official investigators, upon poltergeist activity. According to an independent fire consultant and electrical engineer named Noel Herbiet, whom Mutual and Federal had commissioned to investigate the cause of the 70 or more blazes which had broken out in the affected home, arson could not be blamed and neither could Mrs Dames or her family. In his view, it might all have been down to what he termed "the little-known but not uncommon phenomenon of poltergeist activity". Faced with this unusual assessment, Mutual and Federal initially refused to pay, but a public claims adjuster (a public official tasked with aiding people to make insurance claims) named George Couvaras intervened, with the result that the company eventually ended up paying out Mrs Dames her money. For her own part, however, she now planned to sell the unquiet home, evidently having had enough of the spook [6]. This story seems to imply, of course, that white South Africans who believe in ghosts tend not to speak of tokoloshes but of poltergeists in order to account for such disturbances; but, seeing as both classes of entity apparently go around acting in largely the same way, then what exactly is the difference between the two of them?

Another thing which both tokoloshes and polts apparently like to do is to assault people with pins, or otherwise threaten to do them harm in some way. For example, there was a case of a haunting which was investigated (at some unspecified date, frustratingly) by a man named David Mackie, a former colonial Mining Commissioner. This haunting took place in the town of Paarl, in what is now Western Cape Province, and concerned a black girl who was repeatedly being tormented by having pins stabbed into her flesh by unseen hands, and in whose presence items of furniture would repeatedly dance around. Mackie went out to the haunted house to investigate, and actually witnessed the pins stabbing themselves into the girl's arm of their own accord, causing her to cry out in much pain [7]. Another case of young girls being stabbed and scratched with pins by invisible forces, meanwhile, occurred over a number of years, from 1985 to at least 1992, in a small all-female boarding school in the tiny border village of Rietfontein in Botswana, where, every night, spirits were supposed to appear in both male and female forms, torturing the girls and their teachers by tearing at their clothes, cutting off their hair and scratching their legs. X-rays taken of the affected girls apparently showed needles were embedded beneath their skin, and the police, after much investigation, simply gave up on the case and declared the attacks to be supernatural in nature. In spite of this horror, however - which, if it was all merely down to mass hysteria, seems to have lasted for an extremely long time - the school's pupils refused to simply up sticks and leave, rather touchingly considering a good education to be their only path towards a better life [8].

Tokoloshes were not specifically mentioned in the reports of either of these cases which I examined, incidentally, but we can be pretty certain that these would have been the entities which were blamed for such pranks by black people locally. In the West, though, we would blame poltergeists (or, formerly, fairies); if you wish to read about perhaps the most remarkable instance of a Western poltergeist doing this kind of thing with pins, then you should probably look up an eighteenth-century haunting from Bristol nowadays known generally as the 'Lamb Inn case'.

Amazingly, by way of further comparison, you even get the occasional Western poltergeist-haunting wherein something strange, small and hairy is sighted - something rather like a tokoloshe, in fact. This, for example, is the description of an apparition (which she nicknamed 'Beelzebub') given by an Englishwoman, Jackie Johnson, whose converted farmhouse in Dewsbury, Yorkshire, was the site of much fairly extreme poltergeist activity, which I won't detail here, during the 1990s:

> "It is approximately 3ft 6in tall and hairy like a bear, but with human features … Its back is hunched and its legs are piggy. I know when it's around because there's a dirty, sweaty smell and when it touches you, it feels like an electric shock."

Johnson first saw the entity reflected in her bedroom mirror one day, engaged in an activity which makes it sound even more like a typical tokoloshe: "It had this sly 'I know something you don't know' look on its face ... and this great big erection, which it was making as if to put in its mouth." Perhaps sensibly, upon seeing this beast she hid herself beneath the bedclothes and waited for it to go away, which it eventually did [9]. At no point did Mrs Johnson describe this thing as being a tokoloshe, of course, but if she had been South African, then we may reasonably presume that the case may have been somewhat different.

## Family Issues

One particular case of tokoloshe-haunting which seems to have had many parallels with a poltergeist manifestation was investigated by a South African TV programme named *Carte Blanche* in 2001. A 19-year-old boy named Sunil from KwaDukuza (a town formerly known as Stanga/Stanger, in KwaZulu-Natal Province) was meant - like certain poltergeist victims - to be the subject of states of possession by a tokoloshe, which was described by him as being a small white ape-like creature covered in hair and with long nails. Here, interestingly, the trouble first began when an extension was built for the haunted house in order to accommodate the boy's elderly grandmother four years earlier. Bizarrely, the beginning of building and renovation work in a home is allegedly a known trigger for starting off poltergeist cases, too, for reasons entirely unknown. A 2007 survey of hauntings conducted by the British SPR (Society for Psychical Research), for example, found that 9% of cases reported to them during a certain defined period coincided with such work taking place [10].

Once the extension had been built in Sunil's home and the grandmother moved in, weird things started to happen to her; her bedclothes were pulled off from her during the night, and her lights kept on switching themselves off. Then, phenomena began to spread out from the grandmother's room and into the rest of the house. Messages started to write themselves on walls, heavy furniture began moving around, lights malfunctioned, toilet rolls flew through the air, liquids like body lotion and detergent smeared themselves on walls and mirrors, telephones started constantly ringing people up at random until they ended up having to be disconnected, and the family's food was interfered with, sand ending up being mixed into meals and rice being thrown across the floor. You can find similar examples of every single one of these phenomena simply by flicking through any good book about poltergeist cases. Eventually, the grandmother moved out, but the tokoloshe - and its apparent hatred of pensioners - remained; when the family's other grandmother later came around to visit, she claimed that it spoke to her in Zulu and hit her across her arms and body with some invisible object. Numerous sangomas and assorted other holy men came out to the house and tried various traditional means of exorcism, but to no avail.

When the *Carte Blanche* team arrived at the house to try and do some filming, meanwhile, another common poltergeist trick occurred; their film stopped working. Video tapes suddenly became scrambled as soon as the TV crew entered the house, although they were fine beforehand. Again, this kind of thing happens with Western cases of poltergeist-haunting all the time, suspicious though the fact may at first appear. Spooks, it seems, tend to be rather shy about letting themselves be seen at work; and one other aspect of this particular tokoloshe-haunting appears to be absolutely classic in this respect. According to the mother of the family, the entire household had been pelted with various domestic objects such as eggs, soap, potatoes and tomatoes by the spirit, but "Everything happens from the back, not in front of us." The fact that most poltergeist-missiles are not seen at the beginning of their flight, only during it, is another commonplace of Western poltergeist-lore which seems to have had its parallel in this particular haunting also, then.

A further similarity was that the events apparently had their focus in three young boys in the household, namely Sunil and his 13-year-old and 10-year-old brothers. Sunil even ended up having to move out and spend time with some relatives in the nearby city of Durban, after several notes threatening his life, written on scraps of paper, had been found scattered around the family home by the tokoloshe. The youngest boy, too, ended up being 'possessed' by the tokoloshe, having to take a month off school, rolling around on the floor for hours, and also reporting seeing a white monkey-like thing tormenting him; he said that it growled and could speak Hindi, Afrikaans and Zulu. Whilst possessed, the tokoloshe told the family, through the boy's mouth, that he was "the king" and that they were wasting their time in trying to rid the house of him through exorcism. He also professed to hate children, which is presumably why he took to slapping one of the family's sons in the face with invisible hands and repeatedly pinching another one sharply upon his genitals.

Numerous poltergeist cases in Europe and America also seem to feature one or more adolescents in the household around whom events tend to focus, as well. Many of these adolescents often have some kind of issues relating to family or social tensions going on around them, the theory frequently therefore put forth by Western parapsychologists being that the so-called 'poltergeist' is in fact nothing more than the inadvertent emission of psychic forces from the distressed teenager at their centre. Again in this particular case there is a further similarity, as there appeared to be some real tension going on between different branches of the family involved, a fact reflected by the accusation of Sunil's parents that some estranged relatives were in fact responsible for bewitching them by sending out the tokoloshe against them in order to take revenge. It is not known, incidentally, how or even whether the whole unpleasant situation was eventually resolved [11].

**Pebbles Without a Cause**
Tokoloshes then, it seems, have many habits in common with poltergeists. By way of further example, they also appear to enjoy throwing around pebbles and rocks, one of the most frequently reported of all poltergeist phenomena. One particularly remarkable alleged instance of this was posted by a man named Barry Groenewald on a message-board discussion about the tokoloshe in 2010. Of course, such postings are hardly terribly reliable as regards definite evidence of actual events taking place, but his story is so weird that it surely deserves to be reproduced here. According to Mr Groenewald, his father was something of a psychic who had the ability to see tokoloshes and, one day "many, many years ago" in the city of Bloemfontein, now in South Africa's Free State Province, he went up to a group of people who were all gathered around pointing and staring at something up on a nearby incline. What they were looking at was a large rock or boulder, apparently rolling itself up the incline of its own accord. Mr Groenewald Senior, however, being psychic, could see what was really causing the rock to move; a tokoloshe. The rock then lifted itself into the air, smashing things where it fell, and a policeman who had stopped to try and restore order was then subsequently thrown over his patrol van by the being - allegedly [12].

**In the village of Boqate Ha Sofonia in Lesotho in 2003, more than 400 rocks – including the one pictured here – began to rain down from the sky. In actuality, it was all due to a meteorite breaking up in the atmosphere above, but the villagers blamed a tokoloshe in the form of a poltergeist for causing the incident.**

A more reliable account of flying and falling stones, perhaps, came in July 2003, when there was a panic in the village of Boqate Ha Sofonia in Lesotho. First of all a loud noise was heard in the sky, followed by a shower of stones raining down onto the roofs of the village houses. Uproar followed. Residents blamed a tokoloshe - the BBC reporter on the scene specifically translated this word as meaning "a poltergeist" - and some sprinkled holy water around their residences and on the stones themselves. Of course, the actual cause of the stone-shower was that a meteorite had exploded in the atmosphere above, shattering itself into thousands of small pieces which then rained down across the entire area. But the very fact that residents thought that it was a tokoloshe which was responsible shows quite clearly that the entities are thought of as being able and likely to do that sort of thing in the popular African mind [13].

Certainly, witchcraft and tokoloshes are generally blamed for such things right across the southern part of the continent. In September 2004, for example, the Chigova family, residents of a rented home in the mining town of Zvishavane in Zimbabwe's Midlands Province, were

**Maggie Hendricks, accompanied by a neighbour, holds up some shoes which were allegedly torn apart by a tokoloshe in the form of a poltergeist at her home in South Africa in 1981.**

scared out of their wits when stones began raining down from the ceiling inside one of the rooms of their house. The head of the Chigova family, Caseman, had made news during the 1990s for insisting upon sleeping every night inside a coffin, in order for him to "get a feel for his future home", and had indeed since died. The first phenomenon in the household made reference to this man's demise, a letter dropping down from the roof and alleging that the anonymous authors of the missive were responsible for his death and would soon be "back for more". Immediately after this threat had been received, a large stone materialised somewhere near the ceiling and then fell down to the floor, followed by several others. Then, what is described as being a "hail" of stones began to descend, leading the family to flee and seek assistance from their neighbours, most of whom refused to help for fear of bringing down the curse upon themselves. Police were called out, and had no hesitation in assigning a supernatural cause to events. "It appears to be an issue involving witchcraft," said Superintendant Raphael Mathe, the officer in charge of the police force in Zvishavane [14].

Another case from 2004, meanwhile, centred around a woman from Limpopo Province in South Africa, Miyi Shongi, who was kicked out of her home in the village of Lambani by her family, as she kept on attracting stones to mysteriously fall around her, apparently from thin air. Initially, they called out the police, who kept a nightly watch on the affected household to no avail; stones continued falling down on it "like rain". According to a Captain Ailwei Mushavhanamadi of the local police force, his officers were powerless to help, the Captain saying that "In my personal opinion, this incident has something to do with demonic spirits. The solution might be for the family to pray to God for help." Once the police had proved to be useless, Shongi was thrown out and sent to stay with relatives in the village of Nhombelani, 30km away, but the stones followed her there, too. Professing to be highly "embarrassed" by the phenomena, the woman explained how she thought that an itinerant Zimbabwean trader had cast a spell on her because she had failed to pay for clothes that she had bought from him on credit.

At Nhombelani, once again, the stones began to fall around their victim even within closed rooms. According to Shongi's mother-in-law, "We were shocked to hear a hissing sound and the sound of stones falling on our roof. Some got inside, even though all the windows were closed." Then, a hail of stones suddenly began raining down on them all inside the room, and they had to run for cover, screaming. It appeared that, eventually, Shongi became so mortified at the trouble she was causing everybody that she simply ran away from the village and disappeared. Everyone consulted about the problem, from sangomas to priests to the local police force, blamed evil spirits - presumably tokoloshes - who had been sent out against her as revenge by the wronged trader, who in their view must actually have been some kind of powerful witch [15].

A South African case reported on in 1993, however, was perhaps the most remarkable such instance of supernatural stone-throwing of all. Events centred around a 55-year-old widow named Lydia Phelo and her nine-year-old granddaughter Bathabile, who both lived in the village of Boekenhouthoek in the KwaNdebele region (an old 'Bantustan' - or apartheid-era 'black homeland', in what is now Mpumalanga Province). Lydia was inside her tiny tin-walled house at around noon one day late in 1992, when her peace and quiet were shattered by her paraffin lamp exploding; it appeared that a stone had been thrown at it with some force. According to Lydia, this stone came from out of thin air, inside the room, and moved through space of its own accord. Terrified, Lydia began screaming out for help, and her neighbour, George Masango, ran around to see what was happening - only to be hit on the head by a stone from nowhere himself. Alarmed, he ran away, being pelted by further pebbles as he did so, until he was as far as half a kilometre away, when the assault suddenly ceased.

A week later, the stones still flying, an Apostolic priest, the Reverend Sam Malaza, came around to try and bless the home. As soon as he walked through the doorway, however, he was hit painfully by two stones, one on the side of his face and the other on his thigh. Seemingly unable to exorcise the ghost, he settled for just saying a prayer and then left. Next, Lydia decided to consult an inyanga from the nearby small ex-mining town of Hammanskraal, but the taxi she hired to take her and Bathabile to his house never reached its destination. Stones, it appears, began materialising inside the cab and then flying around dangerously, leading the frightened taxi-driver to cut the journey short and dump them both off at the nearest police station instead.

Inside here, the trouble continued. The officer on duty, Detective-Sergeant Saul Komane, calmed Lydia down and got the full story out of her, when suddenly he saw two golfball-sized stones hurtling to the floor next to Bathabile. The little girl had her hands down by her sides, so could not have been physically throwing them herself, but this did not prevent Komane from then seeing another two stones materialising from out of nothing over the girl's shoulders and then flying towards him. The policeman was shocked. "Do these stones come from your granddaughter?" he asked, puzzled. Upon being asked this question, Lydia started to panic. She thought that Bathabile was being accused of being a witch, and did not want any harm to come to her. Even as she denied that her grandchild was a witch, though, the stones kept on coming.

Eventually, Detective-Sergeant Komane managed to calm Lydia down, dismissed her, and kept Bathabile inside the police station overnight for her own protection. When asked what was going on by the officer, Bathabile denied that she was a witch, and claimed instead that she had been the victim of evil sorcery. She alleged that an unnamed woman who hated her grandmother had decided to curse Bathabile in order to get her revenge. Accordingly, she forced her to dig a hole about a metre away from her grandmother's home, fill it up with stones and then cover it up with soil. Then, the witch rubbed some kind of magical ointment on the child's arms, she said, and hung a bag full of stones on her back. Soon afterwards, the flying rocks began to appear. Whatever the truth of this story, stones were genuinely seen to materialise around Bathabile from out of nowhere by several officers, and the problem was only solved when the child was sent away from Lydia's tin shack back to live with her mother far away [16].

### Stone Me
We would blame a poltergeist for these cases, then, (if we believe in them) but the average southern African might point to witchcraft or a tokoloshe instead. This is purely as a result of prevailing social conditions and beliefs in each region at a specific time. Once, we Westerners too would have blamed witchcraft and imps sent out by sorcerers for such things. In 1682, for instance, during the trial of Joan Butts, (below) a suspected English witch, at Southwark Assizes, a maidservant named Elizabeth Burridge testified that, upon leaving her house one

day stones were cast at her and her mistress "from every side" unaccountably; it was all down to Butts' witchcraft, it was implied [17]. Likewise, in 1661, an English servant girl called Mary Longdon found herself being followed around by showers of small stones that would pursue her from place to place, hitting her on the head, shoulders and arms, before vanishing away into nothing when they touched the floor. In addition, she allegedly found herself being levitated into strange positions, such as inside a chest or up into the rafters, as well as vomiting strange things like pins, needles and bits of wool. A woman named Florence Newton was blamed by Mary for bewitching her because she had refused to give her some beef from her master's tub, and this female was therefore arrested and imprisoned for witchcraft [18].

Once, then, the thought-patterns of people in countries like England towards such matters were similar to those of many present-day Africans. We believe whatever our culture sanctions us to do so, it appears, and a large portion of African culture right now openly sanctions the belief in witchcraft and tokoloshes, whereas modern Western belief-systems tend to allow only the contrasting options of either fraud or genuine poltergeist activity to account for such things as stone-showers occurring within closed rooms inside houses. Presuming that such things really occur, however, it might ultimately prove to turn out that none of these explanations are actually in any way adequate.

One final element of tokoloshe mythology which deserves to be mentioned in relation to the issue of them throwing around stones with unseen hands, though, is that of the tokoloshe's magic pebble, which we referred to very briefly in passing earlier on. This magic pebble, it will be recalled, is meant to be kept by the tokoloshe inside of its own mouth in order to facilitate its becoming invisible - or, to interpret matters another way, in order to enable it to go around playing poltergeist.

Amazingly (or unbelievably, perhaps) there is even an account of some people getting hold of one of these magic pebbles and using it in order to turn themselves invisible, too. It comes from Flora Nthshuntshe, with whose first-hand account of seeing a tokoloshe we opened this book, and it concerns her two younger brothers, named Temba and Tongintaba. Apparently, a tokoloshe had befriended both of these little boys, as he is occasionally said to do with certain youngsters, and regularly came around to the Nthshuntshe home to play with them during the night. One evening, Flora could hear much laughter coming from within her brothers' bedroom, and asked them what was going on. The next morning, they told her; the friendly tokoloshe had paid them a visit and shown them his magic pebble, which was small and very round. He had played a game of 'catch' with them using it; and, each time they did catch it, the boys supposedly turned invisible themselves! Their hairy little friend, however, warned them that, no matter what they did whilst in this state, they should never wander away from him or try to play tricks upon people, otherwise "something terrible" would happen to them [19].

Whatever you think of this tale, the motif as a whole does raise an interesting point for speculation. If tokoloshes are imagined as holding magic pebbles in their mouths when acting like poltergeists, is this idea simply some kind of folk-rationalisation for the fact that, in very many poltergeist cases, stones are hurled around by forces unseen? Maybe, seeing such stones and rocks flying through the air, southern African people just associated the idea of 'magic pebbles' with tokoloshes as a way of trying to 'explain' such bizarre occurrences?

Possibly the idea of children being befriended by invisible tokoloshes, meanwhile, is some kind of means to account for the fact that poltergeist phenomena frequently do centre around young people, for whatever reason, as already alluded to. The further added detail that such childhood friendships are discouraged because it is thought that the kids so befriended will later turn out to be witches also seems salient; because, as we have just seen, many adults who are plagued with poltergeist-like stone-showers are condemned as being witches in later life. As such, the stigma surrounding children having invisible tokoloshe-friends in southern Africa could perhaps be viewed as being essentially an attempt to discourage the child from dabbling in such things in order to prevent him or her from undergoing persecution for 'witchcraft' as an adult. This is all simply conjecture upon my part, of course, but the matter does seem at least worth considering.

### Evil Elves
As we keep on saying, the conception of the tokoloshe keeps on shifting, from poltergeist to demon, to zombie, to incubus. Some people seem to think that they are the same thing as goblins, others do not. Perhaps some others think that they are the same thing as elves, as, during the following case, reported from Malawi in early 2000, those were the creatures which were blamed for the poltergeist-like events occurring at the home of a 62-year-old man, Ribson Mvaro, and his family. Events first occurred in December 1999 when they moved into their newly-built home in the town of Phalombe in the south of the country, an area which is reputed to be well-known for sorcery. According to Mvaro, he and his entire family had been the subject of several peltings from missiles and blows from invisible hands. Neighbours witnessed a young child of the family rolling around on the floor, being attacked by something unseen, and apparently being punched. One time, Mvaro came home and tried to open the front door, but it wouldn't budge; something immensely strong and unknown appeared to be pressing against him from the other side of it. He kept on pushing against it for hours, when it suddenly gave way; inside the house, however, was no sign whatsoever of what had caused the odd incident.

From this point on, the haunting only got worse. Doors kept on opening and closing around the household and invisible footsteps could be heard running about the place. Mvaro called in as many as a dozen witch-doctors, all of them described as being "reputable", but they were not much help. One, who had come from neighbouring Mozambique especially, was chased out of the house by the spirits. From then on, the phenomena began occurring throughout the day as well as the night, and, after dark, became so loud that they were stopping the family from getting to sleep. The explanation finally arrived at for the whole affair was that Mvaro's brother was well-known for keeping what were described as being "elves" to serve him, but died without giving anyone in the family any instructions as to how to care for them once he had passed on. Therefore the elves, hungry and irritated, were simply harassing the Mvaro family for the food which they felt was their right [20]. The word tokoloshe is not directly mentioned in this report, of course, but it does seem that their actions and those of the 'elves' were essentially indistinguishable.

For example, the following recent report, from the small settlement of Mtapa in north-west Zambia, sounds in many ways the same as the above story, except that the hungry elves are here styled specifically as being tokoloshes. Apparently, it seemed that the husband of a certain Mrs Liana Ncube had secretly been keeping some pet tokoloshes in the marital home without his wife's knowledge, in order to ensure the family's prosperity after he had been made redundant six years earlier. According to reports, these tokoloshes - presumably of the chikwambo sub-species? - had facilitated some very lucrative business deals for Mr Ncube, and the family's position had become secure financially.

However, he had died without telling anybody of his tokoloshes, or leaving behind any instructions for how to take care of them, just like Mr Mvaro's brother had done in Malawi, leading to the beings running havoc around the Ncube household in some manner unspecified by the original news report, but presumably essentially poltergeist-like in its nature. Fearing that the tokoloshes might harm or kill her or her five children, Mrs Ncube had called in three different inyangas to exorcise them, but to no avail. Apparently, the tokoloshes had appeared in Mrs Ncube's bedroom one night a fortnight after her husband's death and demanded offerings of meat and isitshwala (cooked corn meal) or they would never leave her alone. Ever since, Mrs Ncube had had no option but to spend her time looking after the tokoloshes as well as her children, a chore made all the worse by the fact that the beasts' appetites were apparently quite "ferocious" [21].

### Infernal Djinn
The further north you head throughout the African continent, of course, the more the prevailing religion changes from Christianity to Islam - and, as such, something strange begins to happen to the tokoloshe. Whilst it is still essentially conceived of as performing the same kinds of acts - acting like a poltergeist, raping people in their beds at night - it ceases to be called a tokoloshe and becomes instead a djinn, one of the generally-invisible 'spirits of the smokeless fire' mentioned in the Koran, some of whom Mohammad himself is actually meant to have converted from evil to Islam. The same thing happens, it appears, amongst Islamic communities living in the predominantly Christian countries further south. For example, in 2004 an anonymous Muslim family of five contacted a South African newspaper pleading for their help in gaining deliverance from a malicious tokoloshe which, they said, had been plaguing them for the past 20 years.

The daughter of the family, it seemed, had started seeing a small African boy sitting next to her around the house when she was about one year old. Nobody else could see the phantom child, but evidence of his apparent reality was provided by strange noises, cold currents of air wafting around the house and making the curtains billow, scratching sounds being heard coming from within a wardrobe, lights switching themselves on and off, and the wife of the family hearing her name being called out of thin air. This woman was the most affected of the household, mysterious bruises appearing on her body from nowhere, together with a feeling of her throat being throttled by invisible hands and, on one occasion, a giant flame shooting out at her from the kitchen stove, which was not even switched on at the time. Furthermore, money kept on mysteriously disappearing from the household of its own accord, which caused the family obvious difficulties.

The family blamed a tokoloshe for all this, as well they might, and tried various sangomas and other witch-doctors to get rid of the thing, without any success. The newspaper contacted the School of Religion and Culture at the University of KwaZulu-Natal upon their behalf, however, and spoke to a Professor Suleman Dangor, an Islamic scholar, who explained his view that it was not a tokoloshe that the family were dealing with at all, but a djinn. Tokoloshes, he said, were not believed in by Muslims, only djinns, but, seeing as both creatures seem in many ways to overlap, essentially this comes across more as a debate about nomenclature than anything else. The probable implication was, however, that only a Muslim holy man, an imam, could get rid of a djinn, and not a sangoma, and so this was the reason why the family's attempts at exorcism had not worked [22].

There are several other similarities present between tokoloshes and djinns, quite apart from their shared manifestation as poltergeist-like entities, though. For one thing, in some parts of the world, such as certain areas of what is now Iraq, the djinn was originally conceived of as being a kind of water-sprite or river-demon, just like the tokoloshe initially was for the Xhosa people [23]. In addition, djinns are meant to favour living in waste areas or liminal places, such as out in the bush or desert, within sewers and rivers or, within a household, inside ovens and toilets [24]. This, again, is not unlike the tokoloshe; the pinky-pinky, we will remember, was meant to live exclusively inside school toilets. The link between schoolchildren and both tokoloshes and djinns is also a strong one, as strange cases of mass hysteria in schools which are often blamed upon tokoloshes by sub-Saharan Africans are blamed upon djinns by Arabs and Muslims further north. Furthermore, some djinns are pictured by their believers as being strange hairy men, just like the tokoloshe; others are meant to have only one arm or one leg, which is also a variant conception of what a tokoloshe looks like. Also, of course, djinns are frequently spoken of as acting like typical poltergeists, doing things such as setting impossible fires, possessing people and hurling stones around through the air.

Another thing which djinns like to do in legend is to shape-shift; and so, of course, do tokoloshes. As such, perhaps we should not be too surprised to find that there are other southern African poltergeist cases on record wherein the apparent identity of the spook does not at first glance appear to belong to either class of being. A 1939 poltergeist haunting in a house near to Western Cape Province's Salt River, for example, featured sightings by witnesses of "a dark shape, sometimes in the form of a large bat and at others like a snake", which wandered around the place disappearing under furniture, whilst a pre-WWII poltergeist-haunting at a house in the Western Cape Province town of Paarl involved reports of "a black object without a head and about seven feet long" and a "big man" who appeared suddenly from out of a bright flash of white light [25].

Even weirder than this case, however, was that of a haunting at the home of a J van Jaarsveld in the town of Uniondale in what is now South Africa's Western Cape Province, which occurred "shortly after the Jameson Raid", apparently (so, sometime after January 1896, then). Here, the usual polt phenomena occurred, much of it seemingly centring around a Miss Meyer, the niece of Mr van Jaarsveld, who kept on having her hair tied up to the bedpost when the lights went out. Some visitors to the home, though, professed themselves able to actually see the entity responsible for all this; it was not a hairy little tokoloshe, but, rather, resembled "a

**South African Sangomas**

phosphorescent crab with two huge pincers" which floated around the room touching people, and, upon other occasions, took the form of "a skeleton hand with two fingers" [26]. Maybe it was because these hauntings all took place within white households, however, that the ghosts were seen in the form of such bizarre apparitions as these instead of tokoloshes; there is some evidence in the poltergeist literature that the people involved in such cases largely see the apparitions that they expect to see. If so, then God knows why some white South Africans once expected to see a spook in the form of a giant glowing crab-ghost, but it might just explain why they didn't see tokoloshes. After all, as we have already seen, they were considered purely to be a superstitious black belief, weren't they?

However, be this as it may, it is only right to note that not all black people in southern Africa have always been minded to blame a tokoloshe for causing poltergeist phenomena. Shortly before the Second Boer War, for example, in March 1897, an affidavit was written out and signed before a white JP and two other witnesses by a black evangelist from the Pondoland region of South Africa, in what is now Eastern Cape Province, named Brown Nombida, about some bizarre poltergeist phenomena which had been occurring on his kraal in the old Ngqeleni district. It seems that, whilst pots were placed on a fire at the haunted place, certain poisonous herbs had mysteriously managed to materialise themselves within the cooking containers despite the fact that their lids had been firmly closed. This made many of the people who ate the food from these pots then become ill and start vomiting. Since then, sticks, stones, clods of earth and farming implements like a plough-share and a hatchet had begun jumping up and down of their own accord and, in some instances, throwing themselves around at people. These paranormal manifestations, it seems, became particularly severe whilst the kraal's occupants were kneeling around and praying for the torments to stop; whilst this activity was going on, stones and clods of earth repeatedly kept on hitting the persons so engaged.

At no point was a tokoloshe invoked by Brown Nombida in order to explain these curious goings-on, however; according to his own sworn statement:

> "I cannot account for the things jumping about in the way they do. I only
> know they are not lifted or thrown by any living person or thing." [27]

However, it must be noted that this account, being as it is more than a hundred years old, dates from a time before the tokoloshe legend had been spread throughout southern Africa as a whole as a result of the labour migration which we examined earlier. Indeed, it does seem as if the practice of black people blaming poltergeist activities upon tokoloshes has actually increased in southern Africa as time has gone on rather than decreased, which might seem at first sight to be surprising until we remember the fact that, of course, the majority of black non-Xhosa or Zulu South Africans simply hadn't really heard of the creatures much before the forced labour migrations of the twentieth century had taken place.

**You Just Can't Get the Staff ...**
Generally, though, in most of the historical accounts which I have examined, there seems to have been a very different approach towards determining what caused poltergeist phenomena in southern Africa, depending upon to which race you belonged. If you were black, then the general answer would be to blame witchcraft or tokoloshes; whereas if you were white, the general answer would be to blame black or coloured people. Houses which were allegedly spokerig (Afrikaans for 'haunted'), then, provided yet another arena within which the old politics of race could be played out, whether covertly or overtly.

Let's view historical southern African poltergeist/tokoloshe phenomena from a possible black point of view, first of all. As is well-known to students of such things, poltergeist activity is often blamed by parapsychologists not upon ghosts, as such, but upon the unintentional emission of some kind of psychic force from a person at the centre of a haunting, termed a 'focus'. Often, the focus is alleged to be a dissatisfied or disturbed person in some way, and the poltergeist phenomena which they inadvertently cause to break out around them hypothesised to be a method through which they unconsciously express their discontent with the way their life is going. This, at least, is one theory about polts; whether the idea fits in with all cases of such hauntings, however, is a matter for some debate.

If this notion is true, though, and the focuses at the centre of events should happen to be black people, then it might reasonably be expected to be the case that, in the past at least, these black people were in positions which afforded them far less power or say over their lives than white people in Africa had. As such, the direction of their resentment would quite likely have been 'projected outwards' onto their oppressors or overlords; with the result that, perhaps, white people would frequently have found themselves being targeted by the poltergeist phenomena in a fashion which acted only to undermine their authority and make them look foolish in some way.

Sometimes, this does indeed appear to have happened. During the pin-jabbing poltergeist case investigated by the high-powered colonial Mining Commissioner David Mackie, which we examined earlier, for instance, Mackie himself went to the haunted house to examine matters with his three brothers, one of whom was greeted as he stepped across the threshold by having a piece of dried cod strike him immediately in the face. He thought that it was a trick, presumably being played by a truculent native, and challenged whoever was responsible for the outrage to dare and do it again; whereupon a roll of tobacco shot itself through the air and straight into his eye. Further threats against the white men followed, including a burning log from the fire moving itself around their feet as if intending to set their trousers aflame, and a bedsheet floating up from off a bed before going around and whipping them all silly with itself. Eventually, the white men decided that there was nothing much they could do in the matter, and fled [28].

It is not hard to see in such actions, surely, the kinds of things that many native black people would have liked to have done to the people who were ruling over them, but dared not really do in actuality, for fear of the repercussions which would inevitably occur. If tokoloshes or poltergeists really are the emissions of repressed psychic forces from certain individuals, then it seems that the 'ghosts' in such instances have the leeway afforded them to be able to perform actions which their black creators could never hope to get away with under similar circumstances.

It is surely not insignificant that many of the 'classic' southern African poltergeist-hauntings from before the end of apartheid seem to have featured black or coloured servant-girls as being the focuses at their epicentre [29]. For example, one of the most celebrated of all early South African poltergeist hauntings occurred at the Cape Town home of the editor of a local German-language newspaper named Adolf Braun, in 1888 or so. Here, the sole phenomena which were experienced centred around our old friends, those familiar invisibly-thrown stones. Pebbles, rocks and, especially, lumps of coal, were hurled into the building and across its roof, smashing windows and hitting a coloured servant-girl living in the house, named Kantas. The police were called out, and surrounded the home in a full cordon, to see where the stones were coming from. Apparently, they were coming from out of thin air; several officers ended up getting black eyes from pieces of coal which materialised before them and then shot right into their faces. The trouble only came to an end for good when the coloured servant, Kantas, packed her bags and left. "The ghost disliked me," she explained, no doubt sadly, and left the house in peace [30].

Here, it does seem obvious enough that the coloured woman caused the phenomena in question; although, apparently, not deliberately, seeing as she too was whacked by the supernatural missiles. However, the notion of dissatisfied servant-girls frequently being associated with poltergeist events is hardly a pattern which is unique to southern Africa; it was well-known throughout Europe and America in times past, too. Indeed, the association between spooks and servants remained a fairly steady one in the West right up until the point that employing servants began to go largely out of fashion during the mid-twentieth century. If European middle-class households still had servant-girls, then it seems plausible to say that they would still have their own poltergeists attendant upon them, too.

Why was there this historical association between serving-girls and spooks, though? According to sceptical writers such as the social historian Owen Davies, who felt that all such polts were merely hoaxes upon behalf of young servants, it was merely an expression of their "insecurities and frustrations" at their lowly way of life. As he says, such domestic employees were:

> "...removed from their families and familiar environments at a formative age, and had to live with strangers and negotiate the inequalities and sexual politics between masters and servants ... [such a maidservant] found expression for her emotional state through a form of displacement activity [i.e. fake poltergeist activity] that enabled the release of pent up frustration through vandalism, whilst at the same time attracting the attention she obviously craved."

Poltergeist activity, he says, can thus be read as a way in which European adolescents:

> "...can and did transform the supernatural into domestic power, radically altering the dynamics of household relationships." [31]

Such pranks, obviously, could be - and no doubt sometimes were - pulled by the black servant-class in places like South Africa upon their white masters. However, it does strike me that, approached from a less sceptical perspective, Owen Davies' reasons for maidservants playing up through fake ghostly phenomena could also be interpreted as being the self-same reasons that servants, albeit unconsciously, might have projected out genuine ghostly phenomena from themselves in order to attack their employers. If so, then the "pent-up frustration" claimed by Davies for white servants over in Europe would also, by definition, have had an added racial element put into the mix in places such as South Africa - where domestic servants were, almost universally, black or coloured. Therefore, whenever a white African householder saw fit to blame their servant for an outbreak of poltergeistry, they were not - unlike in Europe or America, perhaps - picking upon them purely because of their class-status, but also, inescapably, because of their race, too.

### Black Mischief
One stereotype once held by many whites about blacks, for instance, was that, whilst they allegedly had no technical or social intelligence, as expressed by their lack of things such as motorcars, electricity and modern city-settlements, they did have access to certain 'darker',

evil, more primitive, and yet still highly significant, sources of power and intelligence from within the jungle and the witch-doctor's hut. Often, of course, this idea was merely mocked, and black people along with it; except, just sometimes, when the phenomena became so extreme that its existence was no longer practically deniable by those white people who were present near it 'on the ground', as it were.

A good example of this occurred in a small town named Edenville, in what was once the old Boer colony of the Orange Free State (now part of South Africa proper, under the name of Free State Province), at the home of a Mr J Jordaan, probably at some time during the late 1940s. Mr Jordaan had died of a heart attack, which was presumably quite natural, of course, but what occurred soon afterwards certainly was not. Mr Jordaan's son fell ill, and the usual cavalcade of poltergeist phenomena then broke out in the family home; stones fell onto the roof, mysterious lights floated around the place, objects moved about and fell off shelves, knocks and raps were heard, and people were attacked and half-strangled by invisible hands. Eventually, it was discovered that a local native woman - presumably a sangoma - was performing an activity called 'throwing the bones' for her various black clients. Certain muti items were found inside her hut, and she was arrested and charged with practising witchcraft by the authorities (a crime which, in apartheid South Africa, did not in any way mean that the white State actually believed in the reality of witchcraft, of course - it was probably considered to be more a crime of charlatanry than anything else [32]). However, it must be noted in this case that there was actually no real proof that the female sangoma was responsible for sending out the tokoloshe/poltergeist to haunt the Jordaan home at all. After all, 'throwing the bones' is essentially a form of divination, not demon-summoning; rather, it seems likely that the white authorities in this case just wished to find a convenient scapegoat to hang blame for the haunting upon. Apparently, they found one quite easily.

Another good example of this 'if in doubt, blame a black' mentality comes in an account from a Boer named Mr L de Beer, who spent a fortnight sleeping in a haunted farmhouse in the Wepener district of the old Orange Free State sometime in the 1890s. Here, in his bedroom, something very strange would happen each Wednesday night at midnight; namely, the wallpaper would catch fire of its own accord, giving out no smoke, and then suddenly extinguishing itself as abruptly as it had begun, leaving the rest of the night to be spent in total darkness. Other poltergeist phenomena had also occurred inside that same room and - it transpired - the one next to it. A little girl had had her chair pulled from beneath her by forces unknown whilst she was sat at a harmonium many years beforehand, according to Mr de Beer's hosts, and a black man and his child had been thrown off their horse outside by a ghost as well, they said. In order to account for all this, the household involved remembered that, during the building of the farmhouse walls, they had ran out of stone. Therefore, a nearby native headstone had been dug up and used to help build the foundations of the room in question. Presumably, it was suggested, this headstone was cursed somehow, black people allegedly having such powers, leading to the polt phenomena later breaking out as a means of the dead man's revenge [33].

Was this really plausible as an explanation, though? Maybe not, seeing as, apparently, an apparition of the poltergeist was later actually witnessed flitting around the haunted farmhouse; and it was the spectre of a white woman, who seemed to be inordinately interested in the farmer's cups. She was witnessed going into the pantry and picking up and examining these items, apparently. This fitted in rather well with one particular detail of the haunting, namely that the sound of rattling cups and crockery had recently come to be heard emanating from the pantry in the middle of the night when everyone living was safely tucked up in bed [34]. Nonetheless, it was still deemed more appropriate by the family concerned to blame a hypothetical dead black sorcerer for the outbreak of supernatural phenomena, rather than a deceased white lady. That, it seems, would just not have been the done thing.

This appears to have once been a real pattern amongst South African poltergeist-hauntings in the homes of whites. Black and coloured people were ultimately held responsible for causing the events, whether by magic or by returning from the dead, even when the apparitions, which were sighted during these same cases, did not in any way back this hypothesis up. For instance, an early twentieth-century haunting on a white farm near the South African town of Schweizer-Reneke, now part of North West Province - during which abnormally slow-moving stones were thrown, tables moved of their own accord, jugs of water were emptied over the householders' heads and various other assaults perpetrated - featured the intriguing detail that the apparition of a man dressed in rags and a large broad-rimmed hat, with big feet and an odd stooping stride, was sighted walking around the place. In spite of this, however, the poltergeist phenomena were blamed not upon a badly-dressed male, but upon someone termed 'Old Griet'; an old black woman who, the white farmers said, must in fact have been responsible for all the trouble. Perhaps they were influenced in this idea by the bizarre fact that the polt in question used to perform various duties of supernatural housework around the place as well, things such as a kitchen ash-bucket floating around the house and then emptying its contents onto the ash-heap outside being not unknown to take place there [35].

This certainly sounds like the actions of a disgruntled black servant, still performing her old menial duties around the place after her retirement/demise, coupled with attempts being made to humiliate, harm and frighten off her former employers. Was this 'Old Griet' whom they blamed, perhaps, a former member of the farm's domestic staff? If so, had she been mistreated whilst she worked there, the poltergeist thus being interpreted by the victims of its actions as being her means of paranormal revenge against them? We can only speculate; either way, however, it seems definite that, once more, it was a black person who was blamed for causing the haunting by the whites who were actually affected.

Surprisingly, it seems that this kind of thinking is even alive and well in the present day. For instance, the esteemed South African collector of urban legends Arthur Goldstuck, in his book *The Ghost That Closed Down the Town*, reprints a story from the 21st July 1937 edition of the old Afrikaans newspaper *Die Burger*, in which poltergeist phenomena were reported as bothering the white Smuts family in the Lansdowne district of Cape Town. Here, various symbols of domestic order and bliss were ruthlessly shattered and messed-up. Furniture, for instance, was overturned, cushions thrown about from their rightful positions, and crockery continually smashed. The bedclothes in one particular room, however, were the most frequent focus of the ghost's ire. No matter how many times they were made and tucked up under the edges of the mattress nicely, the poltergeist would immediately tear the sheets off, remove the pillows from their cases, and throw the whole lot haphazardly around the room, creating a mess which would then need to be cleared up. After the mess had been tidied, though, the ghost would simply attack the whole lot again, creating a never-ending cycle of tedious domestic chores to be performed by the unfortunate white householders. Now, like Sisyphus, they knew how many black people felt!

Once again, however, together with some unexplained shadows, a full-formed human apparition was seen wandering around the house, whom you would have thought would have been brought in to account for it all. But it was a headless white woman who was seen moving around about a foot off the ground, not a black one, so this fact seems to have been disregarded by some. Furthermore, there was an obvious candidate for the focus-figure in this case, too, namely a family friend, a farmer named only as 'EW', whose arrival in the household coincided exactly with the outbreak of uncanny phenomena. We can presume, quite safely, that this man was white; and that, as such, the poltergeist phenomena probably had nothing to do with any black people. However, according to this 'EW', whilst he was spending his first night at the Smuts home, he awoke in his bed to find a woman at the window, who had threatened him in some way in the past. Then, it seems that he was assaulted by this woman, though she lay no hands upon him; in the report's original words, "suddenly he was held fast and collapsed.[36]"

But what colour was this threatening lady? The original report doesn't actually say, but Arthur Goldstuck, in his 2006 account of the case, seems to be in no doubt whatsoever:

> "The telling clue that this is a poltergeist of a different colour is the presence of the menacing woman, suggesting black magic rather than emotional [re: psychic?] or ghostly energy [is responsible].[37]"

Given that the phenomena that occurred at the Smuts home seemed to involve a kind of ironic inversion of the usual domestic tasks, which would have normally been carried out by a black servant-girl, maybe Goldstuck was right in this speculation of his. Or, then again, maybe he is simply picking up on his knowledge of a well-known aspect of South African folklore often known as 'Malay Tricks'.

## Tricky Characters

And what are Malay Tricks? Put quite simply, it is a term invoked in order to blame poltergeist phenomena upon the actions of Islamic sorcerers, or coloured and Indian people in general - and, specifically, of a class of persons known as the 'Cape Malays'. In order to understand the full implications of this idea, we must first pause for a moment in order to consider what the words 'Cape Malay' and 'coloured' actually once meant in this context in South Africa. Basically, it meant people from South-East Asia and the Indian subcontinent. The Dutch, of course, who were the first real white settlers in southern Africa, used to own colonies in that part of the world, namely those nations once known as the Dutch East Indies; places like Java, Sumatra and Borneo (now mostly parts of Indonesia) and Malacca (now a state in Malaysia). Generally - and often inaccurately - known by the name 'Malays', people from these colonies were, as early as the 1650s, being imported into what we now know as the 'Cape Provinces' for use as slaves, as were indentured labourers from India and Bangladesh from the 1860s onwards.

Over the years, many of these people intermarried with white men of Dutch descent, and later came to be classified under apartheid as either being 'coloured' or 'Cape Malays' for official administrative purposes, although they are still sometimes also known as 'Cape Muslims' colloquially, due to their different religion. Where Indians and persons from the former Dutch East Indies married native black people and produced children, meanwhile, they give birth to yet another ethnic sub-group, the 'Cape Coloureds'. There are quite a lot of these people in South Africa; they are the predominant ethnic groups in Western Cape Province, for example, and the city of Durban in KwaZulu-Natal is sometimes known as the 'biggest Indian city outside India', although many of them have by now lost much of their original cultural identity and have thus become essentially assimilated.

At the time of their first arrival in the Cape, however, these original South-East Asian slaves were actually better educated and more literate than their Dutch (later Boer) masters, who were mostly hardy but unlettered farmer-types. This, combined with their Islamic heritage, gave them a certain sense of mysterious exoticism and, it seems, a certain reputation for both cunning and mysticism, amongst wider white society. It is in light of this long-held reputation, then, that we should probably interpret the whole notion of Malay Tricks.

Cape Malays and Cape Coloureds, it appears, had the reputation of being able to engage in acts of what the Boers called 'goëlery' - or what we might now know as being 'black magic'. And how could you recognise when an act of goëlery had taken place? It was easy; in the words of the son of the famous old white 'ghost-buster', Oom Joubert, "You couldn't see anything ... You would be sitting in a house and pots and things would fall down. Crockery broke and that kind of thing.[38]" In other words, then, you knew when Malay Tricks were being played whenever a poltergeist arrived upon the scene.

Probably the most amazing account of Malay Tricks which I came across whilst researching this book occurred at the home of a white woman, a 'Mrs K van A', in the South African town of Montagu, in what is now Western Cape Province, in 1912. Here, yet again, bricks and stones were thrown around, either hailing down onto the roof or, upon at least one occasion, falling down inside the house itself, without creating any holes in the roof. As per usual, objects fell over and so forth too but, one day, an incredibly disturbing thing happened - whilst the son and daughter of the household were standing in the backyard, a dog came onto the property and looked up at them. This was no ordinary dog, however - as the hound allegedly had human eyes! If this is true, then I think that it could well be one of the most distressing things that I have ever heard ...

In any case, according to the story, the brother, upon seeing the frightening animal, declared out loud his intention to capture it and tie it up to see what would happen. Apparently hearing this, the dog bolted and ran away as fast as it could. This kind of thing, it seemed, went on for the next six months or so, until the haunted family's doctor suggested what could have been causing it. Had anybody in the family angered a coloured person, perhaps? Apparently, they had. A Cape Coloured baker named Jan had called at the house one day and asked Mrs van A if she would care to place an order with him. However, the white woman was talking to another visitor at the time and did not take too kindly to being interrupted by a coloured man. As such, she seems to have told him, essentially, to shut up and wait until he was told to speak. Perhaps understandably, Jan got angry about this and stormed off, after which the haunting began. The doctor, hearing this tale, told Mrs van A that he would sort it all out and marched straight across to Jan's bakery, where he confronted the unruly fellow with the following warning: "Look here, we know that you have bewitched Mrs van A's house. If this does not stop immediately, you will be arrested." The trouble did stop immediately, of course, and all went back to normal. The coloured man had been put back into his proper place, and all was well in the white apartheid world again [39].

Once again, then, dastardly non-whites have been blamed for a poltergeist haunting. I think that the depiction of the race involved in the acts of sorcery here, however, is subtly different than that which was generally used by whites in relation to black people who were meant to be responsible for outbreaks of poltergeistry. Whereas, with the blacks, it seems to have been thought that their alleged supernatural powers were some kind of primitive abilities for causing mischief which more truly belonged in the depths of the dark jungle, coloured persons' supposed magical abilities were thought instead to be a result of deep study and training. Black people, then, were 'natural' magicians, their powers blunt and primal, whereas Malays were 'educated' magicians, and their powers, as such, were more refined and subtle. In the above example, for instance, the coloured magician could apparently change his form into that of a dog in order to surreptitiously and sneakily spy upon the trouble his poltergeists were causing for his enemies in their own household. Blacks might have been feared by some whites as having the potential to rise up against their masters as a kind of disordered mob, perhaps, but the kind of revolution which might have been feared from coloured people would surely have been more cunning and Machiavellian in its nature. Being slightly higher up in status than native black men were, and sometimes even holding relatively respectable positions in society, the Malays were the potential enemy within, and as such might have been trying to rebel in such a way that their supposed white betters would not even be able to notice the fact.

In fact, according to the controversial South African historian Achmat Davids, this is, in a way, what actually did happen; it was his (disputed) contention that the Malays actually did, quite surreptitiously, in many ways transform the white men's culture into that of their own. Apparently, original Asian slaves in the early Dutch colonies could very often read and write in four or more languages, whereas most of the white men who controlled them were illiterate. As such, Davids felt that the Cape Malay people of southern Africa might have influenced the white people's culture as much as the white people influenced theirs. For instance, he noted that the grammatical structure of Afrikaans does not conform to that of Dutch, which is obviously where most of its actual words come from, but to those of Polynesian and Malaysian tongues, and that much traditional Boer music is apparently based upon South-East Asian forms. As such, it appears that, to many white settlers, their early opinion of their slaves was that many of them were in many ways more learned and wiser than they were - or, at least, that their Islamic holy men and sorcerers were. Indeed, it was apparently not uncommon for many Boers to consult coloured conjurors about their problems in a way which they would never have considered doing with the black witch-doctors who also surrounded them [40].

## A Spook by Any Other Name ...

To sum up then, it seems that, whenever poltergeist phenomena were blamed upon black men by whites, it was in a way a kind of condemnation of them as being 'primitive' or 'savage'. Whenever Malay Tricks were invoked as an explanation, however, it seems instead to have been something more by way of a back-handed compliment to coloured people. Such insubordination had to be stopped, for sure, but it was also widely recognised that their sorcerers' alleged magical powers were real and that they in some sense represented a kind of minor racial superiority, in one sphere at least, that coloured people had over their white overlords. Note, for example, how in the story of Mrs van A, her family doctor apparently believed quite firmly in the reality of Jan's magical powers; whereas he, as one of the representatives of Western science par excellence, could pull no such tricks, in spite of his presumably extensive education at a white medical school. Native magic, then, was almost universally condemned - and yet Islamic goëlery was, surprisingly frequently, respected as much as it was feared, even by high-status whites.

As a final coda at this point, however, I must be honest and admit that there are at least a few cases of whites being haunted by poltergeists wherein neither black witch-doctors, coloured sorcerers nor disgruntled domestic staff have been blamed for matters. For example, there was a very curious haunting on a white farm near to the banks of the Little Tugela River in what is now KwaZulu-Natal Province in 1869, wherein none of the usual culprits were accused of being responsible. Here, inside the farmhouse's sitting-room, the usual things went on - stones and cobs of corn materialised from nowhere and were then thrown around at random by unseen hands, for instance. This particular spook, however, did have at least one original trick up its hands. Using a series of oranges, corn-cobs and pumpkins, all of which were attached to one another with hand-made 'chains' of straw, the poltergeist managed, amusingly, to create fruit and veg-based models of wagon-trains, the implication, presumably, being that the family of farmers should jump on their carts and just sod right off from the land which was not rightfully theirs. Given the nature of this apparent message, you might indeed have expected blacks to have been blamed for it all - and yet, somewhat surprisingly, the majority opinion locally was that it was all down to a white woman who had died three years previously, and who wanted revenge upon her husband (presumably the farmer in question?) who had married again not long after [41]. It does have to be said, however, that such cases appear very much to have been the exception; in general, whites were not deemed to have been responsible for such annoyances in the past.

Perhaps some readers at this point will think that we have gone off topic a little here, as it will obviously have been noted that none of the poltergeist cases we have been discussing during the last few pages actually mention tokoloshes anywhere within them. This does not make them irrelevant to our overall concern in this book, however. No doubt the absence of the word 'tokoloshe' in such stories is explicable simply on account of the people who were telling them; namely, white colonialists and Boers. They didn't need to blame tokoloshes for these weird occurrences, as they already had their own convenient scapegoats ready and waiting to be fingered - namely, blacks and coloured people. And yet, it will be noted, the phenomena which they encountered were very substantially the same, in most instances, as the ghostly phenomena which most modern black people now report as taking place within tokoloshe-hauntings. This, surely, can be taken as meaning that both sets of reports are basically describing the same thing, only under a different, more culturally-acceptable name.

To a modern black, a poltergeist is a tokoloshe; to an apartheid or colonial-era white man, meanwhile, it was all just so much Malay Tricks or goëlery. Mankind, it seems, always needs to give the inexplicable a name; and what name you end up choosing to give it generally reflects the nature and underlying assumptions of your own culture rather more than it does the actual underlying nature of the paranormal phenomenon itself which is supposedly being experienced, in my view. Man tends not to see the world through wholly objective eyes, and this, apparently, is as true of poltergeist phenomena as it is of anything else you might care to mention.

# Chapter Ten
## Monkey-Business: Tokoloshes, Baboons and Nandi-Bears

Another way in which it could be claimed that tokoloshes are in fact real creatures - well, sort of, anyway - would be to propose that they are either representatives of some hitherto-undiscovered species of simian or dwarf African bear, or else that they are simply entirely ordinary and well-known indigenous African animals which have just been misidentified by their witnesses in the light of their knowledge of local supernatural folklore. Some eyewitness accounts of tokoloshes are indeed viewable in these terms. For example, probably the first written account of a tokoloshe we have from a white person, that of a Mrs Minnie Martin, the wife of a British colonial official living in Basutoland (what is now Lesotho), which appeared in her 1903 book *Basutoland: Its Legends and Customs* can probably be interpreted in this way if you wish. This account is of much interest, and is worth reproducing here in full:

"Some years ago, before I knew of the existence of Tokoloshe, I was obliged to go to our cowshed rather late one evening to investigate disturbances amongst the cows. The moon was nearly full at the time, and was shining brightly. The shed was at the bottom of our garden, some little way from the house. I went accompanied by my Native nurse girl and our big black retriever. Nothing occurred until we were returning, when suddenly we heard what I took to be a dog running from the Residency through the dead leaves in the garden towards us. I had barely said 'What's that?' when we heard the 'ping' of the wire fence, and saw, crossing the path not a dozen yards in front of us, a little black creature about the size and shape of a boy of six. The night being clear and bright there was no mistaking the fact that it was a human figure of some sort. It ran with a peculiar shuffle, moving its head from side to side, straight through our garden into the darkness beyond. When my girl

OPPOSITE: The witch in the form of a vervet monkey, burnt alive by a rampaging mob in the South African township of Kagiso in 2011. The whole sorry episode illustrates quite clearly the presumed duality which is meant to exist between a witch or wizard and their ape-like familiars.

saw it she caught hold of me in terror, but uttered no word. The dog, on the contrary, gave vent to a sound, half growl, half howl, and tore off to the house, where we followed as quickly as possible, and found him under my little son's bed, from whence he refused to stir. This was to my mind conclusive proof that I had not been 'imagining things,' as was said to me when I described what had occurred; for the dog is a really plucky one, and I had never seen him afraid before. My girl then told me we had seen 'Tokoloshe'.[1]"

This does indeed seem to be impossible to dismiss as being mere imagination upon Mrs Martin's behalf. But, if she really did see a "little black creature" there by her cowshed that fateful night, then what was it? Unfortunately, Minnie's description is not incredibly detailed in its nature, but it is of sufficient quality for at least some speculation to occur about what she saw. To take the most obvious idea first, the fact that the tokoloshe was "about the size and shape of a boy of six" could quite easily be taken as implying that this is all that it was. Perhaps a little black child was simply trespassing upon the Martins' farmstead for some reason, then? Clearly, this must be accepted as being a reasonable possibility; although the dog's reaction and the creature's odd style of movement might just as reasonably be taken as being evidence that this was not in fact the case. Also, the moon, we will remember, was bright that night; surely we might have expected that Mrs Martin and her nursemaid would have been able to tell if the "human figure of some sort" really was just a small human? Nonetheless, the eyes can easily play tricks upon a person after nightfall, whatever the strength of the moon, so the idea that the 'tokoloshe' was merely an infant trespasser can hardly be dismissed outright.

Another, perhaps more likely, option, though, would be to say that the creature was in fact a misidentified monkey or ape of some kind. Minnie Martin was certainly already aware of there being some kind of association between monkeys and tokoloshes in native African myth, as in her book she described the appearance of the beast thus:

"He is not much bigger than a baboon, but is minus the tail, and is perfectly black, with a quantity of black hair on his body. He has hands and feet like an ordinary mortal, but is never heard to speak. [2]"

All of these statements, of course, could be taken as being true about various species of simian. Some do have black or dark fur, some are bigger than baboons, some do have no tails, their hands and feet could be taken as being human-looking, and, as far as I know at least, no monkeys have as yet developed the power of speech. Probably, then, the idea that the tokoloshe loose on the farm that night was simply a stray monkey or ape * of some kind is not an utterly implausible one either. Why would the fierce dog have reacted in the way that it did to a mere monkey, though? Maybe it was because these primates simply didn't usually venture out onto the property, and the dog was put to flight by it purely on account of its unfamiliarity? Dogs can, after all, become scared by the presence of unknown things quite as easily as they can become aggressive in their presence, as most readers will no doubt be aware of from their own experience.

* There is a scientific difference between monkeys and apes – most obviously, monkeys have tails, whereas apes do not – but, in popular speech, the two words have become interchangeable, and it is in this sense that I am using both terms throughout this book. Baboons, incidentally, fall technically into the category of monkeys.

Meanwhile, the black nurse's alarmed reaction to the sighting could just have been down to the tokoloshe's negative reputation in local folklore. After all, Martin describes the creature in her book as being reputed in the minds of the locals to be "the Poisoner, the Evil One, whose deeds are cruel, revengeful, apparently unlimited. He has power to kill, to afflict in every imaginable way, to send mad, or to visit with unknown sickness; but to do good is beyond his power. [3]" Given this unhappy reputation of the tokoloshe locally, it is perhaps no surprise that the nurse girl, suddenly seeing something unexpected in the middle of the night, should have taken it for a tokoloshe, even if it was really just a loose monkey, and become terrified, a reaction which was no doubt only heightened in her by the unusually cowardly behaviour of the farm's guard-dog. Whilst it can hardly be proved that this particular sighting of "the Evil One" was simply down to the nocturnal misperception of a wandering ape, then, it must be considered as at least being a viable hypothesis to account for the event.

Minnie Martin herself, however, seems to have had a leaning towards a different answer as regards the whole affair. Noting that, in local lore, witch-doctors were often thought to be the tokoloshes' masters, she felt that, in her view, these people simply kept what she termed 'bushmen' - presumably meaning either pygmy or dwarf bushmen, or else children, given the tokoloshe's usually-cited stature - whom they employed to go around pretending to be tokoloshes and intimidating the entire community, for their own ultimate gain [4]. In this idea, of course, she is actually quite close to Credo Mutwa's own opinion about the ultimate origin of the very first tokoloshe, cited earlier, albeit without the brain-removal and zombie elements being considered.

Could Mrs Martin have been correct in this theory, however? Is it really possible that witch-doctors could have trained dwarfs to go around pretending to be tokoloshes? Well obviously, yes; it's possible. But is it really likely? I cannot prove that the tokoloshe which Minnie Martin witnessed that night was not a dwarf in hairy-torsoed disguise, but it does seem to me to be a slightly improbable idea. After all, I have never yet come across any reliable news reports of dwarfs or pygmies genuinely going around in the guise of tokoloshes, merely unsubstantiated rumours about the practice. This does not mean that it has never happened, of course - but, equally, I don't think it can be proved that it ever genuinely has. Furthermore, if it was a trained dwarf which had been sent out to bother the Martins' cows that night, then you must query what exactly the sangoma's motivation in all this was. As far as I can tell, he didn't have any. Was he trying to get the tokoloshe to steal some free milk for him? Ultimately, then, I think that Minnie Martin's dwarf-hypothesis must be placed very firmly in the 'probably not' file as regards answers for what she saw.

**Bear Necessities**
One other suggestion as to the possible true zoological identity of the tokoloshe, meanwhile, could draw upon the occasional description of the beast as being somehow 'bear-like' in its nature. Could tokoloshes - including the one that Minnie Martin observed, perhaps - really be some kind of species of tiny bear, observed walking and shuffling around on two feet? Personally I find this idea quite unlikely, as bears are not actually native to countries like Zimbabwe and South Africa; or, indeed, to sub-Saharan Africa as a whole. To this, of course, it could be objected by some that there are really bears in southern Africa, but that they simply

haven't been discovered and classified by science yet. Instead, they are known only to locals, who call them tokoloshes, and treat them with such caution and awe that they have since been imbued, wholly falsely, with various magical and mystical powers in local folklore, a fact which has, quite wrongly, been taken by Westerners as meaning that the beasts themselves are purely fictional. If this were so, then it would not be the first time that such a thing has occurred - but, again, I must say that I find the idea most implausible myself. You really would have thought that animals as curious as 'mini-bears' - for such they must be, if accounts of the tokoloshe's size which we are generally given are correct - would have been officially discovered and catalogued by now.

However, there is at least one mystery bear-type creature known from the African continent, and that is the notorious Nandi-bear - named after the Nandi district of Kenya - of east Africa. Could the tokoloshe be one of these? Well, in order to determine that, we shall perhaps first of all have to examine what exactly a Nandi-bear is in the first place. The answer, sadly, is far from certain.

According to the famed cryptozoologist (researcher into as-yet undiscovered animals) Dr Karl Shuker, whose researches and opinions I am largely following here, the phrase 'Nandi-bear' is actually a kind of umbrella term, which covers a number of alleged cryptids (mystery animals) spoken of, either from myth, legend or direct personal experience, as inhabiting the eastern part of the continent. Confusingly, however, many of these so-called Nandi-bears are not thought of as being actual bears at all! Rather, descriptions of the beasts appear to involve encounters, whether real or fictional, with such diverse animals as anomalous aardvarks, oversized and oddly-coloured hyaenas and, most relevantly for our current purposes, unusual baboons [5].

Baboons, we will recall, are intimately associated with both tokoloshes and their witch-mistresses. Characteristic modern descriptions of the demon, indeed, appear to connect it with this animal more than with any other; typically in modern Africa, the tokoloshe is described as being "like a large baboon, but [it] walks on two legs like a human being", or like a baboon in that it is a "horrible creature with horrible teeth" and prominent genitalia [6].

Might real-life sightings of Nandi-bears, and bear-like tokoloshes, then, really just be down to confused witnesses actually encountering some unusual species of baboon? Maybe there are some baboons which are so big that, standing fully upright on two legs, they could be mistaken for bears or a new, unknown species, later dignified by the name tokoloshe? Perhaps so. According to a 1931 account from a game-warden named Captain Charles Pitman, for instance, whilst working on the Uasin Gishu Plateau in Kenya, he had seen with his own eyes male baboons:

> "of colossal size, capable of killing children with ease; large dogs have been almost torn to pieces [by them], the victim held in its arms. The ape practically disembowels it with downward sweeps of its muscular nail-tipped legs. A great male baboon indistinctly seen in grass or amidst bushland might well be taken for an unknown species. [7]"

Perhaps because of accounts like this, it has been speculated (improbably) in some quarters that a prehistoric species of giant baboon, called Sinopithecus, believed to have been extinct since the ice-age, could actually still have survived in certain out-of-the-way parts of Africa.

Could one of these giant baboons, perhaps, have been mistaken for the "grey polar bear" which was alleged to have assaulted an unnamed white settler in the Trans-Nzoia district of Rift Valley Province in Kenya at some unspecified point during the early decades of the twentieth century? According to Roger Courtney's 1936 book *Africa Calling*, this man had been attacked one night, whilst alone inside his hut, by an animal which "could only have been a Nandi-bear." This eight-foot-tall beast broke down the white man's door to get at him, and was described as having "blazing" red eyes and "slavering" jaws. It chased him around the table until the man managed to pick up a revolver and shoot the creature in the chest with it, at which point it ran away out into the African night, "growling horribly" [8].

However, while these accounts are undoubtedly fascinating in and of themselves, do they really have anything much to do with tokoloshes? After all, whilst tokoloshes might most frequently be said to resemble baboons, they are not said to be giant baboons, although they may be a little larger than the average member of the species, and when they are said to look like bears, they are always alleged to resemble unfeasibly small bears, not huge ones. Many aspects of the supposed behaviour of Nandi-bears also do not really fit in with the tokoloshe-myth. For example, Nandi-bears are often claimed to kill people by biting or clawing open the top of their victims' heads with such force that the top of the skull is shaved right off, leaving the brain entirely exposed. Then, they scoop out the grey-matter with their paws, before eating it.

Interestingly, however, there is at least one fairly recent case of a Chacma baboon (South Africa's most common baboon-type - see below) eating a human being's brain on record, although the reports about it make it clear that this unpleasant event was considered to be very much a one-off. It occurred in the small village of Madipelesa in South Africa's North West Province in 2003, when a large Chacma baboon entered the home of a 34-year-old woman named Lettie Goitsimang Tukane, grabbed her three-month-old son Neo up under one of its arms, and then went back outside into the bush again. Hearing her baby's screams, Lettie rushed out to try and confront the baboon, but it tried to attack her too, and was only scared off when neighbours arrived and started hurling stones at it and setting their dogs loose to attack the creature. However, before it was scared away, the baboon had managed to rip open the baby's skull with its teeth and scoop out a portion of its brain, which it then began to eat in full view of the child's mother once it had got away safely up to the top of a nearby telegraph pole. The Senior Environmental Officer for the region, Richard Gasealahwe, gave his view that the baboon probably thought that baby Neo - who, unsurprisingly, eventually died - was a small goat. Goats, he said, were sometimes attacked by hungry baboons, which would kill them and begin their fresh meal by eating their brains first, and there were indeed some of these livestock being kept inside the house. However, so rare and unexpected was this shocking event that Neo's mother and some other locals felt that they could blame nothing other than witchcraft for the occurrence; presumably recalling associations between witches, tokoloshes and fierce baboons as they did so [9].

In mainstream African mythology, however, tokoloshes, as far as I know, do not eat their victims' brains. Indeed, they are supposed to rape more often than they kill, and I have yet to come across any accounts of people being raped by Nandi-bears, thankfully. Furthermore, there is the rather important fact that Nandi-bears are meant to live in east Africa, in countries like Kenya and Tanzania, not in southern African countries where the tokoloshe is supposed to be native, like South Africa, Namibia, Botswana and Zimbabwe. Tokoloshes then, I think, are not Nandi-bears in baboon-form, even if the occasional baby-eating monkey, as with the case above, does sound positively demonic in its nature.

### Hungry, Hungry Hyaenas

However, there is another possible explanation for what the Nandi-bear actually is; namely, that it is in fact some kind of hyaena. Hyaenas, apparently, really do 'scalp' some of their victims when hunger forces them to attack humans instead of merely scavenging for dead animals, as they usually do. And, when this does happen, they appear to be particularly fond of mutilating human corpses by ripping off various parts of the head and face, often exposing the skull and brains, which I suppose they must also eat. There is one species of hyaena in particular, the brown hyaena or *Hyaena brunnea*, which could, at a stretch, perhaps be referenced in order to account for certain tokoloshe sightings. These animals, it seems, do

actually inhabit southern Africa, as opposed to just the eastern part of the continent, and are a nocturnal species whose habits mean that they are unknown even to most natives. Furthermore, these beasts have long and shaggy hair just like tokoloshes, are much smaller than giant baboons would be, and could maybe surprise and confuse many people if they were to see one out and about at night, particularly if there was little moonlight. Significantly, perhaps, their muzzles are shorter than those of most feliforms (the class of animal to which hyaenas as a whole belong), and could be taken to be bear-like at first glance [10]. Furthermore, their eyes do reflect back light after dark; and tokoloshes, also, are sometimes said to have glowing eyes. To judge by a picture of one which I currently have before me, the fur on their legs is spotted and of a much lighter colour than the fur on the rest of their bodies, too. Perhaps such appendages could be taken by an unwary observer, in very poor lighting conditions, to be human-like legs sticking out from a mass of shaggy hair covering the torso?

There are also numerous evident problems with such an idea, though. For one thing, tokoloshes are universally said to be bipedal, not quadrupeds like brown hyaenas obviously are, and it would take very poor eyesight indeed for a witness to start seeing such an animal as being specifically humanoid in form, as Minnie Martin apparently did. There are other problems with such an identification, too; the ears of the hyaena are prominent, for instance, whereas they are not usually explicitly said to be so in tokoloshes, and the animal's facial characteristics are not remotely goblin-like, either. Ultimately, no doubt there are many smallish, furry creatures which live in the southern African bush that could potentially be 'seen' as being tokoloshes by people who believe in them, whether due to poor lighting conditions or bad eyesight, or simply due to them being glimpsed fleetingly running between trees, bushes and other cover, giving an individual little chance to really be certain of precisely what it is that they had seen. Hyaenas could, of course, potentially have been misidentified by the occasional person as being wild tokoloshes on the loose, then, but so could several other animals, and I don't propose here to examine the potential ability of all of southern Africa's short, furry fauna to be mistaken for tokoloshes. Personally, I think that it is much more likely that Minnie Martin saw an entirely natural animal that night back in the colonial era, rather than a 'real' tokoloshe as such, but precisely what kind of beast it actually was, I suspect we shall never know.

However, we would also do well to consider that we might well be barking up the wrong tree entirely when attempting to classify the tokoloshe as being some kind of flesh-and-blood zoological entity. After all, whilst Minnie Martin's first-hand sighting of a tokoloshe could quite easily be interpreted as being of a biological creature, other eyewitness accounts, such as that of Flora Nthshuntshe, cited right at the start of this book, clearly will not bear such an interpretation. The tokoloshe sighted upon this occasion, we will remember, was "short and fat with a fur cape or animal skin round his shoulders" and whose "eyes were like lights, yellow, shining brightly and looking evil. [11]" Such characteristics are, quite evidently, not those of any actual animal, and neither is the frequently-referenced giant elastic penis which the tokoloshe

**OPPOSITE: A stuffed brown hyaena; could misperceptions of these creatures or some of their relatives be responsible for certain tokoloshe sightings?**

carries everywhere around with him slung over his shoulder (the only actual animal-penis in nature which even remotely resembles that of the tokoloshe is the potentially eight-foot member of the blue whale, and I'm pretty sure that the tokoloshe isn't one of those ...). Instead of trying to classify the tokoloshe as being some kind of mystery cryptid, then, on account of his frequently-mentioned associations with baboons, monkeys and mini-bears, it is my general view that his animal-like qualities would be more usefully viewed as being essentially metaphorical in their nature, as we shall see outlined soon.

### Dial 'M' for Monkey

Whatever we may think of the various attempts that have been made to identify tokoloshes as a whole as being examples of genuine, flesh-and-blood zoological creatures, though, there can be absolutely no doubt whatsoever that there have been at least some occasions wherein innocent monkeys, baboons and other such creatures have been identified by African people as being tokoloshes, and then slaughtered for the 'fact'. Baboons are, after all, widespread in southern Africa - namely, a specific sub-species known as the Chacma baboon (*Papio ursinus*). This beast having, as it does, a fairly short tail, sometimes growing to around three-and-a-half feet in height, and having a long, downwards-sloping face which could, perhaps, be taken to be somewhat human-like in appearance, is obviously occasionally going be mistaken for a tokoloshe under certain circumstances. A specific subcategory of this animal, meanwhile, the Cape Chacma, lives only in the southernmost part of South Africa - the very heart of tokoloshe country - and is the largest type of Chacma baboon of all, having dark brown fur and black feet, making it sound even more like the demonic furry terror of legend. Furthermore, whilst these beasts are fairly plentiful in southern Africa, they will generally flee at the sight of approaching humans, meaning that many people, perhaps, will not be that used to actually seeing them right up close. As such, it is probably no surprise that mistakes sometimes will occur. In 2008, for example, there was widespread panic in Nzhelele, a small settlement in South Africa's Limpopo Province, after it was reported that a tokoloshe in the form of a magical baboon had been raping and molesting women at night.

Eventually the menfolk of the local villages got together and killed the creature, allegedly because they were jealous of the competition they were getting from it for the district's women - a particularly extreme example of penis-envy, perhaps. As an actual real animal was killed by this mob, presumably the beast was actually nothing more than a real flesh-and-blood baboon which happened to have been unlucky enough to be in the wrong place at the wrong time. Or then again, perhaps not, as after it had been slaughtered it was said to have been found in possession of a golden necklace (a gift, maybe, from its witch-mistress) and was

**OPPOSITE: Chacma baboons, the largest of all known baboon species, are common throughout much of South Africa. Could sightings of these animals account for some reports of tokoloshes? Certainly, they can appear vicious and demonic (top) and adopt certain human-like poses (bottom), perhaps giving some credence to the idea. As seen in the second photo, these animals' sex organs are also quite prominent, fitting in with much tokoloshe mythology.**

supposedly wearing a condom, presumably to prevent it from getting AIDS from the women it raped in the night!

Triumphant, the men who butchered it began singing, and took the corpse of the primate to the house of the local traditional tribal chief who, after taking one look at their macabre trophy, told the crowd, perhaps not unreasonably, to "get lost". The dead baboon, he seemed to think, might bring him bad luck. Needing to get rid of the body somewhere, it was decided instead to take it around to the house of the local witch and chastise her for sending the evil monkey-demon out against the village-folk. Unfortunately, this 'witch', named Makwarela Makhalimela, was nothing of the kind, but simply a 60-year-old devout Christian woman who had been singled out by someone amongst the mob as being a convenient scapegoat for whatever reason.

Soon, a hostile crowd had gathered outside Ms Makhalimela's house, singing what she described as being "derogatory songs" about her. Going out to see what was going on, she was subjected to abuse and accused of sending out the tokoloshe against the village women, before being threatened with death by 'necklacing' - the practice of tying a person to a tree with a rubber tyre around their neck before then executing them by setting fire to it, a sadly familiar crime in South Africa over recent decades. All of this, of course, left her and her grandchildren, who happened to be there with her at the time, shivering with fear, a feeling only exacerbated by the fact that the police had also by this point arrived at the alleged witch's home, and seemed to be standing around and doing nothing. Indeed, according to Ms Makhalimela, they appeared to be on the mob's side, not hers. Finally, however, the crowd left without spilling any blood; but that did not mean that the old woman's life had not just been ruined. According to her own words:

> "My good name has been defiled and people will never trust me again. It is painful and it would have been better if they had killed me ... My grandchildren cannot enjoy their schooling as they are labelled as witches. People are no longer visiting us and a lot of strain has been put on my grown-up children. [12]"

Another case of a monkey being murdered, meanwhile, occurred as recently as June 2011, in the black South African township of Kagiso in Gauteng Province. Here, a state of panic broke out after a vervet monkey, which seemed to have become lost and separated from its fellow simians, appeared in the settlement. Apparently not used to seeing lone monkeys wandering through their streets, the residents of Kagiso - which name, ironically, means 'peace' in the local tongue - began chasing it around in the belief that it was a witch in animal form. Supposedly, the creature had been heard to speak, something which led to it being pelted with stones and even shot at by a policeman. Terrified, the animal sought refuge by climbing up into a tree, but the locals gathered around at the bottom of it chanting "Kill that witch!" and a young man named Tebogo Moswetsi volunteered to go up into the branches himself to retrieve it, dropping the frightened animal into a bucket and then passing it down below. Moswetsi claimed that he had captured the beast in this way purely because he was intrigued to see what a talking monkey would sound like, and had no idea what was going to happen to it next. As it turned out, the animal's fate was to be horrific; petrol was poured into the bucket, and someone else then threw on a match. The vervet monkey, aflame, jumped out of the container and then promptly dropped down dead [13].

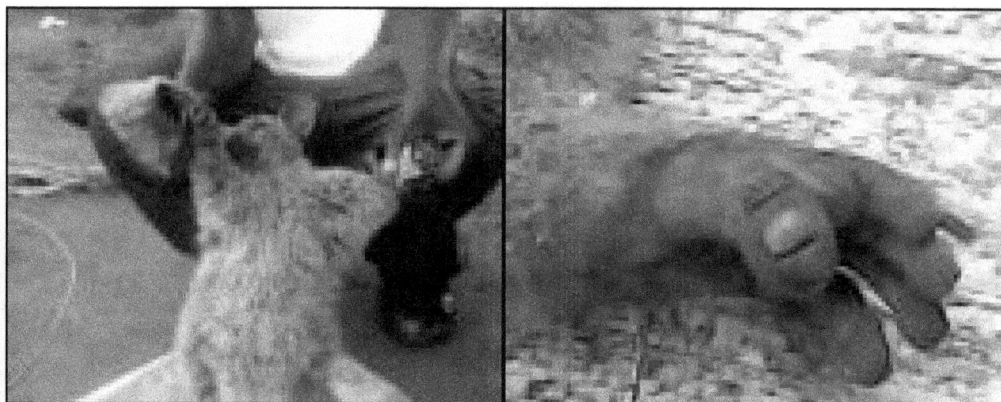

**The thick-tailed bush-baby stoned to death by members of the Ramadzhiela family from South Africa in May 2012; they thought that the animal had human-like fingers (shown here) and genitalia (not shown here!), which, to them, was a dead giveaway that it was a tokoloshe.**

Another animal which is sometimes occasionally mistaken for a tokoloshe, meanwhile, is the bush-baby; a small and rather cute kind of nocturnal lemur-like primate with fairly human-like prehensile fingers which is native to much of southern Africa. In May 2012, for instance, the corpse of a dead tokoloshe was being briefly paraded for the cameras in the small South African village of Tshaulu in Limpopo Province. To judge by the pictures which resulted, however, the 'tokoloshe' in this instance was in fact nothing more than a thick-tailed bush-baby. Apparently, what happened is that several members of the Ramadzhiela family had been awoken in the middle of the night by the sound of some small creature scrambling across the roof of their home. Looking at it, the family were scared, as they felt that it had certain human-like features to it. Alerting the rest of the village, the entire community stood guard outside the house overnight, aiming to prevent the mystery beast from getting away. They tried but failed to capture the animal by enticing it down from the roof, so it seems that one of the men present, Takalani Ramadzhiela, climbed up onto the house and hit the animal on the head with a stone, killing it.

Examining it back down on the ground, it was the general opinion of those present that the beast had hands and genitals like a man, yet was furry like an animal, so must therefore have been a tokoloshe, sent out to do evil by a witch or sorcerer. A local traditional healer, however, was of a different opinion; when asked about the case, he gave his view that the tokoloshe had been sent out to the Ramadzhiela family by their ancestor-spirits, in order to indicate that one of them might be being called to become a shaman.

Zoologists who were shown pictures of the creature, though, implied that it was just a bush-baby; however, no actual corpse was left available for any scientists to examine and make sure of this identification, as the villagers seem to have performed some kind of magical ritual upon it and then hurled it away into a nearby river [14].

**Two Legs Bad**

The case from Kagiso cited above, in particular, demonstrates how widely-held the belief is that witches can transform themselves into various different simians in parts of southern Africa. The association between sorcerers and baboons, especially, is emphasised in many contemporary myths. For instance, one idea about witches is that they are sometimes supposed to ride around naked backwards on the backs of baboons at the 'witching hour' of midnight [15]. More generally however, as we have already discussed, the notion of there being some kind of duality between the witch and the ape is the element of this belief which predominates; when the people in Kagiso burned their monkey, for instance, they appear to have felt that in doing so, they were actually executing the witch, as well. This old 'sympathetic wounding/killing' motif is still alive and well in the modern day in Africa, it seems. For example, it is sometimes said that, if you catch a monkey messing around in your house and give it a whack with a big stick, then you might hear somebody screaming outside. Then, the next day, all you would have to do would be to enquire around to see if anyone is claiming to have been beaten up recently, and you will have found your witch; by injuring the monkey-double, you also hurt his master or mistress, such is the strength of the mystical connection which allegedly exists between the two [16].

At other times, meanwhile, rather than the two souls of the evil-doers being mystically linked, the witch herself is simply said to be able to magically effect the physical transformation of her own human body into that of a baboon (or vice-versa). For example, Isak Niehaus tells an amusing little story about an unnamed South African man who was supposedly woken up at midnight by the sound of his wife's sewing machine being operated. Wondering why his wife was up sewing so late, he went into the living room to investigate; and saw a big baboon sat there at the table operating the thing instead! Scared, he went back to bed but, later on, decided to go back out and investigate further. This time, however, he saw his wife sat at the machine as usual. When he confronted her about all this, she brushed off his concerns quite calmly, telling him that he must simply have been mistaken in what he thought he had seen; it was her who had been sat up all night busy sewing, not a baboon [17].

Once such beliefs are widely accepted, of course, it then becomes quite possible to identify genuine animals incorrectly as being tokoloshes in the form of shape-shifting monkeys or baboons, as occurred in one of the cases we examined initially above. For example, during the widespread witch-hysteria which spread throughout South Africa in the years leading up to the fall of apartheid, many accused 'witches' began setting up shanty-towns, termed 'witch-villages', next to police stations in order to seek protection from angry mobs. These people were, presumably, actually innocent of any crimes, but rumours soon began to spring up in some places that tokoloshe-baboons and monkeys were sneaking out of these villages after dark and stealing food from people to take back to their witch-owners in order to give them sustenance [18].

An absurd idea? Maybe not entirely. It seems to me that such rumours could actually, after a fashion at least, have been based upon fact. Monkeys and baboons will, on occasion, steal food from human settlements, after all, so this kind of behaviour could genuinely have been observed during the period of time when the witch-villages were in operation. It was nothing to do with witches, but merely down to wild animals acting quite naturally. However, pre-existing beliefs about tokoloshe-witch duality, combined with the springing-up of witch-villages in numerous townships, probably simply allowed people to go around interpreting food-theft by apes as being down to increased witchcraft activity in the area when actually it was likely to be nothing of the sort. Because of this kind of reasoning taking place, I personally do not feel that it is in any way necessary to propose that tokoloshe-sightings need be down to encounters with hitherto-unknown species like Nandi-bears. No doubt, if a South African villager saw an abnormally large and uncatalogued type of baboon out late at night, they could claim that it was a tokoloshe; but they could also claim that an entirely ordinary baboon was a tokoloshe out and up to no good too, if they were so minded to.

Even children sometimes hallucinate tokoloshes in the form of baboons, showing that this association is still going strong in the minds of the younger generation. In February 2012, for example, it was reported that yet another case of school-related mass hysteria had broken out at St Sebastian Secondary School in the village of Sigangatsha in the Matabeleland South Province of Zimbabwe. Here, widespread panic had occurred after various female pupils had begun going into trances and encountering what were described in the press either as tokoloshes or chikwambos. Apparently, these entities took the form of baboons. One girl, for example, claimed that she saw her teacher entering the classroom accompanied by some "very short human beings" which then promptly transformed themselves into baboons, whilst another girl fainted and then, after spending time in some kind of trance, began screaming and kicking out at thin air for about five minutes. When she finally came around, she claimed that she had been trying to fight off a baboon which was endeavouring to slap her. Evidently, then, the connection of apes and monkeys with witchcraft will continue on into the future [19].

But why are people so keen to associate witches with baboons in the first place? The standard interpretation seems to be that the connection between them is at root symbolic in its nature, even though it is now generally taken literally by many contemporary witchcraft-believers. The idea that a tokoloshe looks like a baboon has sometimes been interpreted as representing a kind of beast-like caricature of uncontrolled sexuality and an almost childish lack of self-control on their behalf - or, alternatively, as being a result of the tokoloshe's occasionally-claimed origin as the result of sexual liaisons taking place between a witch and a baboon [20]. The fact that a baboon looks relatively human-like, in its basic form at least, means that it is fairly easy to imagine how the actual mechanics of human-animal sex with one would work, which might help to account for the popularity of one portion of this myth. However, there is also the fact that baboons, rather like human infants, tend to display a rather 'childish' or 'unsocialised' sense of morality. They might look a bit humanoid, but they will fight with and sometimes kill one another, or even human beings, will from time to time steal food, and have uncontrolled sexual appetites. The males of some baboon species, for example, keep 'harems' of females for themselves, and female baboons are well-known for courting males by openly displaying their swollen red rumps to them as a sign of their sexual availability.

In Isak Niehaus' view, baboons "are not socialised and lack the restraints culture imposes on their wants and desires.[21]" In other words, then, they are imagined as taking what they want at the expense of others; just like witches are imagined as doing, as we have already discussed. The idea that tokoloshes are created by human witches having sex with baboons is simply yet another way of stating this opinion, in a kind of coded way; after all, what could be more immoral and uncontrolled in its nature than a human being committing and enjoying acts of bestiality? Saying that there is a duality between a baboon-like tokoloshe and a witch or wizard, then, is simply another way for a person to imply that these evil sorcerers are, metaphorically, little better than mere wild animals themselves. Ultimately, then, it is not my opinion that we shall ever see a tokoloshe being placed upon permanent display inside a zoo, regrettably.

# *Conclusion:*

## A Tokoloshe for All Seasons

Tokoloshes, as we have seen throughout this book, are quite protean in their nature; they are always changing their shape, form and behaviour. Nowadays, for example, they have even learned how to pilot UFOs!

It is a curious fact that African conceptions of UFOs are somewhat different than contemporary Western ones are. Here, the average man in the street, probably knowing very little about the subject, would tend to believe either that UFOs are works of fiction or imagination, or else that they are piloted by beings from other worlds. In Africa, of course, it is perfectly true that both of these explanations are available to people. Some Africans do indeed believe that alien beings are visiting our planet. There are, however, other options available for southern African sky-watchers; it is perfectly possible, for instance, for a person to believe that a UFO might be piloted by a witch rather than by a 'Grey' or Venusian.

For example when, in 1999, a Zimbabwean woman named Anna Banda awoke in her house in the suburb of Dzivarasekwa in western Harare, only to find a naked man in her home, babbling on about needing to consume human flesh and blood, Ms Banda had no doubt whatsoever about what must have been happening. The man was clearly a witch, who had flown over a hundred miles to her house in his ruserwa - the Zimbabwean term for a 'flying saucer' - in search of her nephew Tichaona's flesh. Banda let out a piercing scream and doused the man in holy water, and eventually the police came and took him away. They said that he was simply a mad old man, but Anna Banda, who was employed as a 'prophet' by a local Apostolic Church, was very firmly of the opinion that he was in fact an evil UFO-pilot [1].

This initially might seem like an odd idea to us Westerners, but in fact the association of UFOs with witches is merely a kind of extension of a prevailing southern African belief in something that is often termed 'witchcraft technology'; namely, the appropriation of modern mechanical and electronic inventions by witches for use in their own magical practices. The notion of fitting a remote-control unit with a severed tokoloshe-penis as a kind of 'battery' for use in mtshotshaphansi–crimes, explored earlier, is one such example of this; but the idea of so-called 'witchcraft airplanes' is another. Basically, whilst

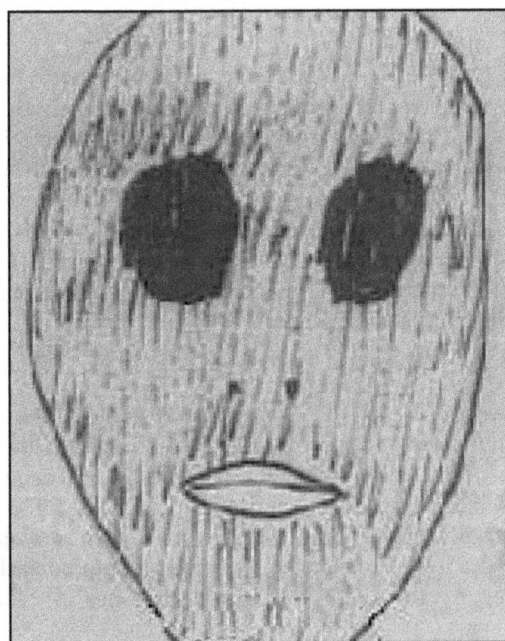

witches were long 'known' by many people to fly through the air, it was often unclear as to how precisely this feat was achieved. Once aeroplanes began to be sighted in African skies, however, a possible answer arose. Why shouldn't witches simply be making use of similar things, albeit much smaller in size and infused with some kind of magical power in lieu of aviation-fuel? It is but a small step from such reasoning to then begin claiming that, as well as 'witchcraft airplanes', witches whizz through the skies inside UFOs as well. Most significant for our present purposes, however, is the opinion that witches sometimes allegedly make use of tokoloshes as co-pilots and crew members inside their magical ruserwas.

**Flying Sorcerers**
It is not always the case, though, that witches have to supervise any tokoloshes inside UFOs. Some of them, seemingly, have now acquired the ability to fly saucers quite independently of their witch-mistresses. Probably the most famous such instance of tokoloshes supposedly being sighted in conjunction with a ruserwa occurred in 1994 at the mixed-race Ariel Primary School in the obscure Zimbabwean town of Ruwa in that country's Mashonaland East Province. Here, during morning break-time on September 16th, 62 pupils were playing outside, being supervised by only one adult, one of the children's mothers, who ran a snack bar inside the school. She, however, did not see the UFOs as, when a boy ran in to tell her about what was happening, she simply did not believe him.

Events began, seemingly, when between three to five saucers (sources differ) were sighted flying along the path laid out for them by some overhead power-cables, one of which either landed or hovered just above the ground near to one particular electricity pylon. A doorway opened in the craft, and two small humanoid figures appeared there. Their description makes them sound not unlike tokoloshes; they were about a metre tall, covered all over in black hair, had hardly any nose, and only small slits for mouths. They were also dressed in tight black shiny diving suit-like gear, and had large black eyes, described by the children as being shaped like rugby balls. The UFO-occupants, then, sounded rather like some kind of a cross between traditional African tokoloshes and contemporary Western descriptions of the now-famous 'Greys' (maybe, if you wish to view this entire episode as being some kind of collective hysteria-induced hallucination, you might want to speculate that these 'visions' assumed this form as a kind of result of the various races of the child-witnesses who were involved?).

The beings jumped out from their craft, apparently, and began running across the bush-covered field which sat next to the school's playground, in a bizarre fashion. Their movements seemed 'confused' somehow, and they also appeared to be moving in slow-motion. The entire cohort of kids stopped what they had been doing and stood there

---

**OPPOSITE: Some schoolchildren's original drawings of the UFO-piloting tokoloshes and their flying saucer, as seen at a school in the Zimbabwean town of Ruwa in 1994 and later investigated by southern Africa's premier ufologist, Cynthia Hind.**

---

191

transfixed by the creatures before them, and particularly by their large, hypnotic black eyes. Whilst in this state, the pupils claimed that they had begun receiving telepathic messages from the aliens; they were being warned, it seems, about the dangers of pollution and the possible forthcoming end of the world. Eventually, the entities returned back to their craft which lifted itself up about three metres into the air and then simply disappeared. It appears that many of the schoolchildren involved interpreted this encounter in terms of it having involved demons, ghosts and tokoloshes, though, rather than extraterrestrials as such, as would surely have happened if such a sighting had been made in the West [2].

However, the question does have to be asked - in what way were these apparent entities really tokoloshes? Sure, they were hairy, but since when have tokoloshes been interested in environmental issues and worn wet-suits? It seems likely to me that the children at Ariel Primary School simply saw something very strange one day - whether it actually had any objective existence to it or not - and then just adapted their later interpretation of it all in order to fit in with their own pre-existing beliefs about creatures from local demonology. These hairy UFO-pilots were seen as being tokoloshes only because they were encountered in southern Africa, I would suggest; if they had been witnessed elsewhere, then they would surely not have been.

**Tokoloshes on Tour?**
This can be proven, I think, as there are actually accounts of very similar entities supposedly being seen stepping out from inside UFOs from various other places in the world, where tokoloshes have not been so much as mentioned, because local people will almost certainly never even have heard of such beings. For example, there was a rash of encounters with little hairy men in South America throughout the 1950s, some of which were quite sensational in their nature.

For instance, on November 28th 1954, two men named Gustavo González and José Ponce were driving a van through some suburbs in the Venezuelan capital of Caracas, when they found the road blocked by a big luminous sphere hovering a few feet off the ground. Getting out to see what it was, González said that he ended up being pulled into a fight with a small, hairy dwarf in a loincloth who had glowing eyes and super-strength. González drew his knife to try and stab the monster, but it merely glanced off the being's body without doing him any harm before another entity then emerged from the UFO and blinded the man with a beam of bright light which he fired out at him from a tube. Ponce said he then saw another two hairy dwarfs run out from the bushes with their arms full of rocks and earth before then jumping up into the sphere with unnatural ease. González having been wounded during his fight with the alien, the two men went to the nearest police station to report what had happened, and ended up being placed under medical supervision. At first, they were not believed. Allegedly, however, one of the doctors who treated the two men later revealed that he knew their story was true as he himself had seen the fracas taking place whilst he was driving past the location in question on his way back from a night-call [3].

A few weeks later on December 10th, on the trans-Andean highway, also in Venezuela, two hunters, Lorenzo Flores and Jesús Gómez, likewise saw a glowing UFO from which super-strong hairy dwarfs emerged. This time, the dwarfs apparently tried to kidnap the two men. Whilst Gómez was being dragged away by them, Florez smacked one of the dwarfs with his shotgun. Reportedly, it had no effect upon the creature, which felt as if it was made from rock, and the gun simply fell apart. It is not quite clear how the two hunters eventually escaped, but they both ran to the nearest police post as soon as they could, where officers reported that they were covered all over in deep scratches and bruises, and their clothing was torn to shreds [4].

On December 16th, meanwhile, yet another hairy dwarf-assault was allegedly perpetrated in Venezuela. A man named Jesús Paz had gone into some bushes to empty his bladder when his friends, who were waiting in their parked car for him, heard a scream. Rushing into the foliage to see what was going on, Paz's friends found him lying unconscious on the ground whilst a little hairy man ran away from the scene and hopped into a flying saucer, which then disappeared with a deafening whistle. Taken to hospital, it was later found that Paz had long and deep scratches all down his spine and his right side, "as though he had been clawed by a wild beast.[5]"

Now, whatever you think of these accounts, you have to admit that the 'aliens' which were involved in them would sound very much, to African ears, like UFO-piloting tokoloshes. They were, after all, vicious and hairy little dwarfs with glowing eyes and precious few clothes on. To South American ears, though, there are no doubt native myths of their own which they could bring in in order to account for these bizarre apparitions. For example, the Tzeltal Indians of Mexico have legends about a race of hairy black dwarfs named ikals, whose appearance is frequently associated with the presence of inexplicable and supernatural balls of light [6]. To many South Americans, no doubt invoking the name of these beings in order to explain some UFOs sightings would be just as acceptable as it would be to an African to mention tokoloshes in order to do the same. Tokoloshes, then, have no monopoly whatsoever upon the idea of being the only hairy dwarfs to have allegedly been encountered flying around planet earth in spaceships.

Even more suggestive in this regard, perhaps, due to the overtly sexual nature of the case, were a series of events reported on in the book *UFO Warning* by the New Zealand UFO researcher John Stuart. In this tome, he detailed a horrifying experience which was supposedly undergone by his female research assistant, Barbara Turner, after the two of them had witnessed a grotesque entity whilst investigating a UFO report in 1954. This being, as depicted in an illustration of the encounter, looked not entirely unlike a gigantic tokoloshe - albeit with the feet of a duck. It was eight feet tall, covered all across its torso and face with hair, and had webbed feet. Apparently, it warned them to stop their research into UFOs as, it said, they were actually Satanic in their nature, not extraterrestrial. Sadly, however, John and Barbara ignored the hairy creature's words. The results were, allegedly, not very pleasant.

First of all, Barbara's personality began to change. Initially, she was described by Stuart as being "sweet, kind [and] innocent" - until she started to suffer from apparent possession states during which she began to spout explicit sexual come-ons to her research partner during their UFO-chat, saying quaintly dirty things like:

> "Gee, I'm glad I'm a girl. I like to be kissed. I like to tease boys, with a partly
> open shirt, brief shorts, all that … I'd like to sit here naked. Like me to?"

The conclusion apparently drawn by Stuart from all this was that Barbara was being possessed by evil entities from the UFOs they were seeking. Matters, however, were soon about to get much worse.

One night not long after she had been visited by the hairy giant, Barbara said, she could detect a phantom smell in her bedroom and thought that she was being watched; after undressing, she felt an invisible hand on her shoulder, followed by total paralysis. For the next two-and-a-half hours, she was raped repeatedly by an unseen being; the next morning, she was covered all over in scratches and her ribs bore two curious brown marks, the size of ten-cent pieces. The whole experience, she later said, was strangely clinical, almost as though the invisible individual was having sex with her more out of professional investigative curiosity than actual passion or desire. Greatly disturbed, she gave up UFO research for good and promptly moved to another city.

A few weeks later, however, her former colleague John Stuart came face to face with the alien rapist in visible form; it sounded horrible.

> "Its body resembled, vaguely, that of a human … Its flesh, stinkingly
> putrid, seemed to hang in folds. It was a grayish color … The slack
> mouth was dribbling, and the horrible lips began to move, but there
> was no sound."

Communicating with him telepathically, the thing told John that his assistant had actually been gang-raped by a group of thirteen of his fellow extraterrestrial beings - three had physically penetrated her, whilst the others just stood around and watched. Eventually, John himself was forced to abandon UFO research after a disturbing encounter with a half-incubus, half-succubus creature that appeared to be male above the waist and female below at one moment and then vice-versa the next [7].

So, then; in this disturbing case we have hairy demons associated with UFOs, gang-rape by invisible entities, and a woman becoming possessed and thereafter expressing her deviant sexual desires. Surely, if this case had occurred in South Africa or Zimbabwe, the conclusion to be drawn would have been obvious? Tokoloshes would have been responsible for it all, evidently! These things being unknown in 1950s New Zealand, however, plain old Satanic hordes were deemed to be worth blaming for matters instead.

**A Question of Reality**

The issue of tokoloshes and UFOs has been dwelled upon finally by me here at length for the simple reason that it shows, in microcosm, how southern African beliefs about the creature are continually changing in order to reflect corresponding alterations in wider society as a whole. After all, before there were thought to even be such things as UFOs, tokoloshes could not, by definition, have been seen flying around in them. Once the idea of the UFO became available to the African mind, however, it seems to have wasted little time in then filling them up with hairy baboon-demons. 'Old Tokoloshe', it seems, has travelled a long way indeed since first being sighted dwelling within lakes and rivers by the Xhosa people. Nowadays, he is even taking trips into outer-space!

When concluding at last our investigation into his centuries-old reign of terror, though, it might naturally occur to the reader to enquire whether or not I myself think that the tokoloshe is a literally real entity or not. Overall, I think that it should seem pretty obvious that I don't. However, I should like to add some fairly significant caveats to this view of mine. Firstly, I would say that, even if tokoloshe-demons are not ultimately real in any physical sense, they certainly occupy a position of social reality. Numerous southern African people, as we have seen throughout, demonstrably act as if he is real, and so, in a certain sense, he is. Take, for example, the issue of tokoloshe-related poltergeist hauntings. Personally, I am willing to accept that some of the phenomena which were spoken of as happening in our chapter about this subject really did occur. But were they down to poltergeists, or to tokoloshes - or to something else altogether, something of which we currently have absolutely no understanding and, as yet, no meaningful words to describe? These are vexed questions which I cannot possibly answer. You say 'tokoloshe', I say 'poltergeist'; maybe we are both wrong in this, or, then again, maybe we are both right. It's all just a matter of perspective and pre-existing prejudice and preference, most likely.

Ultimately, then, it seems to me that the problem of the reality or otherwise of the tokoloshe is slightly meaningless in its nature. Whilst there are certain poltergeist-like hauntings and other odd experiences which might, at face value, be taken as being some kind of evidence of the tokoloshe's actual authenticity, the conception of the spirit overall is so amorphous and constantly-shifting that the question of its literal existence or otherwise is almost a pointless and unanswerable one. If someone were to ask you whether tokoloshes were real, then would he be talking about poltergeist-like tokoloshes, zombie-like tokoloshes, toilet-dwelling tokoloshes or incubus-like tokoloshes? Or, perhaps, might he be inquiring about the level of genuine muti magic present in the bottled chikwambos which are currently on sale openly in the markets of Zimbabwe? The tokoloshe, in its multiplicity of possible and sometimes self-contradictory identities, really is in many senses the common cousin of the European fairy, of whom literally hundreds of local and widely-differing variations were once supposed to exist; if you were to ask a person from the past whether they thought fairies were real, then they might well stop and ask you whether you meant to enquire about leprechauns, pixies, lutins, hobs or brownies by that question? In many ways, in fact, it is my contention that the tokoloshe probably in essence basically is the European fairy, only under a different name, and with the significant further caveat that he is still widely-believed in during the present day, but in a different geographical location.

Overall, then, it is my opinion that the tokoloshe's polymorphous nature is his most significant quality; it is, most likely, what makes him still so useful to the modern African mind. After all, if he is invisible, as he usually is, and can take on any number of different forms, as he frequently does, then he can quite easily be used as a simple, instant, shorthand 'explanation' for phenomena or alleged phenomena as diverse as witchcraft, wet dreams, murder, the birth of disabled children, sightings of UFOs and unusual animals, and a person's success or lack of it in business. So, it must be admitted, could fairies and other spirits in the not-so-very-distant European past. Westerners, perhaps, no longer feel that they need supernaturalised explanations for such things in light of the currently-prevailing materialistic world-view to which we are now all generally brought up to adhere. But many southern Africans, many of whom still live in communities where witchcraft and the supernatural are matters not of superstition but of obvious everyday social reality, quite clearly still do. Fortunately then, for all such needs, they have available to them the strange but fascinating figure of the tokoloshe.

# BIBLIOGRAPHY OF PRINTED WORKS CITED

- Appleyard, Brian (2006) '*Aliens: Why They Are Here*', Scribner: UK
- Bowen, Charles (Ed.) (1974) '*The Humanoids*', Futura Publishing: UK
- Brookesmith, Peter (Ed.) (1995) '*Marvels & Mysteries: Aliens*', Parallel Publishing: UK
- Chambers, Paul (1999) '*Sex & the Paranormal*', Blandford: UK
- Clark, Stuart (2007) '*Vanities of the Eye: Vision in Early Modern European Culture*', Oxford University Press: UK
- Davies, Owen (2007) '*The Haunted: A Social History of Ghosts*', Palgrave Macmillan: UK
- Eliade, Mircea (1992) '*Shamanism: Archaic Techniques of Ecstasy*', Princeton University Press: USA
- Evans, Hilary & Bartholomew, Robert (2009) '*Outbreak!: The Encyclopaedia of Extraordinary Social Behaviour*', Anomalist Books: USA
- Evans, Hilary & Stacy, Dennis (Eds.) (1997) '*UFOs 1947-1997: Fifty Years of Flying Saucers*', John Brown Publishing: UK
- Frazer, Sir James George (1998) '*The Golden Bough: A Study in Magic and Religion*', Oxford World's Classics: UK
- Gaskill, Malcolm (2005) '*Witchfinders: A Seventeenth-Century English Tragedy*', John Murray: UK
- Gershenson, Olga & Penner, Barbara (Eds.) (2009) '*Ladies and Gents: Public Toilets and Gender*', Temple University Press: USA
- Goldstuck, Arthur (2006) '*The Ghost that Closed Down the Town: The Story of the Haunting of South Africa*', Penguin: South Africa
- Harpur, Patrick (2011) '*A Complete Guide to the Soul*', Rider Books: UK
- Harte, Jeremy (2004) '*Explore Fairy Traditions*', Heart of Albion Press: UK
- Holland, Heidi (2005) '*African Magic: Traditional Ideas That Heal a Continent*', Penguin: South Africa
- Hopton, Andrew (1991) '*Anomalous Phenomena of the Interregnum*', Aporia Press: UK

- Hufford, David (1982) *'The Terror That Comes in the Night: An Experience-Centred Study of Supernatural Assault Traditions'*, University of Pennsylvania Press: USA
- Huysmans, Joris-Karl (2001) *'Là Bas'*, Penguin Classics: UK
- Lebling, Robert (2010) *'Legends of the Fire Spirits: Jinn and Genie from Arabia to Zanzibar'*, IB Tauris: USA
- Levi, Eliphas (1995) *'Transcendental Magic: Its Doctrine and Ritual'*, Senate: UK
- McGovern, Una (2007) *'Chambers Dictionary of the Unexplained'*, Chambers: UK
- Mutwa, Credo (1965) *'Indaba, My Children'*, Blue Crane Books: South Africa
- Narváez, Peter (1997) *'The Good People: New Fairylore Essays'*, University of Kentucky Press: USA
- Niehaus, Isak (2001) *'Witchcraft, Power and Politics: Exploring the Occult in the South African Lowveld'*, Pluto Press: UK
- Owen, ARG (1964) *'Can We Explain the Poltergeist?'*, Helix Books: USA
- Price, Harry (1945) *'Poltergeist Over England'*, Country Life Books: UK
- Radin, Paul (1988) *'The Trickster: A Study in American Indian Mythology'*, Schocken Books: USA
- Rosenthal, Eric (1951) *'They Walk in the Night: True South African Ghost Stories and Tales of the Supernormal'*, Dassie Books: South Africa
- Scott, Sir Walter (2001) *'Letters on Demonology and Witchcraft'*, Wordsworth Editions: UK
- Shuker, Dr Karl PN (1995) *'In Search of Prehistoric Survivors: Do Giant 'Extinct' Creatures Still Exist?'*, Blandford: UK
- Steiger, Brad (2008) *'Otherworldly Affaires: Haunted Lovers, Phantom Spouses and Sexual Molestors from the Shadow World'*, Anomalist Books: USA
- Thomas, Keith (1991) *'Religion and the Decline of Magic'*, Penguin: UK
- Vallee, Jacques (1975) *'Passport to Magonia: From Folklore to Flying Saucers'*, Tandem Books: UK
- Wilby, Emma (2005) *'Cunning Folk and Familiar Spirits: Shamanistic Visionary Traditions in Early Modern British Witchcraft and Magic'*, Sussex University Press: UK

# REFERENCES

Please note that some general information about the tokoloshe is repeated so often in the various sources which I consulted that it has not been thought necessary to reference every single element of the beast's description and activities which are 'in the common domain', as it were. All websites were accessed between June 2011 and June 2012, and are given as either tinyurl or bitly addresses for the sake of brevity.


## INTRODUCTION

The word is spelled in a bewildering variety of ways across the source-materials I used – including tokolosh, tokolossi, tokoloshi, thokoloshe, thokolosi, tokolotsi, tikkaloshe, tokkaloss, thikaloshe, othokoloshe, uthokoloshe, etc – but tokoloshe is by far the most commonly-encountered variant, and probably counts as the 'standard' form. As such, where it has been spelled in a different way originally in quoted material, I have altered it to conform to this spelling in the interests of clarity and avoiding confusion. Also, I have consistently pluralised the word as tokoloshes, even though alternative plural forms were available. (Similar methods have been followed by me throughout with other such words drawn from southern African demonology, such as mamlambo, for the same reasons)

1.      Rosenthal, 1951, p.206-207
2.      http://tinyurl.com/6wxpere – 'Mind, gender and culture: A critical evaluation of the phenomenon of Tokoloshe 'sightings' among prepubescent girls in KwaZulu-Natal'; abstract of academic paper by Nhlanhla Mkhize (University of Natal);criticalmethods.org
3.      Holland, 2005, p.151
4.      Radin, 1988, p.xxiv
5.      Radin, 1988, p.18-19
6.      Radin, 1988, p.19-20
7.      Radin, 1988, p.38-40
8.      http://tinyurl.com/5r6566q – 'Tokoloshe the African gremlin?'; Safari Newsreel
9.      Niehaus, 2001, p.51
10.     http://tinyurl.com/3cjqq2p – 'A Christian Perspective on the World of Spirits: A Trans-Ethnic Examination'; 2006 degree paper by Vemon Nicholas Pillay (University of Zululand)

11.    http://tinyurl.com/6eacx9u – 'Tokolosh rape interview gets thumbs-up'; IOL.co.za
12.    http://tinyurl.com/3vytrvv – Posting on GoTravel24.com
13.    http://bit.ly/JKjjbU  -  'Conjured  Lizard  Haunts  Namibian  Farmers'; PhantomsandMonsters.com
14.    Phylis Beard, writing in a 1921 edition of 'The Friend' (a now-defunct Bloemfontein newspaper); cited in Rosenthal, 1951, p.203
15.    Rosenthal, 1951, p.207
16.    http://tinyurl.com/yuu3xr – 'The Tokoloshe: Africa's Brownie?'; vanhunks.com
17.    http://tinyurl.com/yuu3xr – 'The Tokoloshe: Africa's Brownie?'; vanhunks.com & Rosenthal, 1951, p.211
18.    Holland, 2005, p.150
19.    Rosenthal, 1951, p.206
20.    Rosenthal, 1951, p.208-209
21.    Holland, 2005, p.150
22.    See 'Nags to Witches' by Frans Prins and Sian Hall in Fortean Times issue 119, p.30
23.    Holland, 2005, p.151
24.    Niehaus, 2001, p.50
25.    http://tinyurl.com/3gkzxxo – 'TOKOLOSHE!'; Google Images
26.    http://tinyurl.com/6kdz9c3 – 'Daily Sun should stick to witchcraft and tokoloshes – ANCYL'; Klomp Kak
27.    http://tinyurl.com/cumwzjh – 'The R15k Tokoloshe'; Daily Sun online
28.    Goldstuck, 2006, p.124-125

## 1.    A FAMILIAR STORY: TOKOLOSHES AND WITCHCRAFT

1.    http://tinyurl.com/6e5quez - 'Granny beaten up over witchcraft'; SundayExpress.com
2.    http://tinyurl.com/3cjqq2p – 'A Christian Perspective on the World of Spirits ...'
3.    http://tinyurl.com/6q72nh5 – Posting on GoTravel24.com
4.    Holland, 2005, p.227
5.    McGovern, 2007, p.221
6.    Wilby, 2005, p.175
7.    Gaskill, 2005, p.4
8.    Gaskill, 2005, p.210-211
9.    Niehaus, 2001, p.53
10.    Holland, 2005, p.152-153
11.    Gaskill, 2005, p.113
12.    Gaskill, 2005, p.107
13.    Niehaus, 2001, p.49
14.    Wilby, 2005, p.170
15.    Holland, 2005, p.21-22
16.    http://tinyurl.com/yuu3xr – 'The Tokoloshe: Africa's Brownie'; vanhunks.com
17.    Gaskill, 2005, p.285
18.    Rosenthal, 1951, p.204
19.    Niehaus, 2001, p.51
20.    http://tinyurl.com/3cjqq2p – 'A Christian Perspective on the World of Spirits ...'

21.    Levi, 1995, p.405-406
22.    http://tinyurl.com/3cjqq2p – 'A Christian Perspective on the World of Spirits ...'
23.    Niehaus, 2001, p.51
24.    Clark, 2007, p.144
25.    Evans & Bartholomew, 2010, p.338-339
26.    Harpur, 2011, p.3-4
27.    Eliade, 1992, p.93-94
28.    Scott, 2001, p.171
29.    Niehaus, 2001, p.1
30.    http://tinyurl.com/yuu3xr – 'The Tokoloshe: Africa's Brownie'; vanhunks.com
31.    http://tinyurl.com/6lx7a23 – 'Botswana: I Have a Thokolosi for Sale'; allafrica.com
32.    Mutwa, 1965, p.490-492
33.    http://tinyurl.com/6q72nh5 – Posting on GoTravel24.com
34.    Fortean Times issue 289, p.35
35.    Niehaus, 2001, p.26
36.    Niehaus, 2001, p.69-70
37.    Mutwa, 1965, p.492

## 2. SEXUAL POLITICS: TOKOLOSHE-RAPE AND MOLESTATION

1.    Niehaus, 2001, p.94
2.    Niehaus, 2001, p.52-53
3.    Niehaus, 2001, p.177
4.    Holland, 2005, p.153
5.    http://tinyurl.com/3cjqq2p – 'A Christian Perspective on the World of Spirits ...'
6.    Niehaus, 2001, p.53
7.    http://bit.ly/9AuRos; Wikipedia figures
8.    http://tinyurl.com/6fya6vc - 'In parts of Africa, witches are to blame'; Free Press report
9.    http://tinyurl.com/5r6566q – 'Tokoloshe the African gremlin?'; Safari Newsreel
10.    http://tinyurl.com/dx3cudf - 'GAY TOKOLOSHE GAVE ME AIDS!'; DailySun
11.    Holland, 2005, p.152
12.    Chambers, 1999, p.50-51
13.    Thomas, 1991, p.732
14.    Vallee, 1975, p.126
15.    Fortean Times issue 236, p.75
16.    Fortean Times issue 213, p.77
17.    Fortean Times issue 216, p.73
18.    http://tinyurl.com/6q72nh5 – Posting on GoTravel24.com
19.    Niehaus, 2001, p.54
20.    http://tinyurl.com/6ckbotb – 'Long-distance tokoloshe rape'; Cabinet of Wonders
21.    Goldstuck, 2006, p.115
22.    Niehaus, 2001, p.51
23.    Huysmans, 2001, p.123; the source for this detail is a novel, but one which features numerous references to actual demon-lore from the European past, the extensive

research performed by its author quite clearly just being placed into his characters' mouths during their conversations.

24.     Niehaus, 2001, p.51
25.     http://tinyurl.com/63txoxj - 'Bulawayo Mubobobo man masturbated before his victims'; africanaristocrat.com
26.     http://tinyurl.com/3zfdhfl - 'Rapist with supernatural powers of sex arrested in Gweru'; Zimdiaspora
27.     Niehaus, 2001, p.75
28.     Niehaus, 2001, p.76
29.     Fortean Times issue 38, p.24-25
30.     http://tinyurl.com/69zv6sf – 'Notorious tokoloshe raping Bulawayo women'; Zimdiaspora
31.     Goldstuck, 2006, p.115
32.     Niehaus, 2001, p.54-55 & 61
33.     http://tinyurl.com/5wnymka – 'Tokoloshe is brought to court'; newzimbabwe.com
34.     http://tinyurl.com/3cjqq2p – 'A Christian Perspective on the World of Spirits ...'
35.     Lebling, 2010, p.206-207
36.     Fortean Times issue 202, p.54
37.     Streiber cited in Appleyard, 2006, p.68

## 3. PHANTOM PREGNANCIES: TOKOLOSHES AND MISCARRIAGE, INFERTILITY AND DISABILITY

1.     Niehaus, 2001, p.53
2.     Niehaus, 2001, p.177
3.     Niehaus, 2001, p.55
4.     Holland, 2005, p.17
5.     Niehaus, 2001, p.53
6.     Frazer, 1998, p.702-703
7.     Fortean Times issue 205, p.24
8.     http://tinyurl.com/ydk5uha; 'Bizarre creature born with features of man and goat' – The Daily Telegaph.com.au
9.     http://tinyurl.com/6q72nh5 – Posting on GoTravel24.com
10.     Gaskill, 2005, p.22
11.     Hopton, 1991, p.4
12.     Harte, 2004, p.108
13.     http://tinyurl.com/deyj8g; 'My future wife impregnated by the tokoloshe?'; discussion thread on Yahoo! Answers
14.     http://tinyurl.com/6jfjf7w – 'Man who cried 'tokoloshe' guilty of murder'; IOL.co.za
15.     Harte, 2004, p.112-113
16.     http://tinyurl.com/3cjqq2p – 'A Christian Perspective on the World of Spirits ...'
17.     Susan Schoon Eberly, 'Fairies and the Folklore of Disability' in Narváez, 1997, p.232
18.     Richard P Jenkins, 'Witches and Fairies: Supernatural Aggression and Deviance Among the Irish Peasantry' in Narváez, 1997, p.321-323

## 4. THE SPIRIT OF THE LAW: TOKOLOSHES IN COURT

1.  http://tinyurl.com/3pwlzc2 – Post by Michael Osborne on 'Constitutionally Speaking' website
2.  http://tinyurl.com/3q7a49m – 'The Cultural Defence in Criminal Law: South African Perspectives' by Peter A Carstens et al; p.9
3.  http://tinyurl.com/3q7a49m – 'The Cultural Defence in Criminal Law: South African Perspectives' by Peter A Carstens et al; p.9-10
4.  http://tinyurl.com/3q7a49m – 'The Cultural Defence in Criminal Law: South African Perspectives' by Peter A Carstens et al; p.9
5.  Compiled from http://tinyurl.com/6jfjf7w – 'Man who cried 'tokoloshe' guilty of murder; IOL.co.za & http://tinyurl.com/5u3y97q – 'Tokoloshe baby' killer gets life'; News24.com & http://tinyurl.com/3ld8jhw – 'I didn't kill a baby – I killed a tokoloshe'; IOL.co.za & http://tinyurl.com/3nb7esr – 'Tokoloshe killer' tells of resurrection plan'; IOL.co.za & http://tinyurl.com/43gfj5j – 'Tokoloshe exorcist fed baby paraffin, herbs'; IOL.co.za
6.  http://tinyurl.com/3qrx4mv – 'Tokoloshe killer vanishes as if by magic'; IOL.co.za & http://tinyurl.com/3ewdmja – 'Tokoloshe killer turns up – in jail'; IOL.co.za
7.  Compiled from http://tinyurl.com/668ql2c – 'Tokoloshe murder accused to stay in custody'; IOL.co.za & http://tinyurl.com/6bmewtv – 'Sanele's family prepare for final goodbye'; IOL.co.za & http://tinyurl.com/4ytx6va – 'Jilted lover killed my son'; IOL.co.za & http://tinyurl.com/3kmt6an – 'Boy dies after man allegedly goes berserk'; IOL.co.za
8.  http://tinyurl.com/3fvwg5b – 'Man up for killing tiny tokoloshe'; DailySun & http://tinyurl.com/6c7fssh – 'Tokoloshe'; paranormalmysteriesblogspot.com
9.  http://tinyurl.com/4yjmxkf – 'Tokoloshe mom killer goes free'; IOL.co.za
10. http://tinyurl.com/3kmt6an – 'Boy dies after man allegedly goes berserk'; IOL.co.za
11. http://tinyurl.com/3r3ya4y - 'State blamed for teen's prison death'; IOL.co.za
12. http://tinyurl.com/5uecaph – 'Tokoloshe steals dockets: court evidence'; mybroadband.co.za
13. http://tinyurl.com/bt9r4mg – 'Macheso's 'Chikwambo' breaks family apart?'; Bulawayo24News.com
14. http://tinyurl.com/3hldr3t – 'Rapist blames 'tokoloshe' for crime rampage'; IOL.co.za
15. http://tinyurl.com/3cjqq2p - 'A Christian Perspective on the World of Spirits ...'
16. Holland, 2005, p.152
17. Compiled from Fortean Times issue 286, p.4-5 & http://tinyurl.com/cxsdwfz – 'Zombies threaten me, 'Mgqumeni' tells court; The Sowetan & http://tinyurl.com/78c4rms – 'South African 'back-from-dead singer Mgqumeni' detained'; BBC Online & http://tinyurl.com/d3hxuz5 – 'S Africa police charge Mgqumeni 'imposter' with fraud'; BBC Online
18. http://tinyurl.com/y8bv7b8 – 'Tokoloshe Murders'; TIME Magazine online
19. http://tinyurl.com/6gyh6gj – 'Money spinning GOBLIN starts stealing from owner'; Zimbabwe news online
20. http://tinyurl.com/5u9ogr2 – 'Men caught with body parts'; IOL.co.za
21. http://tinyurl.com/6aenh74 – ''Tokoloshe' dad fingered in court'; IOL.co.za

**5. A COMMON SUPERSTITION?: ATTITUDES OF AUTHORITY TOWARDS THE TOKOLOSHE**

1.   http://tinyurl.com/yuu3xr – 'The Tokoloshe: Africa's Brownie?'; vanhunks.com & http://tinyurl.com/6q72nh5 – Postings on GoTravel24.com
2.   http://tinyurl.com/y8bv7b8 – 'Tokoloshe Murders'; TIME Magazine online
3.   Holland, 2005, p.150
4.   Holland, 2005, p.152
5.   http://tinyurl.com/5vkddhe – 'Row over chief rages as councillor is freed'; Sowetan Live
6.   http://tinyurl.com/3cjqq2p – 'A Christian Perspective on the World of Spirits ...'
7.   http://tinyurl.com/6fya6vc – 'In parts of Africa, witches are to blame'; Free Press report
8.   http://tinyurl.com/5rhgg4s – 'Namibia: Tokoloshe-Battling Priest Loses Appeal'; allafrica.com
9.   http://tinyurl.com/ycuczdo – 'Religion: Tikoloshe in Church'; TIME Magazine online
10.  Compiled from http://tinyurl.com/yuu3xr – 'The Tokoloshe: Africa's Brownie?'; vanhunks.com & http://tinyurl.com/2wng6vc – 'What is a Tokoloshe?'; Strange News Daily
11.  http://tinyurl.com/7otrh – 'Zimbabwe traditional healer burnt by goblins'; newzimbabwe.com
12.  http://tinyurl.com/6cojbnz – 'My encounter with a tokoloshe'; New Zimbabwe.com
13.  http://tinyurl.com/6bh2dt3 – 'Woman relives rape ordeal by 'prophet''; Sowetan Live
14.  http://tinyurl.com/6lbxjox – 'What Thokolosi?'; The Voice
15.  Compiled from http://tinyurl.com/6x8hqj5 – 'Tokoloshe 'may be a mind thing''; The Namibian online & http://tinyurl.com/5sadozf – 'The tokoloshe homunculus'; letter in the South African Medical Journal, Vol.99, No.5, available in an online.pdf

**6. A MATTER OF BLACK AND WHITE: TOKOLOSHES AND RACE**

1.   http://tinyurl.com/6y62hc5 – 'Charlize Theron - Biography'; talktalk.co.uk
2.   Scot cited in Harte, 2004, p.3
3.   Compiled from http://bit.ly/uzcqpE – 'Nicolette Lotter tells of sorcery, rape'; Times LIVE & http://tinyurl.com/cksdqd6 – 'I was Satan'; IOL.co.za & http://tinyurl.com/bsbtfl3 – 'Lotter didn't want to sound crazy'; News24.com & http://tinyurl.com/cnndj8k – 'Naidoo was possessed by an evil force'; Times LIVE & http://tinyurl.com/br5jlcn – 'Lotter son knew killing was wrong'; Sowetan LIVE & http://tinyurl.com/dyu95sw – 'Third Son of God, Lotter siblings convicted of murder'; ReligionNewsBlog.com & http://tinyurl.com/dy3sn4e – 'Nicolette Lotter was programmed to kill'; News24.com
4.   Rosenthal, 1951, p.209-210
5.   Goldstuck, 2006, p.125-126
6.   See http://tinyurl.com/3eqqrop for a good selection of relevant Madam and Eve cartoons
7.   Goldstuck, 2006, p.127-128

## 7. GHOUL SCHOOLS: TOKOLOSHES AND MASS HYSTERIA AMONGST SCHOOLCHILDREN

1.   Goldstuck, 2006, p.313-314
2.   http://tinyurl.com/65rdcf3 – 'GOD HELP YOU'; The Voice
3.   http://bit.ly/Lx5Y18 – 'Naked female Chikwambo severely attacks primary school girls in the toilet in Bulawayo'; myzimbabwe.co.zw
4.   http://tinyurl.com/3eocxpb – 'Tokolosh fever back'; posting by 'Pianist' on myDIGITALLIFE
5.   Goldstuck, 2006, p.248
6.   Penny Siopis quoted in Claudia Mitchell, 'Geographies of Danger: School Toilets in Sub-Saharan Africa' in Gershenson & Penner, 2009 p.62
7.   http://tinyurl.com/4lnnty7 – 'Corrective Rape: Fighting a South African Scourge'; TIME magazine online
8.   http://tinyurl.com/kwo4ag – 'South African rape survey shock'; BBC online
9.   Mitchell in Gershenson & Penner, 2009, p.64
10.  'Outrage over gang rape of disabled girl' by Jonathan Clayton in The Times (London), 20.04.2012
11.  Mitchell in Gershenson & Penner, 2009, p.69
12.  Mitchell in Gershenson & Penner, 2009, p.72
13.  http://tinyurl.com/69cpoar – 'PASSIONS & PANICS – a new exhibition by Penny Siopis'; Google docs
14.  http://tinyurl.com/3l8awk7; posting by 'OldTimeRadio' on Fortean Times message board
15.  'Elves in the toilet' in Fortean Times issue 98, p18
16.  Compiled from http://tinyurl.com/yblmdru – 'Children Attacked by Hairy Sex Dwarf'; The Morning Starr & http://tinyurl.com/6dlwklx – 'Is a Horny Thokolosi Terrorizing Botswana?'; Monster Island News
17.  http://tinyurl.com/676tow9 – 'Headmaster flees as hysteria grips school'; Zimbabwe Daily News
18.  Evans & Bartholomew, 2009, p.752-753
19.  http://tinyurl.com/3cthoez - 'Makande rural clinic'; Zimbabweghosts.blogspot
20.  http://tinyurl.com/3v3hkp2 – postings on niggermania.net

## 8. GOBLIN FOR SALE!: CHANGING CONCEPTIONS OF THE TOKOLOSHE

1.   Goldstuck, 2006, p.281
2.   http://tinyurl.com/6fya6vc – 'In parts of Africa, witches are to blame'; Free Press report
3.   http://tinyurl.com/6gllzbk – 'Zimbabwe: Open Market for Goblins'; allafrica.com
4.   http://tinyurl.com/6kyjmlo – 'Zimbabwe: 'Goblins' Demand Outstrips Supply'; Zimbabwe Herald
5.   http://tinyurl.com/6zxpycj – 'Residents Shocked by Goblin'; Bulawayo24News
6.   http://tinyurl.com/6om55pv – 'Goblin thrown out of Mabvuku Kombi'; NewsdzeZimbabwe
7.   http://bit.ly/LDDqCG – 'Goblins Terrorise Women in Zimbabwe'; WeirdWorldNews

8.  http://tinyurl.com/6q72nh5 – posting on GoTravel24.com
9.  http://tinyurl.com/cumwzjh – 'The R15k Tokoloshe'; DailySun.com
10. Holland, 2005, p.154-155
11. Holland, 2005, p.156
12. Niehaus, 2001, p.56-57
13. Niehaus, 2001, p.58
14. Niehaus, 2001, p.56
15. Niehaus, 2001, p.58
16. Holland, 2005, p.114
17. Niehaus, 2001, p.58-59

## 9. HAIRY GHOSTS: TOKOLOSHES AND POLTERGEISTS

1.  Compiled from 'Smearing Tokoloshe' in Fortean Times issue 138, p16 & http://tinyurl.com/2wng6vc – 'What is a Tokoloshe?'; Strange News Daily
2.  Beard quoted in Rosenthal, 1951, p.203
3.  http://tinyurl.com/3vytrvv – 'I fought with invisible TOKOLOSHE'; posting on gotravel24.com
4.  http://tinyurl.com/yuu3xr – 'The Tokoloshe: Africa's Brownie?'; vanhunks.com
5.  http://tinyurl.com/3cjqq2p – 'A Christian Perspective on the World of Spirits ...'
6.  Goldstuck, 2006, p.258-259
7.  Rosenthal, 1951, p.56-57
8.  Fortean Times issue 69, p.8
9.  See 'Fortean Bureau of Investigation' by Christine Wood in Fortean Times issue 117, p24-25
10. See 'Renovation Hauntings' by Peter A McCue in Fortean Times issue 268, p30-35
11. http://tinyurl.com/3g2xbxh – 'I See Dead People'; MNET.co.za & Goldstuck, 2006, p.252-255; Please note that certain aspects of either report simply did not correspond with one another, so I have attempted to reconstruct what were in my view the most likely sequence of events and main cast of people involved from comparing the reports, though I may of course have made some minor errors whilst doing so. As such, I can say that the basic outline of my summary of this case is correct, though certain small details may not be.
12. http://tinyurl.com/3vytrvv – 'Tokkelos'; posting on GoTravel24.com
13. http://tinyurl.com/a7Ix – 'Meteor caused Lesotho 'poltergeist''; BBC online
14. http://tinyurl.com/3bhwk9t – 'Witchcraft blamed as stones fall on family'; newzimbabwe.com
15. Compiled from http://tinyurl.com/6f786al – 'Mystery stones plague family' & Untitled Report; Fortean Times Message Board
16. Goldstuck, 2006, p.275-277
17. Owen, 1964, p.271
18. Price, 1945, p.15-16
19. Rosenthal, 1951, p.207
20. 'Fortean Times issue 138, p16
21. http://tinyurl.com/6ckbotb – 'Hungry tokoloshes'; Cabinet of Wonders

22. http://tinyurl.com/5ut2384 – 'Strange spirit has put us all through hell'; IOL.co.za
23. Lebling, 2010, p.128
24. Lebling, 2010, p.135
25. Rosenthal, 1951, p.55-56
26. Rosenthal, 1951, p.138
27. Brown Nombida quoted in Rosenthal, 1951, p.197-198
28. Rosenthal, 1951, p.56-57
29. Rosenthal, 1951, p.51
30. Rosenthal, 1951, p.53-54
31. Davies, 2007, p.176-177
32. Rosenthal, 1951, p.41
33. Rosenthal, 1951, p.126-127
34. Rosenthal, 1951, p.128
35. Goldstuck, 2006, p.270
36. Goldstuck, 2006, p.267-269
37. Goldstuck, 2006, p.269-270
38. Goldstuck, 2006, p.282
39. Rosenthal, 1951, p.51-53
40. Goldstuck, 2006, p.34-37
41. Rosenthal, 1951, p.129-130

## 10. MONKEY-BUSINESS: TOKOLOSHES, BABOONS AND NANDI-BEARS

1. Minnie Martin quoted in Rosenthal, 1951, p.205
2. Minnie Martin quoted in Rosenthal, 1951, p.204
3. Minnie Martin quoted in Rosenthal, 1951, p.204
4. Minnie Martin quoted in Rosenthal, 1951, p.205
5. Shuker, 1995, p.153
6. Niehaus, 2001, p.50
7. Captain Charles Pitman quoted in Shuker, 1995, p.153
8. Shuker, 1995, p.153-154
9. http://n24.cm/d8f5RO – 'Witchcraft, says baby's mom'; News24.com
10. Shuker, 1995, p.154-155
11. Rosenthal, 1951, p.206-207
12. http://tinyurl.com/5smtnv7 – 'Tokoloshe Baboon Killed'; zoutnet.co.za
13. http://tinyurl.com/3tlhoov – 'Monkey 'witch' slain'; IOL.co.za
14. http://tinyurl.com/bvl9d8p – 'It is a tokoloshe'; Zoutnet.co.za
15. See 'Nags to Witches' by Frans Prins and Sian Hall in Fortean Times issue 119, p.28
16. Goldstuck, 2006, p.284-285
17. Niehaus, 2001, p.49
18. Niehaus, 2001, p.179
19. http://tgr.ph/zD9VGC – 'Girls at Zimbabwe school attacked by goblins'; Telegraph online & http://bit.ly/ylmW5R – 'Goblins attack secondary school girls';Bulawayo24News
20. http://tinyurl.com/3cjqq2p – 'A Christian Perspective on the World of Spirits ...'

21.     Niehaus, 2001, p.53

**CONCLUSION: A TOKOLOSHE FOR ALL SEASONS**

1.     http://tinyurl.com/6fya6vc - 'In parts of Africa, witches are to blame'; Free Press report
2.     Cynthia Hind, 'UFOs in Africa: Changing Ways in Changing Days' in Evans & Stacy, 1997, p.195-196
3.     Bowen, 1974, p.93-94
4.     Bowen, 1974, p.95-96
5.     Bowen, 1974, p.96-97
6.     Vallee, 1975, p.61
7.     Brookesmith, 1995, p.29 & Steiger, 2008, p.131-132

STILL ON THE TRACK OF UNKNOWN ANIMALS

The Centre for Fortean Zoology, or CFZ, is a non profit-making organisation founded in 1992 with the aim of being a clearing house for information, and coordinating research into mystery animals around the world.

We also study out of place animals, rare and aberrant animal behaviour, and Zooform Phenomena; little-understood "things" that appear to be animals, but which are in fact nothing of the sort, and not even alive (at least in the way we understand the term).

Not only are we the biggest organisation of our type in the world, but - or so we like to think - we are the best. We are certainly the only truly global cryptozoological research organisation, and we carry out our investigations using a strictly scientific set of guidelines. We are expanding all the time and looking to recruit new members to help us in our research into mysterious animals and strange creatures across the globe.

Why should you join us? Because, if you are genuinely interested in trying to solve the last great mysteries of Mother Nature, there is nobody better than us with whom to do it.

Members get a four-issue subscription to our journal *Animals & Men*. Each issue contains nearly 100 pages packed with news, articles, letters, research papers, field reports, and even a gossip column! The magazine is Royal Octavo in format with a full colour cover. You also have access to one of the world's largest collections of resource material dealing with cryptozoology and allied disciplines, and people from the CFZ membership regularly take part in fieldwork and expeditions around the world.

The CFZ is managed by a three-man board of trustees, with a non-profit making trust registered with HM Government Stamp Office. The board of trustees is supported by a Permanent Directorate of full and part-time staff, and advised by a Consultancy Board of specialists - many of whom are world-renowned experts in their particular field. We have regional representatives across the UK, the USA, and many other parts of the world, and are affiliated with other organisations whose aims and protocols mirror our own.

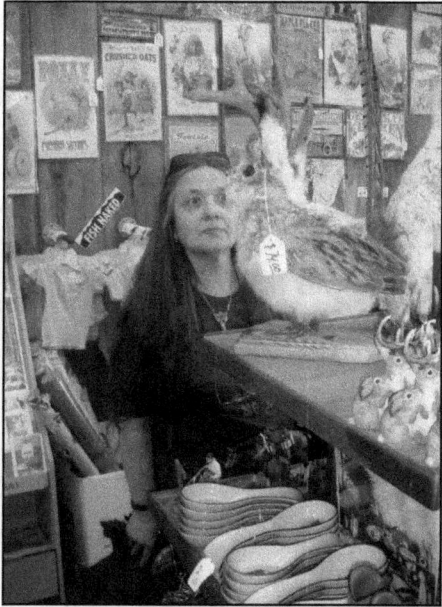

You'll find that the people at the CFZ are friendly and approachable. We have a thriving forum on the website which is the hub of an ever-growing electronic community. You will soon find your feet. Many members of the CFZ Permanent Directorate started off as ordinary members, and now work full-time chasing monsters around the world.

Write to us, e-mail us, or telephone us. The list of future projects on the website is not exhaustive. If you have a good idea for an investigation, please tell us. We may well be able to help.

We are always looking for volunteers to join us. If you see a project that interests you, do not hesitate to get in touch with us. Under certain circumstances we can help provide funding for your trip. If you look on the future projects section of the website, you can see some of the projects that we have pencilled in for the next few years. In 2003 and 2004 we sent three-man expeditions to Sumatra looking for Orang-Pendek - a semi-legendary bipedal ape. The same three went to Mongolia in 2005. All three members started off merely subscribers to the CFZ magazine. Next time it could be you!

We have no magic sources of income. All our funds come from donations, membership fees, and sales of our publications and merchandise. We are always looking for corporate sponsorship, and other sources of revenue. If you have any ideas for fund-raising please let us know. However, unlike other cryptozoological organisations in the past, we do not live in an intellectual ivory tower. We are not afraid to get our hands dirty, and furthermore we are not one of those organisations where the membership have to raise money so that a privileged few can go on expensive foreign trips. Our research teams, both in the UK and abroad, consist of a mixture of experienced and inexperienced personnel. We are truly a community, and work on the premise that the benefits of CFZ membership are open to all.

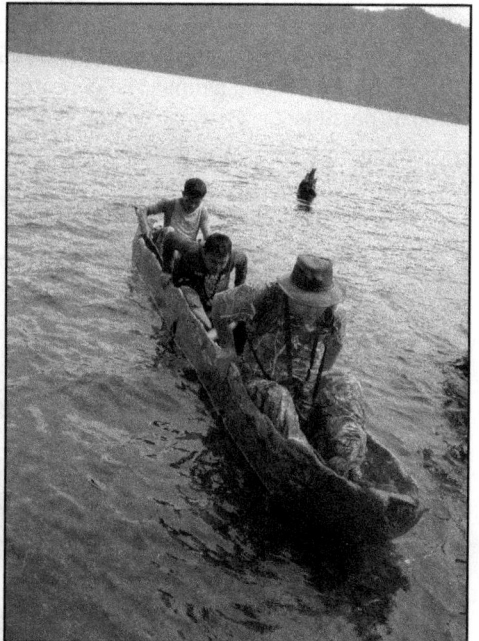

Reports of our investigations are published on our website as soon as they are available. Preliminary reports are posted within days of the project finishing. Each year we publish a 200 page yearbook containing research papers and expedition reports too long to be printed in the journal. We freely circulate our information to anybody who asks for it.

We have a thriving YouTube channel, CFZtv, which has well over two hundred self-made documentaries, lecture appearances, and episodes of our monthly webTV show. We have a daily online magazine, which has over a million hits each year.

Each year since 2000 we have held our annual convention - the Weird Weekend. It is three days of lectures, workshops, and excursions. But most importantly it is a chance for members of the CFZ to meet each other, and to talk with the members of the permanent directorate in a relaxed and informal setting and preferably with a pint of beer in one hand. Since 2006 - the Weird Weekend has been bigger and better and held on the third weekend in August in the idyllic rural location of Woolsery in North Devon.

Since relocating to North Devon in 2005 we have become ever more closely involved with other community organisations, and we hope that this trend will continue. We have also worked closely with Police Forces across the UK as consultants for animal mutilation cases, and we intend to forge closer links with the coastguard and other community services. We want to work closely with those who regularly travel into the Bristol Channel, so that if the recent trend of exotic animal visitors to our coastal waters continues, we can be out there as soon as possible.

© Undergroundimages2007

Apart from having been the only Fortean Zoological organisation in the world to have consistently published material on all aspects of the subject for over a decade, we have achieved the following concrete results:

- Disproved the myth relating to the headless so-called sea-serpent carcass of Durgan beach in Cornwall 1975
- Disproved the story

of the 1988 puma skull of Lustleigh Cleave
* Carried out the only in-depth research ever into the mythos of the Cornish Owlman.
* Made the first records of a tropical species of lamprey
* Made the first records of a luminous cave gnat larva in Thailand
* Discovered a possible new species of British mammal - the beech marten
* In 1994-6 carried out the first archival fortean zoological survey of Hong Kong
* In the year 2000, CFZ theories were confirmed when a new species of lizard was added to the British List
* Identified the monster of Martin Mere in Lancashire as a giant wels catfish
* Expanded the known range of Armitage's skink in the Gambia by 80%
* Obtained photographic evidence of the remains of Europe's largest known pike
* Carried out the first ever in-depth study of the ninki-nanka
* Carried out the first attempt to breed Puerto Rican cave snails in captivity
* Were the first European explorers to visit the `lost valley` in Sumatra
* Published the first ever evidence for a new tribe of pygmies in Guyana
* Published the first evidence for a new species of caiman in Guyana

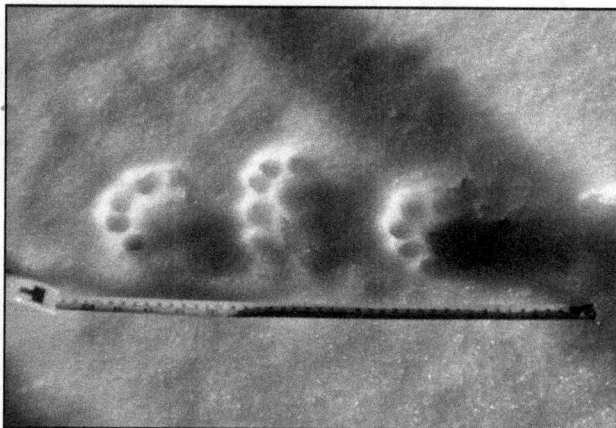

on a monster-haunted lake in Ireland for the first time

• Had a sighting of orang pendek in Sumatra in 2009

• Found leopard hair, subsequently identified by DNA analysis, from rural North Devon in 2010

• Brought back hairs which appear to be from an unknown primate in Sumatra

• Published some of the best evidence ever for the almasty in southern Russia

CFZ Expeditions and Investigations include:

• 1998 Puerto Rico, Florida, Mexico (Chupacabras)
• 1999 Nevada (Bigfoot)
• 2000 Thailand (Naga)
• 2002 Martin Mere (Giant catfish)
• 2002 Cleveland (Wallaby mutilation)
• 2003 Bolam Lake (BHM Reports)

- 2003 Sumatra (Orang Pendek)
- 2003 Texas (Bigfoot; giant snapping turtles)
- 2004 Sumatra (Orang Pendek; cigau, a sabre-toothed cat)
- 2004 Illinois (Black panthers; cicada swarm)
- 2004 Texas (Mystery blue dog)
- Loch Morar (Monster)
- 2004 Puerto Rico (Chupacabras; carnivorous cave snails)
- 2005 Belize (Affiliate expedition for hairy dwarfs)
- 2005 Loch Ness (Monster)
- 2005 Mongolia (Allghoi Khorkhoi aka Mongolian death worm)

- 2006 Gambia (Gambo - Gambian sea monster , Ninki Nanka and  Armitage's skink
- 2006 Llangorse Lake (Giant pike, giant eels)
- 2006 Windermere (Giant eels)
- 2007  Coniston Water (Giant eels)
- 2007 Guyana  (Giant anaconda,  didi, water tiger)
- 2008 Russia (Almasty)
- 2009 Sumatra (Orang pendek)
- 2009 Republic of Ireland (Lake Monster)
- 2010 Texas (Blue Dogs)
- 2010 India (Mande Burung)
- 2011 Sumatra (Orang-pendek)

For details of current membership fees, current expeditions and investigations, and voluntary posts within the CFZ that need your help, please do not hesitate to contact us.

The Centre for Fortean Zoology,
Myrtle Cottage,
Woolfardisworthy,
Bideford, North Devon
EX39 5QR

Telephone 01237 431413
Fax+44 (0)7006-074-925
**eMail** info@cfz.org.uk

**Websites:**

www.cfz.org.uk
www.weirdweekend.org

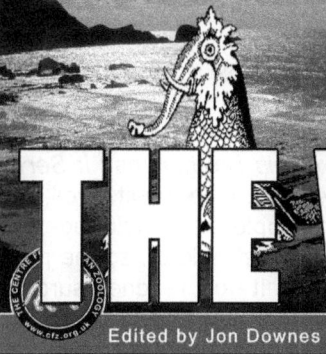

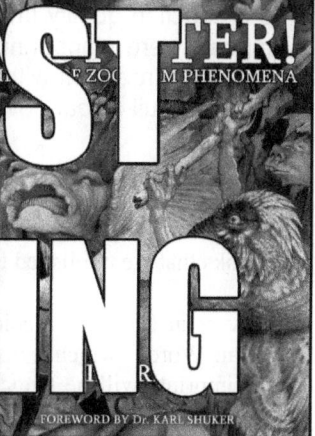
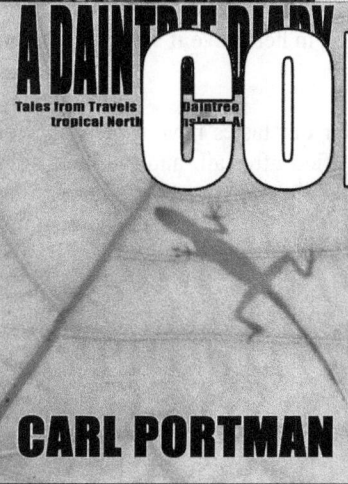
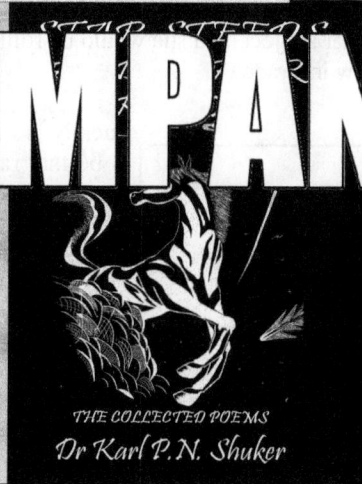

# THE WORLD'S WEIRDEST PUBLISHING COMPANY

# HOW TO START A PUBLISHING EMPIRE

Unlike most mainstream publishers, we have a non-commercial remit, and our mission statement claims that "we publish books because they deserve to be published, not because we think that we can make money out of them". Our motto is the Latin Tag *Pro bona causa facimus* (we do it for good reason), a slogan taken from a children's book *The Case of the Silver Egg* by the late Desmond Skirrow.

WIKIPEDIA: "The first book published was in 1988. *Take this Brother may it Serve you Well* was a guide to Beatles bootlegs by Jonathan Downes. It sold quite well, but was hampered by very poor production values, being photocopied, and held together by a plastic clip binder. In 1988 A5 clip binders were hard to get hold of, so the publishers took A4 binders and cut them in half with a hacksaw. It now reaches surprisingly high prices second hand.

The production quality improved slightly over the years, and after 1999 all the books produced were ringbound with laminated colour covers. In 2004, however, they signed an agreement with Lightning Source, and all books are now produced perfect bound, with full colour covers."

Until 2010 all our books, the majority of which are/were on the subject of mystery animals and allied disciplines, were published by `CFZ Press`, the publishing arm of the Centre for Fortean Zoology (CFZ), and we urged our readers and followers to draw a discreet veil over the books that we published that were completely off topic to the CFZ.

However, in 2010 we decided that enough was enough and launched a second imprint, `Fortean Words` which aims to cover a wide range of non animal-related esoteric subjects. Other imprints will be launched as and when we feel like it, however the basic ethos of the company remains the same: Our job is to publish books and magazines that we feel are worth publishing, whether or not they are going to sell. Money is, after all - as my dear old Mama once told me - a rather vulgar subject, and she would be rolling in her grave if she thought that her eldest son was somehow in `trade`.

Luckily, so far our tastes have turned out not to be that rarified after all, and we have sold far more books than anyone ever thought that we would, so there is a moral in there somewhere...

Jon Downes,
Woolsery, North Devon
July 2010

# Other Books in Print

*Giant Snakes - Unravelling the coils of mystery* by Newton, Michael
*Mystery Animals of the British Isles: Kent* by Arnold, Neil
*Centre for Fortean Zoology Yearbook 2009* by Downes, Jonathan
*CFZ EXPEDITION REPORT: Russia 2008* by Richard Freeman *et al*, Shuker, Karl (fwd)
*Dinosaurs and other Prehistoric Animals on Stamps - A Worldwide catalogue*
by Shuker, Karl P. N
*Dr Shuker's Casebook* by Shuker, Karl P.N
*The Island of Paradise - chupacabra UFO crash retrievals,*
*and accelerated evolution on the island of Puerto Rico* by Downes, Jonathan
*The Mystery Animals of the British Isles: Northumberland and Tyneside* by Hallowell, Michael J
*Centre for Fortean Zoology Yearbook 1997* by Downes, Jonathan (Ed)
*Centre for Fortean Zoology Yearbook 2002* by Downes, Jonathan (Ed)
*Centre for Fortean Zoology Yearbook 2000/1* by Downes, Jonathan (Ed)
*Centre for Fortean Zoology Yearbook 1998* by Downes, Jonathan (Ed)
*Centre for Fortean Zoology Yearbook 2003* by Downes, Jonathan (Ed)
*In the wake of Bernard Heuvelmans* by Woodley, Michael A
*CFZ EXPEDITION REPORT: Guyana 2007* by Richard Freeman *et al*, Shuker, Karl (fwd)
*Centre for Fortean Zoology Yearbook 1999* by Downes, Jonathan (Ed)
*Big Cats in Britain Yearbook 2008* by Fraser, Mark (Ed)
*Centre for Fortean Zoology Yearbook 1996* by Downes, Jonathan (Ed)
*THE CALL OF THE WILD - Animals & Men issues 11-15*
*Collected Editions Vol. 3* by Downes, Jonathan (ed)
*Ethna's Journal* by Downes, C N
*Centre for Fortean Zoology Yearbook 2008* by Downes, J (Ed)
*DARK DORSET -Calendar Custome* by Newland, Robert J
*Extraordinary Animals Revisited* by Shuker, Karl
*MAN-MONKEY - In Search of the British Bigfoot* by Redfern, Nick
*Dark Dorset Tales of Mystery, Wonder and Terror* by Newland, Robert J and Mark North
*Big Cats Loose in Britain* by Matthews, Marcus
*MONSTER! - The A-Z of Zooform Phenomena* by Arnold, Neil
*The Centre for Fortean Zoology 2004 Yearbook* by Downes, Jonathan (Ed)
*The Centre for Fortean Zoology 2007 Yearbook* by Downes, Jonathan (Ed)
*CAT FLAPS! Northern Mystery Cats* by Roberts, Andy
*Big Cats in Britain Yearbook 2007* by Fraser, Mark (Ed)
*BIG BIRD! - Modern sightings of Flying Monsters* by Gerhard, Ken
*THE NUMBER OF THE BEAST - Animals & Men issues 6-10*
*Collected Editions Vol. 1* by Downes, Jonathan (Ed)
*IN THE BEGINNING - Animals & Men issues 1-5 Collected Editions Vol. 1* by Downes, Jonathan
*STRENGTH THROUGH KOI - They saved Hitler's Koi and other stories*
by Downes, Jonathan
*The Smaller Mystery Carnivores of the Westcountry* by Downes, Jonathan
*CFZ EXPEDITION REPORT: Gambia 2006* by Richard Freeman *et al*, Shuker, Karl (fwd)
*The Owlman and Others* by Jonathan Downes
*The Blackdown Mystery* by Downes, Jonathan

TRADE MARK

BEWARE OF IMITATIONS

CFZ CLASSICS

CFZ Classics is a new venture for us. There are many seminal works that are either unavailable today, or not available with the production values which we would like to see. So, following the old adage that if you want to get something done do it yourself, this is exactly what we have done.

Desiderius Erasmus Roterodamus (b. October 18th 1466, d. July 2nd 1536) said: "When I have a little money, I buy books; and if I have any left, I buy food and clothes," and we are much the same. Only, we are in the lucky position of being able to share our books with the wider world. CFZ Classics is a conduit through which we cannot just re-issue titles which we feel still have much to offer the cryptozoological and Fortean research communities of the 21st Century, but we are adding footnotes, supplementary essays, and other material where we deem it appropriate.

*Headhunters of The Amazon* by Fritz W Up de Graff (1902)

# Fortean Words

The Centre for Fortean Zoology has for several years led the field in Fortean publishing. CFZ Press is the only publishing company specialising in books on monsters and mystery animals. CFZ Press has published more books on this subject than any other company in history and has attracted such well known authors as Andy Roberts, Nick Redfern, Michael Newton, Dr Karl Shuker, Neil Arnold, Dr Darren Naish, Jon Downes, Ken Gerhard and Richard Freeman.

Now CFZ Press are launching a new imprint. Fortean Words is a new line of books dealing with Fortean subjects other than cryptozoology, which is - after all - the subject the CFZ are best known for. Fortean Words is being launched with a spectacular multi-volume series called *Haunted Skies* which covers British UFO sightings between 1940 and 2010. Former policeman John Hanson and his long-suffering partner Dawn Holloway have compiled a peerless library of sighting reports, many that have not been made public before.

Other books include a look at the Berwyn Mountains UFO case by renowned Fortean Andy Roberts and a series of forthcoming books by transatlantic researcher Nick Redfern. CFZ Press are dedicated to maintaining the fine quality of their works with Fortean Words. New authors tackling new subjects will always be encouraged, and we hope that our books will continue to be as ground-breaking and popular as ever.

*Haunted Skies Volume One 1940-1959* by John Hanson and Dawn Holloway
*Haunted Skies Volume Two 1960-1965* by John Hanson and Dawn Holloway
*Haunted Skies Volume Three 1965-1967* by John Hanson and Dawn Holloway
*Haunted Skies Volume Four 1968-1971* by John Hanson and Dawn Holloway
*Haunted Skies Volume Five 1972-1974* by John Hanson and Dawn Holloway
*Haunted Skies Volume Six 1975-1977* by John Hanson and Dawn Holloway
*Grave Concerns* by Kai Roberts

*Police and the Paranormal* by Andy Owens
*Dead of Night* by Lee Walker
*Space Girl Dead on Spaghetti Junction* - an anthology by Nick Redfern
*I Fort the Lore* - an anthology by Paul Screeton
*UFO Down - the Berwyn Mountains UFO Crash* by Andy Roberts
*The Grail* by Ronan Coghlan
*UFO Warminster - Cradle of Contract* by Kevin Goodman
*Quest for the Hexham Heads* by Paul Screeton

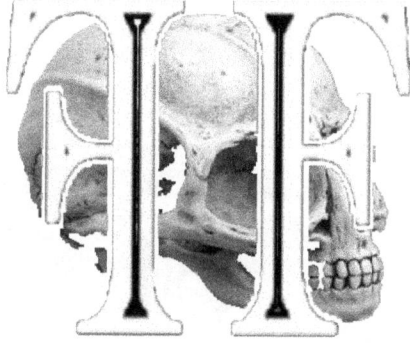

# Fortean Fiction

J ust before Christmas 2011, we launched our third imprint, this time dedicated to - let's see if you guessed it from the title - fictional books with a Fortean or cryptozoological theme. We have published a few fictional books in the past, but now think that because of our rising reputation as publishers of quality Forteana, that a dedicated fiction imprint was the order of the day.

We launched with four titles:

*Green Unpleasant Land* by Richard Freeman
*Left Behind* by Harriet Wadham
*Dark Ness* by Tabitca Cope
*Snap!* By Steven Bredice
*Death on Dartmoor* by Di Francis
*Dark Wear* by Tabitca Cope